Pious Citizens

Modern Intellectual and Political History of the Middle East
Mehrzad Boroujerdi, *Series Editor*

Democracy and Civil Society in Arab Political Thought: Transcultural Possibilities
MICHAELLE L. BROWERS

The Education of Women and The Vices of Men: Two Qajar Tracts
HASAN JAVADI and WILLEM FLOOR, trans.

Globalization and the Muslim World: Culture, Religion, and Modernity
BIRGIT SCHAEBLER and LEIF STENBERG, ed.

*A Guerrilla Odyssey: Modernization, Secularism, Democracy,
and the Fadai Period of National Liberation in Iran, 1971–1979*
PEYMAN VAHABZADEH

International Politics of the Persian Gulf
MEHRAN KAMRAVA, ed.

The Kurdish Quasi-State: Development and Dependency in Post–Gulf War Iraq
DENISE NATALI

*Modernity, Sexuality, and Ideology in Iran: The Life and Legacy
of Popular Iranian Female Artists*
KAMRAN TALATTOF

The Politics of Public Memory in Turkey
ESRA OZYUREK, ed.

Religion, Society, and Modernity in Turkey
ŞERIF MARDIN

The Urban Social History of the Middle East, 1750–1950
PETER SLUGLETT, ed.

Pious Citizens

Reforming Zoroastrianism
in India and Iran

Monica M. Ringer

Syracuse University Press

Part of this volume first appeared in "Reform Transplanted: Parsi Agents of Change among Zoroastrians in Nineteenth-Century Iran," *Iranian Studies* 42, no. 4 (2009): 549–60, available at http://informaworld.com, reprinted here with permission. Chapter 8 appeared in Persian translation in *Irannameh* 26, no. 2 (2011).

∞ The paper used in this publication meets the minimum requirements of the American National Standard for Information Sciences—Permanence of Paper for Printed Library Materials, ANSI Z39.48–1992.

For a listing of books published and distributed by Syracuse University Press, visit our Web site at SyracuseUniversityPress.syr.edu.

ISBN: 978–0–8156–3264–1

Library of Congress Cataloging-in-Publication Data

Ringer, Monica M., 1965–

   Pious citizens : reforming Zoroastrianism in India and Iran / Monica M. Ringer. — 1st ed.

      p. cm. — (Modern intellectual and political history of the Middle East)

   Includes bibliographical references and index.

   ISBN 978-0-8156-3264-1 (cloth : alk. paper) 1. Zoroastrianism—India—History

2. India—Religion. 3. Zoroastrianism—Iran—History. 4. Iran—Religion. I. Title.

BL1530.R56 2011

295.0954'09034—dc23   2011040056

Manufactured in the United States of America

For my daughter, Soraya

And a branch of cypress from Paradise they brought
Which he planted before the gate of Kashmar

—FERDOWSI, *SHAHNAMEH*

Monica M. Ringer studied with Hossein Ziai and Nikki Keddie at UCLA, receiving an MA in Islamic studies (1992) and her PhD in modern Middle Eastern history (1998). She is the author of numerous articles and a book titled *Education, Religion, and the Discourse of Cultural Reform in Qajar Iran*. She teaches Middle Eastern history at Amherst College.

Contents

Illustrations

Acknowledgments

It would be only a slight exaggeration to say that this project was inspired by the story of a tree: the legend of the Cypress of Kashmar, Zoroaster's cypress, planted in commemoration of King Goshtasp's acceptance of "the good religion." The event, memorialized in Ferdowsi's *Shahnameh*, appears in various histories. According to Qazvini, the famous cypress existed into the ninth century until it was felled on orders of Abbasid Caliph Mutawakkil. The demise of the magnificent tree caused great dismay among people, birds, and animals, and the caliph was murdered before the tree could be transported back to Baghdad, suggesting divine retribution for the sin of ordering it cut. A. V. Williams Jackson, touring Iran in 1907, met Iranians who confirmed that the cypress had grown in the vicinity of Torbat, Khorasan. This legend and its subsequent echoes inspired my attempts at uncovering the interplay of history, memory, and meaning in the reexamination and reconstruction of tradition, history, belief, and practice undertaken by Zoroastrian reformers in nineteenth- and twentieth-century India and Iran.

I also like to think that this project began with a casual question on my first evening in Iran. The late professor Kasra Vafadari asked why I had omitted any discussion of Zoroastrian schools in my first book on educational reform in nineteenth-century Iran. This omission seems all the more glaring now in retrospect, but at the time it piqued my interest, and struck me as needing both response and redress. I was privileged to have Kasra's assistance that summer and the next as I began hunting for sources. Although this project developed into something quite different along the way, I am indebted to Kasra for launching the idea of working on the Zoroastrian community of Iran.

There are many others whom I wish to acknowledge. To my daughter, Soraya, I recognize all the ways in which work on this project kept us apart, and hope that in as many ways or more, it has brought us together. To the many friends and colleagues whose own expertise and insight continues to inspire and educate me, helping me move from unconscious suspicions and roughly formed ideas to articulation and focus, I cannot thank you enough. Several individuals in particular have given generously of their time and knowledge, most especially John Hinnells, whose advice made an enormous difference. Mohammad Tavakoli-Targhi, Margaret Hunt, Chris Dole, Rudi Matthee, Holly Shissler, Alan Babb, Eric Hooglund, and Jon Armajani also read some or all of the manuscript and shared their recommendations. Thanks to Andrew Dole and David W. Wills for conversations about Christianity, and to Philip Stern who assisted with sources on the British in India. Yuhan Vevaina shared hard-to-find source material as well as his own published and unpublished work, as did Afshin Marashi, Dinyar Patel, and Mitra Sharafi. Talinn Grigor allowed me permission to use a couple of her photographs of Pahlavi government buildings.

Over the years I presented ideas from this book in conference form. I owe special thanks to Berna Turam, who organized three conferences with me—two in Amherst and one at Bogazici University in Istanbul. The working group that grew out of these conferences facilitated many fruitful conversations, and I hope that this will continue, regardless of our future projects. To this group, Holly Shissler, Berna Turam, Ben Fortna, Carole Woodall, Yesim Bayar, and Irvin Schick, heartfelt thanks.

I also wish to thank my Amherst students for propelling me to keep learning through teaching. Special thanks to my research assistants, Laura Alagna and Karl Teo Molin. Michael Kasper at Frost Library helped me with sources, and Rhea Cabin, unofficial head of the Amherst College History Department, helped me with too many things to properly list. Thanks also to President Tony Marx, Dean Gregory Call, and the Trustees of Amherst College for awarding me funding during my critical junior sabbatical year, and to the Mellon Foundation for two years of funding while I was teaching at Williams College. Mary Selden Evans and the editorial staff of Syracuse University Press have been simply marvelous.

Last, my own teachers. My appreciation is due to Nikki Keddie for her honest and frank advice that is not always easy to hear, but in the end always spot-on. I also have never properly thanked Hossein Ziai for introducing me to Iranian history. My interest in Iran, and in religion more specifically, dates from my senior year as an undergraduate at Oberlin College when I wrote a seminar paper on Shi'ism under the direction of Professor Ziai. I hope that my attempts at understanding the transformation of Zoroastrianism in nineteenth- and twentieth-century India and Iran in part acknowledge that debt.

Pious Citizens

1. "Tombeau de Cyrus," lithograph. First appeared in Ernest Breton, *Monuments de tous les peuples, décrits et dessinés d'après les documents les plus modernes* (Brussels: Librarie Historique-Artistique, 1843).

Introduction

Modernity, Religion, and the Production of Knowledge

> What is often assumed to be opposite is in fact deeply entangled, and what is
> seen as unconnected is in fact the product of close encounters.
>
> —PETER VAN DER VEER, *Imperial Encounters:*
> *Religion and Modernity in India* (2001)

Even before the infamous reelection of Iranian president Ahmadinejad in
2009, the Zoroastrian symbol of the *Fravahar* enjoyed currency among opponents of the Islamic Republic, Muslim and Zoroastrian alike. Sporting the
Fravahar on a necklace or pinned boldly on a chador established a certain ideo-
logical distance from the Islamic Republic—the *Fravahar* signifying an alternative—not a Zoroastrian Republic, but rather a secular republic grounded on
the pre-Islamic grandeur of Cyrus the Great. Certainly, since Ahmadinejad's
reelection and the intensification of opposition to the Islamic Republic, the *Fravahar*, like Cyrus the Great's tomb and other symbols of ancient Iran, has come
to express growing antipathy to the Islamic Republic. During *Nowruz*, Persian
New Year, Iranians pilgrimage to Cyrus the Great's tomb for picnicking and
New Year merrymaking. There is even a recent photograph on the Internet of a
man prostrate before the tomb, praying. Yet should we find this surprising, or
accept as natural and inevitable the positing of an Islamic/pre-Islamic binary,
of current "Islamic" Iran juxtaposed by Cyrus the Great? I would argue that to
view this correlation as inevitable is to ignore the origins of these connections,
and to see them as eternal rather than as the results of a specific reimagining
of the past and its curious connection to Zoroastrianism. Why, for instance,
is the pre-Islamic past understood as an authentic national past claimed by all
Iranians, regardless of religious affiliation, devoid of religious (Zoroastrian) or

ethnic (Persian) content? How has the Zoroastrian religious ceremony of *Nowruz* become a secular *national* holiday? The answer, of course, is tied to the emergence of modern Iranian nationalism. But the reimagining of the ancient Iranian past and its construction as a *national Iranian* past *and* as an *authentic Zoroastrian* past occurred within the specific context of Zoroastrian religious reform. So although the story is an "Iranian" story, it is equally a Zoroastrian story, one that cannot easily be disentangled from the ways in which religion and the religious past were reimagined as part of a larger process of religious reform in nineteenth- and early-twentieth-century India and Iran. Zoroastrian religious reform, which began first among the Parsis in India and was then transplanted to and thrived among the Zoroastrians in Iran, is at the origin of these connections: between the Zoroastrians of India and Iran, between social change and religious reform, between religious beliefs and the creation of modern pious citizens. It is also at the origin of how conceptions of history were scripted onto maps of modernity. This book winds its way through the tangle of these threads, teasing out the multiple strands of Zoroastrian religious reform in India and Iran over the course of a century, roughly from 1830 to 1940.

Zoroastrian religious reform constituted a serious theological project that involved the radical reconceptualization of religious beliefs and practices. This transformation was intimately tied to the promotion of social and political reform. Reformers concurred that modern states derived their strength from constitutional government, rule of law, and the formation of citizens. Reformers believed that rational and enlightened religion, characterized by social responsibility and the interiorization of piety, was critical for the development of modern individuals, citizens, secular public space, and popular sovereignty. The promotion of social and political change, consistently articulated as the quest for progress and civilization, depended on religious reform.

Zoroastrian reform was initiated in India by Parsi merchant elites. These elites initially sponsored religious reform in order to counter British Protestant missionary attacks on Zoroastrianism. However, these elites were also closely allied commercially and politically with the British (particularly so in Bombay) and found themselves drawn to British cultural sensibilities. Parsi merchants were thus most acutely aware of British imperial power and its accompanying social and political values. British missionaries denounced Zoroastrianism as a false religion and denigrated Zoroastrian religious practices as absurd superstitions. Missionaries also attributed British ascendancy to Protestantism. The close causal relationship between religion and civilization was proffered as a reason for Indian backwardness and a liberal rationale for colonialism.[1] The Parsis engaged in intense and prolonged dialogue with these Protestant missionaries. As each side entered the fray, they were forced to articulate and clarify their own positions toward religion. This constitutes a unique dialogue, which, owing to proselytization restrictions, does not exist between Protestantism and Islam.

From the outset, therefore, social and political vitality was understood as a function of religious "truth." As Parsis were increasingly attracted by British social and political values, they began to see a need for religious reform. The impetus for change thus came not from within the Zoroastrian religious establishment, but from the wealthy merchant community leaders. There was also a strong internal theological dimension behind the Zoroastrian reform movement. If, as Parsis insisted, their religion was true and valid, then it must necessarily be compatible with scientific truths and be able to defend itself against theological challenges. Priests were seen as incapable of responding to the missionary attacks, and their "ignorance" was blamed for the prevalence of superstitions. Theological debates concerned the viability of Zoroastrianism in a new age and its ability to support if not promote new ideas and values; in short, debates circled around Zoroastrianism's capacity to generate progress and civilization. Religious reform was a solution, a means of engendering modernity.

This early generation of Parsi reformers also initiated new contacts with Iran and sought to regenerate the Zoroastrian community there. Reform took root in Iran in the context of centralization, modernization, and secularization measures sponsored by the Qajar and, later, Pahlavi shahs. In India the first generation of Parsi merchant reformers was replaced by a second generation of scholars and Zoroastrian priests who emerged from new, reformed educational and religious institutions. They engaged in intimate dialogue with the emerging field of religious studies scholarship in the West and took up religious reform, no longer primarily as a defense against missionary attacks, but in order to reconcile Zoroastrianism with ideas of evolutionism and historicism prevalent in international scholarly circles.

The question of instrumentalism is a complicated one. It is not as simple as identifying which came first, desire for social reform or genuine theological reexamination. The question itself presupposes a false binary. It is true that reformers were deeply concerned about religion's effect on society, but this is not to say that they took an instrumentalist approach to religious reform. Reformers were absolutely convinced that religion itself was not only the cornerstone of change, but also the cornerstone of individual morality and community health. They also firmly believed in the truth of their religion and that this truth had become overlaid with false accretions, owing largely to the exigencies of survival in a predominantly Hindu milieu, but partly also as a result of the evolution of human society. Reformers engaged in serious theological reconsideration in order to recover their original, true religion and believed that such a resuscitation of "true" beliefs and practices would result in progress and civilization. It would be artificial to insist on a distinction between a genuine theological project and social reform—one simply cannot untangle the two. So while new social values may have prompted the internal criticism of religion, it was reformers' commitment to the centrality of religion, as a belief system, as a repository of eternal truth, and as the fountainhead of morality, that they believed must be resuscitated in order to generate progress and civilization.

Rational Religion

Religious reform entailed the transformation of the nature and function of religion in society, not the elimination or marginalization of religion. It was characterized especially by the rationalization of religion. Rational religion as it was then defined eliminated external mediation between individuals and God. The personal relationship of an individual with God was expressed as consciousness of God and led to the interiorization of piety. As a result, sacred texts gained in importance as the sites of God's intentions that could be understood through human reason and empirical readings. Texts were thus the only mediators between God and individuals. God's intentions were embedded in, and ultimately retrievable from, sacred texts. This "discernability of intent" meant that individuals were empowered to try to discern God's intent—and in so doing to develop their own consciousness of God. The privileging of texts over practices also led to the categorization and systematization of religions that did not have a sole authoritative text akin to the Bible or the Quran. Here I am thinking of the well-known example of the systematization and consequent reconceptualization of Hinduism. Zoroastrianism experienced a similar refashioning. In both instances, European scholars played seminal roles in determining new canons for these religions and in positing categories based on a Christian template that both explicitly and implicitly shaped Zoroastrianism in new ways.

Another consequence of the rationalization of religion was the denunciation of ritual as irrational. Rational religion, with its emphasis on individual knowledge of the Divine, rejected religious ritual performance as the manifest failure to understand underlying intent. Ritual thus lacked any intrinsic value. The *discernability of intent* made ritual superfluous at best, and at worst an obstacle to spiritual consciousness. Moreover, the performance of ritual implied a specific location of the sacred in both time and space. In other words, ritual, as performed in certain prescribed ways, places, and times, was thereby limited to those ways, places, and times. Rational religion de-emphasized ritual as circumscribing the sacred. As in Calvinism, the location of the sacred in individual consciousness freed the sacred from spatial and temporal constraints.[2] The sacred became unlimited and unbounded. The sacred was embodied in individual piety and as such informed all actions; all behavior was thus a function of piety and imbued with moral content.

Historicism and the Destruction of Tradition

Religious rationalization was linked to a new understanding of tradition. In the late nineteenth century, reformers and scholars alike developed a new awareness of historical context. They believed that the history of human society was a function of changing contexts, that change over time was socially dependent. Historicism shattered the myth of tradition, rendering it impossible to see it as natural, inevitable, or unchanging. Rather, tradition itself was constructed—a product of social and historical context. Religion was no longer "Truth" as continuously practiced since the time of the Prophet Zoroaster but instead the product of human understanding—which in turn was influenced by changing political, intellectual, and social contexts. Only sacred text(s) were authoritative. The constructed nature of tradition, as opposed to its eternal truth value, meant that the future and past were malleable. As a result, the past and the future emerged as sites of construction. Historicism enabled the conception of the modern through a reconstruction of the past. This consciousness of tradition through the embrace of historicism led to the positing of "modern" as tradition's binary. Modernity was conceived of in opposition to tradition *by definition*. I believe that for this reason, historicism is thus the intellectual hallmark of modernity in the Middle East and South Asia.[3]

Religious reform was posited not as modernizing religion, but as a return to an original "true" religion. Religious reform involved identifying "true" religion as the intent of God, rather than as currently practiced and/or dictated by tradition. Reformers insisted that "true" religion was the original, pure essence of religion, not something new. Reform thus was not presented as a process of inventing or modernizing religion, but rather as a rescue mission, a resuscitation of an obscured "truth" from the accretions and distortions of tradition. Yet in this process religion was certainly reimagined and reconceptualized along new lines with novel modes of practice. Reformers' appropriation of the claim to discern intent in sacred texts enabled fresh and often radical reinterpretations. For Zoroastrian reformers, it was not a question of *which religion* was conducive to "progress and civilization," but rather "how can a religion modify itself *to assume certain forms* that would be conducive to progress and civilization." Reformers were remarkably consistent in their articulation of the form that "true" religion should take.

The reevaluation of religious tradition entailed a two-pronged approach.[4] Reformers thought that religion was both an impediment to the promotion of "progress and civilization" and conducive of it. Religion *as currently understood and practiced* was a hindrance to "progress and civilization." Yet religion, if *reconceived and differently practiced,* would promote "progress and civilization." On the one hand, religious reform was reactive. It aimed to remove religious institutions, ideas, and practices that were believed to be obstacles to "progress and civilization." On the other hand, religious reform was also proactive. Most reformers did not want to eliminate religion. Rather, they were convinced that if religion were reformulated and differently practiced, it would turn into an engine of modernity.

One important consequence of the historicization of tradition and the associated emphasis on the individual's rational ability to retrieve the essence of religion in sacred texts was a profound anticlericalism. This anticlericalism assumed both intellectual and institutional forms. Intellectually, rational, scientific textual analysis replaced the former authority of tradition and canonical interpretations of texts. With individuals asserting the ability, and thus implicitly the *authority* to interpret texts, the religious establishment was accused of upholding false religion and of being unscientific and irrational. The religious establishment was divested of its monopoly on the mediation of divine intent and interpretation of texts.[5]

Enlightened Religion, the Individual, and Social Change

In the nineteenth century, reformers understood that the individual was at the center of any substantive social or political change. The establishment of a modern state and society revolved around the citizen. The citizen was *both the subject and the agent of change.* Citizens were the principal prerequisite of modern state and society and, at the same time, generative of it. Religious reform, as entailing the creation of a private individualized consciousness manifest in public morality, emerged as the sine qua non of larger social and political reform. Reformers articulated their programs as "character" transformation.[6] Religion and society were indissolubly connected. Not only must reform be *accompanied* by religious reform, but reform itself was in fact a *product* of religious reform. Religious reformers believed that religion was causally generative of "progress and civilization." Interiorized piety emphasized individual social responsibility and thus the formation of modern citizens. It also created new relationships between the individual, religion, and society.

Change required new institutions and laws, but also new political and social cultures that depended on educating citizens about their new relationship to state and society. Religious reformers, as social reformers, were thus very interested in the sorts of individuals formed by religion. They were concerned about creating specific sensibilities and dispositions that they believed were themselves productive of social responsibility and, ultimately, progress. Rational religion, characterized by monotheism, the individual's spiritual relationship to God, and the downplaying of ritual over the interiorization of piety, was believed to be conducive of just the sort of sensibilities and dispositions required in the modern age to generate social progress, women's rights, modern science, and, ultimately, citizens in secular states. Religion was the cornerstone, the sine qua non of any other substantive change and the beating heart of progress.

The relationship of religion to private and public space also changed fundamentally. The shift in piety from the public demonstration of sectarian identity to individual consciousness of God led to both the privatization of religion and, at the same time, the secularization of public space. As ritual performance gave way to private contemplation of God, worship itself moved from the public space to the private space of individual consciousness. The *practice* of rituals was privatized, whereas civic responsibility came to be "performed" in public.

Religious difference became a function of a historicized understanding of tradition, rather than essential, truth-based difference. In other words, difference became merely historical, not essential. Such religious universalism de-emphasized sectarianism and facilitated the emergence of new secular public spaces that were shared equally between citizens, regardless of religious affiliation. Citizens thus were theoretically equal in relationship to the state, in terms of both rights as well as social and political responsibilities. In this sense, the modern citizen emerged alongside a modern, secular public. This was not uniform across the Middle East and India, however, and remained stunted in Iran owing to incomplete secularization of the legal system.

Secularism should not, therefore, be understood as the elimination of religion from society. In the Middle East and Indian contexts, secularization meant the elimination of a religion of state, legal equality of citizens regardless of faith, and state control of law and education. Secularization of the public sphere and the privatization of religion profoundly altered but, I would argue, did not diminish the role of religion in society. Rather, reformers aimed to imbue *all* actions with religious meaning. Reformers believed that the internalization of piety would lead individuals to recognize that God's intent was for them to behave morally in this world. Ethics was a matter of conscious moral behavior, rather than the correct performance of specific, and thus parochial religious rituals. "True" religion broke down barriers between private and public realms, claiming both as stages upon which the conscious moral individual acted. The moral individual, not the dutiful performer of religious ritual, was the desired object of reform.

The debates over religion initiated by reformers gradually created new public spaces where texts and traditions were debated and reconstructed and where definitions and assumptions about religion were crystallized and propagated. Individual citizens participated in debates in journals and reform societies and laid claim to an individualized understanding of God through their readings of sacred texts. The moral citizen that resulted was conscious of God and of his or her own social responsibility. Benedict Anderson's famous theory concerning the severing of mediation between individuals and states and the construction of horizontal ties between citizens as a prerequisite of modern states applies well to this process.[7] As a result, corporate identities, primarily defined as religious identities, were dismantled to make way for national identities that transcended religious differences.

The privatization of particularism and the public performance of common commitment *as citizens* also facilitated the construction of national identities and solidarities. The individualization of subjectivity created the modern citizen and popular sovereignty, further marginalizing the religious establishment and promoting secular states. Public space emerged as national space rather than spaces fractured by religious identities. The resultant public sphere was a secular one, but inhabited by religious individuals. As Pamela Voekel has noted in conjunction with Catholic Reformism in Mexico, the interiorization of piety led to the formation of pious citizens with "divinely illuminated consciences."[8] The modern state emerged as one based on a virtuous citizenry. There thus were theological premises behind ideas of equality, citizenship, secular space, and individual civic cum pious consciousness.

Modernity and the Production of Knowledge

Religious reform is part of the larger story of reform and modernization in India and the Middle East, and the non-West more generally. The West has long claimed ownership of modernity and with it "progress and civilization." The West's ability to define modernity rests on claims to have generated it. These claims are based in part on the creation of a dichotomy between the West and the non-West, one that appropriates desirable qualities to the West and, in so doing, rejects undesirable qualities as belonging to the non-West.

It follows that modernization necessarily involves Westernization. The West's claim to have originated modernity explicitly means that other societies seeking to modernize must follow the path blazed by the West—they must imitate the West in order to become modern. Such claims legitimize colonialism as a "civilizing" mission and argue that it was only through Western agency that "other" societies could be pushed along the linear path to modernity. Thus, as Uday Mehta points out, there is no fundamental inconsistency between British Liberalism and British imperialism. Liberalism is not just a whitewashing or what he calls "a ruse and gloss of the empire"—something fundamentally contradictory to empire—but is inseparable from the patrimonialism implicit and explicit in Liberalism.[9]

Reformers struggled with the seductive power of the West's powerful definition of modernization, already well established by the mid-nineteenth century, as well as its practical implications. Some did accept the equation of modernization with Westernization and advocated large-scale adoption of Western institutions and ideas. In India, S. Bhattacharya terms this equation the "pupil's progress" paradigm, which posits Indian stasis and passivity as opposed to Western progress and agency. Only through imitation of the West can India develop "progress and civilization."[10] This view was even more widely accepted in the post–World War I Middle East when the defeat of the Ottomans by European powers seemed to confirm Western claims to define modernity and power. Of course, not all non-Western reformers accepted the equation of modernity with the West. Nonetheless, these claims affected their own understanding of modernity, and of its prerequisites. The Western claim to having *originated* modernity explains the frequency of non-Western counterclaims to their own origins of modernity. Claiming prior origins was fundamentally a way of insisting on the universality of modernity, and multiple paths to its achievement, as opposed to the imitative "adoption" of Western forms. Ironically, these very counterclaims contributed to the validation of the *importance* of origins, which reinforced the essentialization of culture and delegitimized adaptation as "inauthentic."

More recent scholarship on the relationship of the non-West to Western claims to modernity has emphasized its complexity. In particular, contemporary modernity theorists such as Mohamad Tavakoli-Targhi, Ali Behdad, and Peter Van der Veer argue eloquently for a more faceted and nuanced relationship between the West and the non-West.[11] They point to the internal heterogeneity and discontinuities as well as reciprocity that have characterized the non-West's relationship with the West. They have shown that the relationship was both interactive and contemporaneous, with influence moving in both directions, not simply unilaterally. The idea of reciprocity is crucial in explaining the fashioning of images and tropes of self and other by both the West *and the non-West* and how they were employed to legitimate and delegitimate different reform programs.[12]

This book seeks to uncover the hidden mechanics of the modernization paradigm and the West's claims to define "progress and civilization" as it interacted with Zoroastrian reform movements. As emphasized by Tavakoli-Targhi and Van der Veer, construction and influence went in both directions. The larger story is thus equally about *Western construction of self and other* through interaction with the non-West *and* about *non-Western construction of self and other* through interaction with the West. Both sites were "laboratories" for imagining modernity, although the West's political and military power enabled it to deny the interactive and constructed nature of this process.[13]

In this book, I focus on how Western definitions of "modernity" and modern religion were variously interpreted, accepted, rejected, and modified by Zoroastrian religious reformers.[14] In so doing, I emphasize reformers' interactive dialogue with these definitions, their diversity of opinions, and the arguments they used to legitimize their claims. The intellectual project of determining the path to modernity was one of profound agency, reciprocity, and contemporaneity with the West.[15] It was also fundamentally an exercise in the power of definition. In this undertaking I am deeply influenced by Bourdieu's notion of the intellectual field and the constant jostling for centrality expressed as "intellectual orthodoxy."[16] These ideas are particularly useful in this study where so much of the debate concerns the power to define and categorize as a way of producing knowledge and "truth." To take one example, reformers universally denounce "superstition." Yet there is no a priori definition of superstition. Rather, it is the ability to *define* a practice as superstitious—and the *centrality of evaluative criteria*—not the practice itself that explains the assignation of "superstition." *Superstition* is a delegitimizing term, just as *authenticity* is a legitimizing term. In particular, I explore the ways in which imagining modernity and its prerequisites involved the production of knowledge. Western colonialism and the construction of the myths of self and other were deeply implicated in the production of new disciplines of knowledge. It is no coincidence that the period of Western colonialism witnessed the emergence of the academic disciplines of anthropology, linguistics, comparative religious studies, and others. As pointed out by Edward Said, the Orientalist became the central authority *for* the Orient.[17] These fields produced knowledge of the self and other and were complicit in legitimizing colonialism as the bestowing of "civilization" on the non-West.

Scholarship on the effects of Orientalism on the non-West has primarily focused on the *outcome* of Orientalism, namely, the legitimization of colonialism. Yet I am more interested in exploring the ways in which religion was at the center of the Orientalist projection of self and other. Peter Van der Veer's scholarship on Britain and India has convinced me that religion was actually the *principal criterion* in the Western creation of modernity.[18] Religion was a central battleground for the Western creation and claim to modernity and, conversely, in its assignation of backwardness to the Middle East and India. Religious antipathy, cloaked or uncloaked, is obvious in much of the European travel writing to the Middle East and India. But I would argue that this antagonism is more symptomatic of a fundamental religious outlook than simply the result of an "anti-Hindu" or "anti-Islamic" bias. Rather, it is indicative of the Western (largely Protestant) formulation of *modern religion through the scholarly discipline of religious studies* and the related process of claiming modern religion as quintessentially Protestant and the attribution of backward religion to "others"—not only to Hinduism, but to Zoroastrianism and Islam as well. James Mill's influential *History of British India* (1817) exemplified the belief that religion defined civilization. He wrote that "everything in Hindustan was transacted by the Deity. The laws were promulgated, the people were classified, the government established, by the Divine Being. The astonishing exploits of the Divinity were endless in that sacred land. For every stage of life from the cradle to the grave; for every hour of the day; for every function of nature; for every social transaction, God prescribed a number of religious observances."[19]

For Mill and others, religion was *the* defining difference between civilizations. And since civilization resulted from religion, religious difference embodied and reinforced the dichotomy of modern versus traditional, rational religion versus irrational religion, morality versus immorality, civilized versus backward. In this way, a causal connection was claimed between rational religion and the moral citizen. The non-West, defined by its civilization and irrational religions as backward, thus needed religious reform in order to claim modernity. To be modern was to modernize religion. Non-Western reformers concurred with the causally generative role of religious reform in the construction of modern citizens. Religious reform *was* social reform, just as civilization *was* modernity. Their project was to create new individual subjectivities, modern citizens, secular space, and a new public.

The relationship of Protestantism to Zoroastrian religious reform is a slippery one. Akin to the Western claim to modernity, Protestantism in particular has claimed paternity of the promotion of science, rationalism, individualism, and thus modernity. Religious reform movements that focused on an interiorization of piety, anticlericalism, and anti-ritualism consciously looked to Protestantism as an example of "progressive" religion. More important, Protestant definitions of "true" religion had a profound impact on the rearticulation of Zoroastrianism. Yet like larger questions of Orientalism, one must not allow Protestantism's own claim to modernity to obscure the impetus and drive of other religious reform movements. Religious reform that promoted religious rationalism and consequent individualism, secularism, and the modern citizen are not facile imitations or de facto Protestantizations. Rather, I concur with religious historian Pamela Voekel who argues that similar religious reform movements can and do emerge in non-Protestant religions.[20] Religious reform, based on new readings of sacred texts, cannot be claimed as either a product of or a process unique to Protestantism. Religious reform movements in Europe, whether Protestant, Catholic, or Orthodox, all tended to reinforce notions of individualism that led to the emergence of citizens. Early modern European reform movements "sought to reform or purify the self by espousing a simplified, internalized piety. Out of this reformed Christian self emerged the idea of a new kind of political subject, one who had enough self-regulated discipline to become a tacit participant in the state."[21] From *consciousness of God* emerged *individual moral consciences* necessary to participatory citizenship and popular sovereignty. Individualism thus has profound theological premises. Zoroastrian reformers themselves understood the causal relationship between rational religion and the modern citizen and were firmly convinced that their own religion was intrinsically rational and could, like Protestantism, be the agent of progress and civilization.

Chapter Outline

Our story begins in Bombay, in the midst of British governance and the rapid rise of the wealthy Parsi merchants to prominence. Chapter 1 contextualizes the impetus and shape of the Zoroastrian reform movement and discuss how, from the beginning, religious and social reform were linked. Chapter 2 charts the stormy dialogue between Protestant missionaries and Zoroastrians in India as a means of exploring early ideas concerning "true" religion as they were both contested and shared. Parsi reform ideas are the exclusive focus of Chapter 3, where I examine the emerging contours of Parsi ideas concerning religious reform, from

Reformists to more orthodox defenders of tradition. Chapter 4 looks at the international religious studies scholarship that dominated the intellectual climate and largely supplanted earlier, missionary-driven, religious dialogue. Western religious studies scholarship relied heavily on historicism and evolutionism to explain the nature and function of evolved, progressive, enlightened religion. In this chapter, I examine the ideas of a number of scholars who either formulated the field of comparative religious studies, were themselves engaged in Zoroastrian studies, or both. This analysis provides a broad intellectual context for the second generation of Zoroastrian scholars and reformers that are the focus of chapter 5. This second generation included both Reformists and orthodox who, despite important differences, shared many premises about the nature and function of religion, as well as intellectual tools for recovering "true" religion from history. Chapter 6 charts the beginning of a new relationship between the Parsis and the Zoroastrians in Iran, as the former committed themselves to religious and social reform in Iran. It also looks at how the Parsi "rediscovery" of ancient Iran influenced ideas concerning the Zoroastrian historical tradition and its relationship to an Iranian homeland. Chapter 7 takes up the story of Zoroastrian reform in Iran from the mid-nineteenth century through the early Pahlavi period. The chapter focuses on the Iranian experience of religious reform, particularly regarding the powerful role of merchant community leaders. It also situates Zoroastrian reform in Iran in the context of modernization movements in an Islamic state. The chapter investigates Iranian Zoroastrian reform's special relationship to state-sponsored Iranian nationalism. Zoroastrian identity, and the scripting of modernity onto the ancient Zoroastrian past, made Zoroastrian reform, and the new ideas of the generative capacity of religion in society, community, and state, an essential component of the Iranian construction of modernity. Chapter 8 explores the religious reformist writings of the most prominent Iranian Zoroastrian of his generation, Kay Khosrow Shahrokh. A man of his age, Shahrokh's life spanned the transition of the Zoroastrian community from rural to urban, from agricultural to mercantile and from uncertain status as a religious minority to prominence in the court. Though predominantly recognized as a political leader, Shahrokh was deeply engaged in rethinking religion and intimately aware of the generative possibilities implicit in rational religion for the promotion of national identity, equality of citizenship, and secularism in Iran. In the conclusion to the book I argue that religious reformers were involved in an intellectual revolution of reshaping religion and that the creation of the pious citizen was intended to generate modernity, secularism, and national identity. I also insist on the centrality of religious reform to the project of modernity in the Middle East and South Asia and consider reasons that has not been reflected in the historiography.

A Preliminary Introduction to Zoroastrianism in Iran and India

Zoroastrianism is an ancient religion that originated with its namesake, the Prophet Zoroaster, in northeastern Iran between 1700 and 1000 BCE. Zoroaster is believed to have received revelations from God, which he communicated to his followers. After many years of little conversion, Zoroastrianism gained a large following after the successful conversion of King Gushtasp.[22] Zoroastrianism claims a large number of religious texts, collectively titled the Avesta.[23] They are written in the Avestan language, a close relation of Sanskrit. Much of the commentary on scriptures is written in the Pahlavi language, the language of pre-Islamic Sassanian Iran, and many of them date from this period (224 BC to AD 651). Accurate dating of the texts in the eighteenth and nineteenth centuries challenged previous acceptance of the texts as scriptures. It is now generally accepted that only a small part of the Avesta, the Gathas, or hymns of Zoroaster, date to the time of Zoroaster himself. The Gathas are now believed to be the only extant part of the Avesta actually composed by Zoroaster. Much of the remainder of the Avesta is of later, and unknown, provenance.

Zoroastrianism, like all religions, has been variously understood and practiced over thousands of years. Constant are the belief in a primary god—Ahura Mazda—and of man's participation in the divine struggle between good and evil. Leading the forces of good is God himself—Ahura Mazda—symbolized by light, honesty, truth, and justice. Evil, led by the evil spirit Angra Mainyu or Ahriman, represents darkness, deceit, falsehood, and injustice. Zoroastrian theology is woven around the principal core of "good thoughts, good deeds, good words." Zoroastrian ethics consists of man's conscious choice to align him- or herself with God and the forces of good against evil. Belief in the ultimate triumph of good over evil, resurrection, and the existence of heaven and hell is fundamental.

Zoroastrian devotion places a heavy emphasis on ritual behavior and purification. These foci are manifested in daily prayers and ritual cleanliness. There are strict prohibitions against pollution—both ritual and physical—of the basic elements of earth, fire, air, and water. Two of the most distinctive Zoroastrian practices are the keeping of a sacred fire and the manner of disposal of the dead on mountaintops or in man-made towers called *dakhmeh*s. The existence of fire in worship ceremonies led to the Zoroastrians being accused by their monotheistic Islamic detractors of worshiping fire. Zoroastrians have consistently denied this allegation, arguing that fire serves as a symbolic orientation toward God, much like the direction of prayer for Muslims. It is difficult to determine the nature of beliefs concerning fire from the inception of Zoroastrianism to the present, since evidence of beliefs in some periods is scarce. Some scholars have argued that fire has always been symbolic, others that it was in fact worshiped. Certainly, with the hegemony of Islam in Iran and the associated pressures on the minority Zoroastrian community, it is feasible that monotheism became more firmly accepted in Iranian lands following the Arab invasion.

Zoroastrianism probably influenced the later religions of Judaism, Christianity, and Islam as well as strains such as Manichaeanism. Scholars remain intrigued with the idea of Zoroastrianism as the possible originator, or at least the earliest known example, of notions of resurrection, heaven, and hell. Zoroastrianism is often presented as the first monotheistic religion, especially since the nineteenth century when nonmonotheistic religions suffered charges of evolutionary "backwardness." The possibility of finding the "ur-religion" (or originating religion) prompted intense scholarly inquiry into Zoroastrianism by European linguists and theologians beginning in the eighteenth century and flourishing in the nineteenth century.

The dispute concerning whether Zoroastrianism is dualistic or monotheistic continues, unresolved. Different theories, and of course (mis)understandings of Zoroastrianism over the ages, make the debate particularly difficult to settle. The principal issues in the debate concern historicism, the definition of dualism, and the perennial problem of sources. Zoroastrianism, as one of mankind's oldest religions, was understood and practiced differently in different times. It is possible, therefore, that it may have been dualistic in some periods and not others. The appellation of dualism itself is problematic, since the Zoroastrian emphasis on the cosmic battle between good and evil may obscure recognition of the existence of a fundamental monotheism. Our understanding of how Zoroastrianism was practiced and understood is also colored by the sources and the difficulty in ascertaining how these sources were interpreted in different times. The emphatic accusation of dualism by Muslims was certainly influenced by antagonism, and probably influenced European travelers' understandings of Zoroastrianism as well.

The principal theories are, first, that Zoroastrianism is and has always been monotheistic and that Zoroaster was the first to preach monotheism in a polytheistic religious landscape. Some scholars, however, believe that after Zoroaster's death, Zoroastrianism reincorporated elements of the premonotheistic religious conception and thus was essentially misunderstood by the Zoroastrians themselves. Advocates of these two positions insist on an unchanging essence of Zoroastrianism as monotheistic. Proponents of this position include nineteenth-century philologist Martin Haug, twentieth-century missionary and New Testament scholar James Hope Moulton, and, more recently, Professor Mary Boyce.[24]

Another group of scholars stresses the changing nature of Zoroastrianism, rather than positing an enduring essence. These scholars range from insisting on Zoroastrianism as a form of polytheism—often detractors of Zoroastrianism such as nineteenth-century missionary John Wilson[25]—to others such as modern scholar Susan Maneck who emphasizes change over time. Maneck points to the fact that it was in the Islamic period that monotheism was embraced and dualism downplayed and argues that Zoroastrianism, however conceived of by Zoroaster himself, was practiced as a form of dualism and only gradually morphed into a primarily monotheistic religion.[26] In the same vein, William Darrow has illustrated that in the Islamic period there emerged a marked tendency to pattern Zoroaster after an Islamic model of prophetic activity.[27]

Zoroastrianism was practiced, although possibly not exclusively, in the Achaemenid period in Iran (553–330 BC). After the reconquest of Iran by the Sassanians on the heels of the invasion of Alexander the Great (334 BC) and the subsequent Parthian Empire (247 BC–AD 224), Zoroastrianism was adopted as the state religion. Most of Zoroastrian religious writings derive from this period up until the Arab conquest that overthrew the Sassanians in the mid-seventh century (AD 651). With the Arab invasion and spread of Islam in the former Sassanian Empire, many Zoroastrians were converted or killed and many fire temples destroyed and religious texts lost. The status of Zoroastrians as "people of the book" remained questionable, and as a result, Zoroastrians incurred greater pressure to convert than did Christians and Jews. Over the course of the centuries, the Zoroastrian community declined, eventually coming to reside primarily in the southern towns of Yazd and Kerman.

Zoroastrians in Iran

The condition of Zoroastrians in Iran until the secularization policies of the late nineteenth and twentieth centuries was largely determined by their status as non-Muslim minorities in an Islamic state. The Islamic legal code (shari'a) stipulated that non-Muslim monotheists be accorded protected yet inferior status in an Islamic state and society. The shari'a specifically protected non-Muslim "peoples of the book" (adherents of other monotheistic faiths who had received revelations from earlier prophets than the Prophet Muhammad) from harassment or persecution. They were accorded the right to practice their faith, the right to state protection, and the prerogative of regulating their own personal status laws (such as marriage, death rites, and so on). However, they also suffered serious restrictions and limitations. These constraints included inferior legal status relative to Muslims (and thus handicaps when dealing with Muslims and the state) as well as various occupational, physical, and sartorial barriers. Non-Muslims could not, for example, ride horses or build houses higher than Muslim houses and were limited to simple, unadorned clothing. Legally, socially, and symbolically, non-Muslims were inferior subjects in an Islamic polity.

The Zoroastrians suffered the further ignominy of their tenuous place in the monotheistic fold—often being considered polytheists, fire worshippers, and not fellows in the Abrahamic tradition. Although they consistently insisted on their monotheism and even went so far as to claim that their prophet, Zoroaster, was one and the same as Abraham, Muslims typically considered them idolaters.[28] Their position vis-à-vis the shari'a was thus more tenuous than the Christians and Jews, which made them particularly prone to persecution and harassment.[29] Napier Malcolm, a missionary who spent five years in Yazd, commented on the complicated religious status assigned to Jews and Zoroastrians: "[The Jews'] religion of course is held in much greater respect than that of the Parsis, for they are people of the Book, and although the Persian Shiahs granted the Zoroastrians a certain share in this status, when they allowed them to continue in the country on the same terms as Jews and Christians, the ordinary Yezdi of to-day hesitates considerably before he allows that Zoroaster was in any sense a prophet."[30]

2. "Idealized Portrait from a Sculpture Supposed to Represent Zoroaster," in *Zoroaster: The Prophet of Ancient Iran,* by A. V. Williams Jackson (New York: Macmillan, 1899), following p. 289, as originally included in Dosabhai Framji Karaka, *History of the Parsees* (London, 1884). Used with permission from Elibron Classics reprinted edition of Jackson, 2005.

In practice, the implementation of the shari'a depended on local and state authorities, as well as on the inclinations of local Muslim populations, ulama, and rulers. The local population could and did ignore the shari'a—either by imposing harsher restrictions or by ignoring them—and the relationship between the authority of the local governor and the shah determined the extent to which this defiance was permitted to occur. Much of the story of the persecution of non-Muslims was thus a function of their place in the contests between local and state authorities and the result of the particular inclinations of the rulers themselves.

Much of the information concerning the conditions of the Zoroastrians prior to the mid-nineteenth century comes from European travel literature. Until this time, no statistics were kept, either by the Iranian government or by the Zoroastrians themselves. Information provided by European observers, however, is often shaped by the tendency of Zoroastrians to dissimulate as well as by general Muslim prejudices and misinformation. There is enough information, however, to suggest that Zoroastrians were significantly better off prior to the assertion of ulama authority under Shah Hosayn Safavi (r. 1694–1722). The fall of the Safavid dynasty to the Afghan invaders in 1722 and the ensuing turmoil placed an already weakened population under severe strains.

Travelers to Iran in the time of Shah Abbas I (r. 1588–1629) and Abbas II (r. 1642–46) reported that there was a Zoroastrian quarter in the capital city of Isfahan. Figueroa noted in 1618 that there were as many as three thousand Zoroastrian houses in the city, the Zoroastrians there having only ten years previously been forcibly moved to the capital by Shah Abbas I.[31] During the same period, Pietro Della Valle also described the Zoroastrian quarter, called "Gauristan" after the pejorative *gaure* or *guebre*, as Zoroastrians were labeled. He wrote that "the streets [were] very wide, straight and much handsomer than those of Chiolfra [Julfa]. . . . [N]one of the houses however have more than a ground floor."[32] Tavernier spent three months in Kerman in 1654 purchasing wool. He observed that the Zoroastrians monopolized the wool trade and that the community was made up of ten thousand individuals who were "now" allowed to "live in quiet" by the king of Persia.[33] Chardin, traveling in Iran during 1664–78, reported that the Zoroastrians were all laborers, workmen, fullers, or woolen operatives and that none were involved in trade.[34]

Many of the European travelers to Iran in the seventeenth century reported in their narratives that the Zoroastrians were monotheists. For example, Father

Gabriel agreed with his predecessors Tavernier, Della Valle, and Raphael Du Mans that the Zoroastrians did not in fact worship fire: "The Gaures do not render to this fire the honours we imagine they defer to it, idolatrous beliefs. They affirm that they only recognize one God, Creator of Heaven and earth, whom they adore with an adoration which is special to him, and as for this fire which they maintain it is but an honour they bear it in recognition of the great miracle of the deliverance of their Prophet."[35] With the rising authority of the ulama in the later seventeenth century, Zoroastrians came under increased state pressure and were further restricted in occupation, dress, and freedom of religion. Father Sanson wrote in 1683–91 of the Zoroastrians that "[they] groan under a cruel Slavery: They are forbid the Liberal Arts, and exercise only the mand [*sic*] Drudgery of Labourers, Gardeners and Porters: They are always put upon the vilest and most painful Works. . . . [T]he modern Persians . . . treat 'em worse than they do the Jews: they accuse 'em of worshipping the *Sun* and the *Fire*."[36] A few years later, Gemelli noted that the Zoroastrians no longer lived in the spacious suburbs of Isfahan described by Tavernier some forty years previously.[37]

Persecution of the Zoroastrians intensified with the accession of Shah Sultan Hosayn to the Safavid throne in 1699. The shah signed a decree of forcible conversion of the Zoroastrians in Isfahan, who were subsequently converted to Islam or massacred for refusing. Their fire temple was destroyed. Le Bryn, visiting Isfahan in 1703, wrote, "The Guebres of this age are a set of poor ignorant creatures who . . . have lost the true knowledge of their ancestors manner of worship, of which they retain nothing but the letter."[38] He contrasted their current status with that in the heyday of Safavid central authority: "In the reign of King Abbas they enjoyed the same liberty as was granted the Armenians and Christians . . . [but now are] reduced to a low degree of poverty."[39]

The Afghan invasion of 1722 and demise of the Safavids launched Iran into civil war for more than fifty years, before the Qajar dynasty claimed the throne and gradually asserted its sovereignty over the country. Not surprisingly, the Zoroastrians suffered greatly during this period of instability and lack of central government control. Some European travelers to Iran many decades after the invasion reported that the Zoroastrians assisted the Afghan invaders. Zoroastrian tradition maintains that the community was caught between the ebbs and tides of Afghan and Safavid fortunes and suffered devastation as a result.[40]

The reconquest of Iranian lands and consequent extension of central government authority by the Qajars (1898–1924) ushered in a period of stability. Still, by the turn of the nineteenth century the Zoroastrians were found almost exclusively in the southern cities of Yazd and Kerman and their surrounding villages. As described by many travelers, Kerman and more especially Yazd were geographically isolated and difficult to reach. Napier Malcolm described Yazd as "a solitary object rising abruptly out of a vast desert that is about the nearest thing to a vacuum which Nature has yet produced."[41] Even in the 1920s it took as many as three weeks to reach Yazd from Tehran.[42] The protection afforded by their isolation allowed the Zoroastrians there to survive the chaos and destruction of the long eighteenth century more successfully than elsewhere. Population figures for the mid-nineteenth century give the number of Zoroastrians in Yazd and surrounding villages as 6,483 and in Kerman as much lower at 1,756, with a total Zoroastrian population in Iran not exceeding 7,000–8,000 individuals. Other cities in Iran had only a handful of Zoroastrians. By the turn of the century, the total Zoroastrian population had probably reached 11,000.[43]

The Zoroastrians in Yazd and Kerman had no formal community leadership or official intermediaries with the Muslim population or city governor. Sometimes individual Zoroastrians gained the respect of the governor and enjoyed a certain amount of access to the court, but such standing was personal and never formalized. Yazd retained its religious prominence as the traditional Zoroastrian ecclesiastical center, however, and there were important fire temples and pilgrimage sites in the vicinity. The religious establishment—the *mobeds*—served the community in their religious functions and maintained a rotating parish system in order to do so.[44]

Zoroastrians continued to be affected by the shari'a restrictions. The majority lived in separate parts of the city or in different surrounding villages than their Muslim neighbors. The community was further separated from the larger Muslim population by language barriers. The majority of Zoroastrians in Yazd and Kerman spoke Dari as their mother tongue, and typically only the men had a rudimentary knowledge of Persian.[45] Zoroastrians mostly worked as farmers on large Muslim landholdings, although there were some Zoroastrian landowners as well. Travelers report that they were not allowed to engage in trade, and those merchants who disobeyed this ban were located in the caravanserai, not the bazaar.[46] Zoroastrians were theoretically forbidden to ride horses, travel abroad, and to have schools, all of which strictures were rarely defied.[47] Zoroastrians continued to wear shari'a-specified clothing, usually described as yellow or undyed.[48] E. G. Browne described their clothing on a visit to Yazd and Kerman in 1887–88: "They are compelled to wear the dull yellow raiment already alluded to as a distinguishing badge; they are not permitted to wear socks, or to wind their turbans tightly and neatly, or to ride a horse; and if, when riding even a donkey, they should chance to meet a Musulman, they must dismount while he passes, and that without regard to his age or rank."[49] In addition to general intolerance and persecution, the Zoroastrian community was burdened by an onerous tax on non-Muslims, the *jazieh.*

However, the centralization policies pursued by the Qajar shahs, combined with growing international pressures, directly benefited the Zoroastrian communities in Iran. The assertion of central authority by Naser al-Din Shah (r. 1848–96) and Mozzafar al-Din Shah (r. 1896–1907) and their reformist ministers meant not only their increased willingness to intervene in provincial matters, but also their ability to force governors to implement their policies in tax, military, and legal matters. In line with the shahs' centralizing measures were the beginnings of secularization in legal and educational spheres. Schools influenced by European curricula sprang up in the capital and many of the provincial cities to educate a new cadre of government employees and elites with new skills and a growing appreciation of European political systems.

The nineteenth century also witnessed an enormous growth in European penetration of Iran—politically, economically, and on a local level—through the experience of missionary schools and medical dispensaries. European officials encouraged the shahs to regularize and facilitate commercial exchange and also urged the protection of non-Muslim minorities. The British in particular took an interest in the Zoroastrian community, even appointing a Zoroastrian as the British agent in Yazd. Browne observed the hopes that hung on this appointment at the time: "This was what the Zoroastrians so earnestly desired, for they believed that the British flag would protect their community even in times of the gravest danger."[50] Sometimes the increasing identification of Iranian minorities with Christian European protectors led to fearmongering and persecution, but for the most part minority communities benefited from outside interest and protection.[51]

The most significant international relationship as far as the Zoroastrians were concerned was with the Bombay Zoroastrian (Parsi) community. Beginning in the mid-nineteenth century, Parsis from Bombay urged British intervention on behalf of their coreligionists in Iran, funded the establishment of schools and the refurbishment of religious temples and sanctuaries, and developed a trade network of significant proportions. As a direct result, British and other European officials actively lobbied Naser al-Din Shah to abolish the despised *jazieh* tax on the Zoroastrians. He eventually did so in 1882, although it nonetheless continued to be collected in Yazd for years.[52] British officials Sir Percy Sykes and Lord Curzon both noted the enormous changes in the Zoroastrian community in Yazd and Kerman as a result of the Parsi connection. Curzon wrote, "It was about fifty years ago that the Parsis of Yezd [*sic*] began that trade with India which has since reached such considerable dimensions, and has added to the always great commercial reputation of the city. They occupy a position here not unlike that of the Chinese compradors and agents in the Treaty Ports of Japan, the bulk of the foreign trade passing through their hands, and a good deal of the home industry being likewise under their direction."[53] The Parsis were the instigators in Zoroastrian community organization, as well as religious, educational, and social reform. Parsis often enjoyed British citizenship, which gave them added leverage in dealing with local and court officials.[54]

Even with the increased stability and protection afforded the Zoroastrians later in the century, the community continued to suffer kidnappings, forced conversions (usually of marriageable girls), and even unpunished murders.[55] Browne attested to Zoroastrian status at the bottom rung of minorities, writing, "Though less liable to molestation now than in former times, they often meet with ill-treatment and insult at the hands of the more fanatical Muhammadans, by whom they are regarded as pagans, not equal even to Christians, Jews and other 'people of the book.'"[56] Acute observers such as Browne, Curzon, and Malcolm in the latter part of the century drew a clear causal connection between persecution of the Zoroastrians and weak central government. Browne explained, "Occasionally, when there is a period of interregnum, or when a bad or priest-ridden governor holds office, and the 'lutis' or roughs, of Yezd [*sic*] wax bold, worse [than sartorial restrictions] befalls them. During the period of confusion which intervened between the death of Muhammad Shah and the accession of Nasiru'd-Din Shah, the present king, many of them were robbed, beaten, and threatened with death unless they would renounce their ancient faith and embrace Islam; not a few were actually done to death."[57] Sometimes the governor was unable or unwilling to keep intolerance or the authority of the ulama in check. The Zoroastrians depended for their lives and livelihoods on the protection of the local governor, but occasionally had recourse to the shah's protection when the governor failed them.[58]

Even with increased wealth and protection later in the century, Zoroastrians still suffered from intolerance and acts of violence. Curzon attested to this fact on a trip to Yazd in 1890:

> In spite of their riches and respectability, the community is one that has always suffered, and is still exposed to, persecution. Severe disabilities are inflicted upon them in the transactions of daily or mercantile life. . . . [W]ithin the last twenty years a wealthy Parsi has been murdered in the open streets at the instigation of the mullahs, and his murderer has escaped scot-free; they are compelled to wear sober-coloured garments, and may not ride, or keep open shops, or possess high or handsome houses in the city. When they purchase property, a higher price is exacted from them than from Mohammedans; they are forced to conceal their means, and to restrict their commercial operations for fear of exciting hostile attack; while in the streets they are constantly liable to insult and personal affront.[59]

Napier Malcolm astutely summed up the context of persecution: "As a matter of fact, the so-called fanaticism of Yezd [sic] was two-thirds of it non-religious in character. There was an element of turbulency, produced by a series of weak governors; there was a real religious element; and there was an element of insularity, utterly unconnected with creed and doctrine."[60] Writing in the early twentieth century after significant improvements in Zoroastrian legal status, Malcolm correctly pointed out that "the great difficulty was not to get the law improved, but rather to get it enforced."[61]

Zoroastrians in India: The Parsis

The Zoroastrians of India, called the Parsis because of their Iranian origins, moved to India in successive migrations in the Islamic period. [62] The initial migration following the Arab conquest of Iran has been canonized as a story of religious persecution by invading Muslims. According to the account, Zoroastrians suffered at the hands of Muslims and, in order to protect themselves and safeguard their religion, escaped first to northeastern Iran, then to the island of

Hormuz, and finally to the shores of India. This generally accepted narrative of the Zoroastrian migration emphasizes Muslim religious persecution and injustice and thus identifies the Parsis as religious refugees. Recently, scholars have questioned this explanation of Parsi origins. There is a remarkable scarcity of sources on this migration. Historians are forced to rely almost entirely on two narrative accounts, the *Qisseh-ye Sanjan,* written in 1599 by a Parsi priest, and the *Qisseh-ye Zartushtian-e Hendustan,* written more than two hundred years later.[63] The story should be complicated by the fact that there were already Zoroastrians in India in the Sassanian period. Scholar Andre Wink has theorized that the Zoroastrian immigrants to India, both before and after the Muslim conquest of Iran, were primarily merchants—since evidence suggests that it was only sometime after their arrival that religious experts and priests were sent for to join them in India. He argues that competition over trade routes between the Muslims and the Zoroastrians may also have contributed to the decision to immigrate to India.[64]

Subsequent migrations, especially resulting from Safavid rulers' attempts to convert their subjects to Shiism in the sixteenth century, added to the Parsi population and cemented their close association with their Iranian "homeland." Indian princes allowed the Parsis to settle in India, where they enjoyed a great degree of community autonomy and religious freedom. The Parsis adopted the local Gujarati language and much of local dress and customs.[65] Religious syncretism, which included the veneration of the cow and bull and the abandonment of Persian, further distinguished the Parsis from their Iranian coreligionists over time.

The earliest detailed description of Parsi religious practices is found in a travel account of a French Dominican monk to India in 1322. Friar Jordanus wrote, "There be also other pagan-folk in this India who worship fire: they bury not their dead, neither do they burn them, but cast then into the midst of a certain roofless tower, and expose them totally uncovered to the fowls of heaven. These believe in two First Principles, to wit of Evil and of Good, of Darkness and of Light, matters which at present I do not propose to discuss."[66] Jordanus emphasizes Zoroastrian practice as pagan, fire worshipping, and dualistic, accusations that usually went hand in hand with and were replicated in much of the European travel literature to India and Iran over the centuries.

3. "Grand Prêtre des Gaures ou Perses devant le Feu ajant à la main son Rituel." Copper engraving from Thomas Hyde, *De Vetere Religione Persarum*, 1700.

Zoroastrians were also conspicuous at the Mughal court (1526–1857), usually as traders, craftsmen, and servants. Emperor Akhbar (1542–1605), famous for his interreligious dialogues, incorporated elements of Zoroastrianism into his syncretistic religion: *Din-i Ilahi* (the Divine Religion).[67] Akbar is reported to have kept a sacred fire in his palace and to have worn the Zoroastrian sacred cord, the *kusti*. He named a Parsi priest of Navsari as high priest of all Parsis.[68] The family of this Bhagarian priest, Meherji Rana, came to be regarded as the principal religious and political leaders of the Parsi community by subsequent rulers.[69]

Throughout this period, the principal link between the Parsis and their coreligionists in Iran remained their shared religious heritage. This relationship is memorialized in a series of written theological inquiries sent from India to

Zoroastrian priests in Iran roughly between the years 1478 and 1773. Twenty-six major questions and answers, or *rivayats,* were compiled, testifying to the ongoing religious authority of the Iranian Zoroastrian priests in Yazd and Kerman.[70] This dialogue contributed to a revival of learning among the Parsi priesthood in Navsari, India, which by the sixteenth century managed to assert political and religious hegemony over the Zoroastrian community.[71]

The gradual centralization of religious authority and associated political power of the Navsari Parsi priesthood over the community was a result of the sacking of Sanjan, India, during the Mughal conquest of the Deccan in the sixteenth century and the subsequent relocation of the sacred fire (*Atesh Bahram*) to the town of Navsari.[72] This place then became the religious center of the Parsis, serving as a site of pilgrimage, as well as the repository of a Zoroastrian manuscript library and center of learning.[73] The Navsari priests organized into an assemblage called an *anjoman* for decisions on religious matters.

Priestly authority did not go uncontested, however. In 1642 members of the Parsi laity formed a council that included both priest and lay members. This council, called a *panchayat* after the Hindu institution of a village council of elders, served as the supreme Parsi governing body in Navsari. For centuries, the *panchayat* enjoyed authority over community affairs and possessed the power of excommunication.[74] The *panchayat* remained in contest with the priesthood for ultimate authority over the community. *Panchayats* would later be established in the cities of Surat and Bombay, with differing degrees of success in supplanting the dominance of the priesthood.

Between the sixteenth and eighteenth centuries, the Parsis increasingly moved from agricultural occupations to trades related to commerce, especially shipping, trading, weaving, and carpentry, eventually coming to dominate the textile and shipbuilding industries. By the eighteenth century, few Parsis still engaged in farming, and most resided in urban areas, primarily port cities on the coast.[75] Their willingness to work with Europeans and breadth of commercial operations enabled them to become the principal brokers of the East India Company by the end of the seventeenth century. This close reciprocal relationship between the Parsis and the British would expand over the next two centuries and would deepen to include not only commercial ties, but political and cultural ties as well.[76] In 1744 the Parsi population of Surat was estimated as one hundred thousand persons, approximately one-fifth of the entire city population.[77]

Just as Surat rose to dominate trade in the sixteenth and seventeenth centuries, it would gradually be eclipsed by the rise of Bombay in the mid-eighteenth century.[78] By this time, Bombay reigned supreme as the major trade center of West India. The Parsis, so tied into the European trade networks, immigrated to Bombay as it rose in prominence and became the principal partners of the British and British East India Company there. By the turn of the nineteenth century, Parsis in Bombay were described as dominating "the Indian groups of Bombay in terms of wealth, numbers and generosity."[79] Parsi gentlemen also adopted British manners, holding European-style balls and riding through town in Western carriages.[80]

The rise of Bombay as the heart of the Parsi community deeply affected the nature and leadership of the Parsi community. Large merchants arose as the principal leaders of the community. Their prominence soon led to the marginalization of the Parsi priesthood. This shift in authority, together with the impact of the British in India, would have far-reaching consequences for the Parsis in India and would lead to the emergence of a religious and social reform movement among the Parsis.[81]

1

Bombay and Murmurs of Reform

Religion as "Civilization" and "Progress"

> We want the English language, English manners, and English behaviour for
> our wives and daughters, and until these are supplied, it is but just that the
> present gulf between the Englishman and the Indian should remain as wide
> as ever.
> —Statement by the Parsee Society, 1863

The Parsi community in India initiated reforms in the nineteenth century
largely as a result of British impact in the region. The rise of Bombay as the premier port on the western littoral and the unique relationship between the British
and the Parsis in that city had profound effects on the Zoroastrian community
itself and on their attitude toward society, tradition, and religion. A powerful Parsi
merchant class developed and assumed community leadership. British secularization policies, together with the political and economic incentives to adopt British
education and cultural sensibilities, lent a particular character to the Parsi community in Bombay. The British-style schools established in Bombay emerged as
breeding grounds for the first generation of Parsi reformers. The powerful connection between "civilization" and European knowledge and forms of religion that
guided British education led to the inseparability of social and religious reform.

The Rise of Bombay

The Zoroastrian Parsi community was fundamentally transformed by increasing
British involvement in India over the course of the eighteenth and nineteenth
centuries. Leadership of the community passed to the new class of large merchants, and the Parsis became deeply associated with British commercial and

political interests. Their close relationship also led to the adoption of British notions of modernity, "enlightened" religion, and social reform agendas. These changes spawned the Zoroastrian reform movement.

From the outset, the emergence of Bombay as a leading commercial center in India was intimately tied to both British rule of the island and the relationship between the British and the Zoroastrian merchant community that emigrated there.[1] Bombay's harbor and potential as a trading hub were noted by the very first British visitor to India, the Jesuit priest Thomas Stephens in 1579.[2] Nearly a century later, in 1662, Bombay was acquired from the Portuguese.[3] Increased British control over the area catapulted Bombay into a leading commercial center in India beginning in the 1730s.[4]

Bombay, as the only city virtually "created" by the British in India, was unique.[5] In addition to the commercial opportunities in this new port city, Bombay offered religious neutrality and the practice of legal impartiality, something rare on the mainland, particularly in Portuguese-controlled territory.[6] Bombay was a destination for those fleeing the insecurity of the mainland.[7] The British policy of religious neutrality often in practice connoted tolerance. For example, in 1792 as a result of complaints by the Parsi community of British intrusion into a burial site, the East India Company threatened to expel anyone from "the Honourable Company's service" who failed to respect local religious customs.[8]

As minorities in Indian society, the Parsis were not closely associated with the Indian ruling classes and were profoundly attracted by British-controlled Bombay. Parsis allied themselves with the British government in India in order to protect themselves from local Indian rulers. Many Parsis worked for the British, sometimes even becoming British subjects. As astutely pointed out by John Hinnells, the attraction was mutual: "It was not only the Parsis who respected the British but the British also respected the Parsis because in them they saw, in a strange and foreign land, people who shared similar morals, principles, and even a physical similarity."[9] This mutual regard intensified as a result of Parsis' adoption of Western customs. The Europeanization of Parsis was frequently remarked upon by travelers. Lieutenant Moore, writing in 1794, commented:

> Some of them have two or three country houses, furnished in all the extravagance of European taste; with elegant and extensive gardens, where European gentlemen are frequently invited, and where they are always welcome to

entertain their own private parties. . . . [W]e have seen Parsee merchants give balls, suppers, and entertainments to the whole settlement; and some of them ride in English chariots. . . . The Parsees have been often known to behave to English gentlemen, respecting pecuniary concerns, in a manner highly liberal. . . . A Parsee beggar was never known; and their women, who are fair as Europeans, are proverbially chaste; so that a harlot is as rare as a beggar. Upon the whole they are a very handsome race of people.[10]

As a result, the Parsis became favored trading partners and political go-betweens with the British.[11] The British deliberately fostered the Parsis' intermediary role as part of their larger ruling strategy. Political and educational policies deepened British association with Indian minorities, particularly the Parsis. The intertwining of British political interests with the inculcation of British culture was exemplified in the famous speech on educational policy by Lord Macaulay in 1835 where he declared that the British actively sought to create a class "who may be interpreters between us and the millions whom we govern; a class of persons, Indian in blood and colour, but English in taste, in opinions, in morals and in intellect."[12]

The Demise of Clerical Authority

The rise of Bombay as a center of international commerce and Parsis' close association with British political and cultural interests led to the rise of Parsi merchants as the leaders of their community. Through the process of immigrating to Bombay, Parsis left social and religious structures behind. By the mid-nineteenth century, more than half of the Parsis in Bombay were involved in commerce—as bankers, merchants, or brokers.[13] These new mercantile elites were bound up in British commerce and were more receptive to the advantages that connections to the British, as well as British education and accoutrements of lifestyle, had to offer.

Prior to the eighteenth century, the Parsi community had no fixed written code of laws. Internal civil and religious affairs and the administration of justice were in the hands of the Zoroastrian clergy, the *dasturs*. The *dasturs'* authority within their community was based on their religious duties and the social and political authority associated with them. As unofficial heads of their community, the *dasturs* also functioned as intermediaries with Indian state authorities.

In keeping with the general British policy of honoring native customs, the British governor of Bombay, Gerald Aungier (1669–77), encouraged various Indian communities to form organizations (*panchayats*) to regulate their internal affairs.[14] In 1673 the Parsi Panchayat was established with five members, all from elite merchant families originally from Surat.[15] The Panchayat functioned as a governing body to assist Parsis moving to Bombay and to resolve civil disputes within the growing Parsi community there.[16] Although membership was hereditary, in the 1740s membership was expanded to include other, newer, elites, primarily individuals associated with shipbuilding and the China trade.

Some years later, the *panchayat* appealed to the British to officially recognize their authority.[17] They also requested permission to take punitive measures against Parsis who defied *panchayat* rulings. The then governor of Bombay, Williams Hornby, granted their request, although restricting the *panchayat*'s authority to the nonpriestly Parsis. The declaration read: "To the Parsees, not of the Priest Caste, You are hereby empowered to meet and inquire into all matters that are committed by your Caste, contrary to what has been agreed to by the majority of the Caste, and to punish the offender agreeably to the rules of your Caste, so far as not permitting them to come to your feasts, or beat them with Shoes, but no other corporal punishment."[18]

Although religious issues were still referred by the *panchayat* back to the priests, the lay merchant leadership gradually expropriated this authority. The *panchayat* enjoyed the ability to expel Parsis from the community through a series of economic, social, and religious boycott options. Possible punishments included forbidding priests to enter the house of the offender, forbidding access to Zoroastrian religious sites (including burial), exclusion from participation in festivals, and the symbolic degradation of being forced to beat oneself with a shoe.[19] Not only thus were laymen given the power of communal and religious excommunication, but they were given these authorities *by the British*. The Zoroastrian priests accordingly lost power to the large merchants even as the *panchayat* became dependent for its authority on the British government. Zoroastrian priests were further marginalized by the growing attention of the *panchayat* to religious affairs.

One such instance was *panchayat* involvement in the religiously charged issue of marriage. In 1777 the Panchayat called an *anjoman*, which passed a decision prohibiting the marriage of lay family women into priestly families.

This decision was viewed as retaliation for an earlier priestly decision prohibiting marriage of their daughters to the laity. The ruling caused so much defiance
that the British were called in to mediate. The British Commission charged to
investigate the matter reported in 1786 that they had been unable to determine
the intent of the Parsi scriptures on the issue of marriage.[20] Furthermore, the
report found that among the Parsi priests, very few could "read their Law in
the original language" and that translations left much room for interpretation.
The report went on to state that "it appears that the Parsees . . . have lost much
of their ancient knowledge and have been in their rigid observation of the Laws
of their religion assuming and exercising a great latitude of dispensation."[21]
Although the commission found in favor of both exclusionary marriage rulings, this controversy illustrated the need for more clarity in Parsi custom and
practice. The British accordingly requested that the community draw up a code
that could be used for the British to administer Parsi community issues such as
marriage and inheritance. Such a code was eventually drawn up by laymen in
1865. As Great Britain increasingly took over the Indian legal system and inter-
fered in Parsi communal affairs, they imposed their understanding of the pur-
view of religion within the Zoroastrian community, defining "religious" issues
as those "usages and customs" based on "sacred texts."[22] Religion increasingly
implied the private sphere of activities, rather than the larger legal and communal sphere that had included marriage and inheritance. The British Commission on the marriage controversy also found that the Panchayat only had the
authority to govern the laity, not the priests. Accordingly, the British called for
the establishment of a new *panchayat* whose membership included both laity
and priests and that would have the authority to regulate the entire community
(including the priests). The Parsis nominated twenty-four persons, of which the
British government chose six priests and six members of the laity to form this
new body. Although the priests had official representation in the new *panchayat*,
they were also subject to its authority.

Due to their power within the community, the lay leadership maintained
overall control. The Panchayat subsequently attempted to regulate priestly affairs.
On one occasion in 1796, the Panchayat ruled that some priests had performed
religious ceremonies in an impure state. As punishment, the Panchayat barred
them from performing any ceremonies for an entire year, thereby excluding them
from an important source of income. The Panchayat further marginalized the

priests' autonomy by ruling that they be allowed to file suits only with the Panchayat, not in civil courts.[23] The authority of this newly constituted *panchayat* was enormous and extended well outside of Bombay, even excommunicating Parsis living as far away as Surat.[24] By the early nineteenth century, however, changes in the Parsi community would spell the swift demise of the Panchayat.

By 1820 it was clear that the Panchayat had lost its former prestige, and with it its authority in the community. This was primarily a function of the rapid growth and changing nature of the community itself. Since 1780 the Parsi community had grown threefold. There emerged new elites, many of them as a result of the enormous increase in the China opium trade. Their wealth, together with the impact of British-style education and culture, led them to challenge the leadership of the older elites as well as the social and cultural mores they represented. In a letter written in 1832, a British official emphasized the growing independence, financially, socially, and culturally, of the new elites:

> The Court of Directors expressed an anxiety to restore the power formerly exercised by the higher classes of Parsees over their inferiors, by means of their Punchayets. It was found impracticable. Indirect influence, moral estimation and long habits of voluntary acquiescence in the will of others when once interrupted, were not easily restored. . . . The difficulty arose out of the increase of the tribe, the numbers now possessed of wealth, their independence turn of mind, and from want of a good understanding among the leading families. . . . [T]he second class of rich Parsees wish to live and expend their money as they please, without troubling or being troubled by Punchayet.[25]

The new elites were self-made and had much weaker ties to the older elite families. They also tended to display different attitudes toward the social issues of the day, including religious tradition and the status of women. They were attracted to European customs and ideas, which the older generation viewed as immoral and threatening to community maintenance. Rather than accepting the authority of the Panchayat, the new elites preferred the adjudication of the British courts.[26] These new elites would take over leadership of the Parsi community, but would never restore the power of the now moribund *panchayat*. The British government sealed its demise in 1838 by refusing to grant it any more coercive power.[27] The Panchayat formally ceased to exist and was revived only later in the century as a purely charitable foundation, with no legal or communal jurisdiction.[28] In the words of a historian of the Panchayat, "Since the 18th Century, no authority existed any more in the Parsee community that could decide internally, as the superior authority, on law and order. The clergy's loss of authority is the result of a beginning emancipation of the Parsee laity due to its rising economic prosperity. This laity was no longer willing, with its newly won self-consciousness, to subject itself to the jurisdiction of the—frequently uneducated—priests."[29]

The Parsi Priesthood

The Zoroastrian clergy presented a contradictory problem. On the one hand, the new commercial elites enjoyed their authority with the community and did not want their views challenged by the priests. This situation was particularly true once these commercial elites began to sponsor religious, social, and educational reforms within the community. On the other hand, the community as a whole also suffered from the increasing marginalization—intellectually, socially, and politically—of the priests.

The Zoroastrian priesthood was traditionally hereditary and required the memorization of large quantities of Avestan language liturgies that were often poorly understood. Priests were thus unable to respond effectively to rising Christian missionary and scholarly challenges in the nineteenth century. The rising economic dominance of the merchant classes also made the poorly remunerated priesthood unattractive, even to sons of priests, who increasingly entered other professions. It was thus that leadership of religious reform, as well as socio-political reforms, was dominated by the laity. An article in the *Indian Spectator* summed up the dismal status of the Zoroastrian priesthood in the late nineteenth century:

> Social change and secularization had led, in the 19th century, to the Parsee clergy's having lost on influence and prestige in spite of its numerical strength. After it had been relieved of traditional secular functions by the laws of 1865 and by the Panchayat dominated by laymen, it limited itself only to its ritual tasks. With the establishment of an educational system that took place without the participation or the influence of the clergy (the clergy had actually never practiced the function of transmitting knowledge to the laity), the clergy was

surpassed in the field of education and pushed into a position in which it was hardly taken seriously anymore intellectually. It had to endure sarcastic articles in Parsee newspapers that overwhelmed it with mockery of its uncultured state and "parasitic existence."[30]

The weakness and lack of authority of the Parsi priesthood vis-à-vis the merchant elites had many long-term ramifications. First among them was that religious reform was primarily conducted by the laity, rather than by priests. The laity was not always fluent in the Parsi religious texts and traditions and had social and political interests that affected their position on religious issues. Religious reformers thus heralded from among the laity, while often more traditionalist articulations of Zoroastrianism were left for priests to undertake. Certainly, the creation of new British-style educational institutions emphasized English and Western curricula. New educational systems also led to the further demise of the Parsi priesthood, as social prestige, cultural capital, economic opportunity, and political influence were increasingly a function of these new schools.

Educational Reforms

The Parsis' connection with the British through shared commercial interests and political identification prompted an interest in British-style education. Zoroastrian merchants' status was in large part a product of their relationship to the British, so it is not surprising that they were the first to flock to British schools and to socialize with the British more freely and openly than either Hindus or Muslims.[31] British education cemented the connection between political and social reforms and British concepts of "progress" and "civilization." It also forged a link with emerging notions of "true" or "progressive" religion and its role in generating change that was subsequently adopted by the Zoroastrian reformers.

European-style schools were established in India both by missionaries and by local communities. In 1815 the English founded the Society for Promoting the Education of the Poor in the Government of Bombay.[32] The school administered by the society taught reading, writing, arithmetic, and Protestantism. The schools, designed to educate the poor, quickly became popular, however, with a wider segment of the Indian population—especially Parsis. The annual report of 1819 stated, "By far the greater part of the native children in these schools are

Parsees."[33] Scottish missionary John Wilson established the Ambrolie English School in 1832, which would later become the General Assembly's Institution. Only ten years later, the college of the General Assembly's Institution boasted a student body of 1,446 students.[34]

The attraction of the British curriculum of these schools, combined with concerns over missionaries' proselytization intentions, prompted representatives from the Hindu, Muslim, and Parsi communities to establish their own schools. Members of these communities established the Native School and School Book Committee, later reestablished as the Bombay Native Education Society. The most famous and influential of the schools established by this group was the Elphinstone Institute, named after Mountstuart Elphinstone, British governor of Bombay (1819–27). Classes at the Elphinstone were conducted in English, with the intention of training Indian teachers in European-style education, who could then serve as teachers in local schools, teaching in the vernacular languages. Elphinstone also hoped to convince local elites to send their sons into service with the British and, more generally, to encourage their loyalty to the Crown.[35] Parsis enthusiastically welcomed the opportunity and contributed a full half of the funds to establish chairs at the Elphinstone in "English language, the Arts, Science, and Literature of Europe."[36]

The Elphinstone and other European-style schools were initially populated with middle- and lower-class Parsi children, with the upper-class merchant families preferring to provide English tutors for their children or to send them directly to England to study. However, by midcentury, even the merchant elites came to value the European-style schools in India and began to send their children in large numbers. By midcentury the Zoroastrian community began establishing similar schools on its own initiative and expense. Particularly prominent was the Sir Jamsetjee Jeejeebhoy Parsee Benevolent Institution, founded by its namesake in 1849. Only six years later, this institution had as many as 1,294 boys attending its schools.[37]

The popularity of these new British-style schools derived from two sources. First, since they taught English, graduates were well placed to work for British firms. Second, the Parsis' close commercial ties with the British and their minority status in the Indian context made them receptive to British culture, as well as to British education more generally. British-style schools reinforced these ties. The Parsis, alone among the merchant communities of Bombay, sent their sons

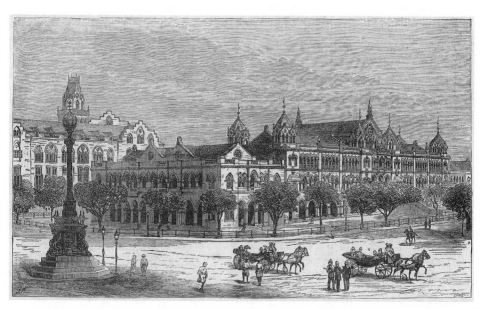

4. The David Sassoon Building of the Elphinstone Institute, Bombay, *Illustrated London News* (1881).

to receive English education.[38] Palsetia also notes the strong political impetus behind educational initiatives: "The involvement of men like Jamsetjee Jejeebhoy and Framji Cowasji Banaji in educational efforts reflected as much a desire to participate in the leadership of Bombay society alongside the British as an appreciation of the value of an education for Parsis and other Indians. The small number of Parsis associated with educational efforts in Bombay reflected a political culture that viewed the support for education as an elite undertaking in the promotion of a civic culture. The opportunity for contact with the British [that] . . . education afforded was not lost on these men."[39] Not surprisingly, it was these very same two gentlemen who entertained European guests English-style and were among the first to socialize publicly with their wives. In her memoirs, D. C. Jessawalla, who claims to be the first Parsi girl educated in a British school, remembers the crossing of Parsi religious and social barriers in order to entertain Europeans. Referring to the 1840s she writes that "in those days no Parsee would eat in the presence of aliens nor appear at a table where prohibited food . . . was served. . . . Sir Jamsetjee and Set Cursetjee Cowasjee Banajee were amongst the first to invite

Europeans to their houses, and on several occasions the then Governors of Bombay, with their staff, graced with their presence the supper tables, but the host was a mere spectator at the feast or at most served his guests with wine, and perhaps once or twice pledged their health but did nothing further . . . the ladies of the house merely enjoyed the sight through the venetian blinds of the adjoining rooms."[40] By the latter part of the century, these boundaries had ceased to function, at least among the upper-class Parsi merchant families in Bombay.

The value of European-style education, both in terms of career opportunities and in the more implicit accumulation of cultural capital it conferred, was further enhanced with the British government's new educational policy announced in 1835. Prior to this time, the British had, like the Mughals before them, continued to conduct business in Persian or Urdu and to sponsor institutions that taught "classical" Indian learning (Sanskrit, Arabic, and Persian). Those individuals in favor of this policy, the "Orientalists," argued that it was better to support "traditional" Indian learning than to alienate the population by forcefully promoting British education. A gradual process of injecting Western education into the Indian system had the tactical advantage of maintaining religious "noninterference" even while encouraging gradual receptivity to Western education. Their opponents, the Anglicists, countered that British education was the surest means of adding "useful knowledge" to the Indian curriculum, both to train Indian civil servants and, more important, to inculcate Indians with British values.[41] They were also reticent to lend additional status to Indian elites whom they viewed as invested in maintaining a backward and "superstitious" society.[42] The East India Company's 1813 Charter stated that "the Company had a positive duty to provide for the introduction of 'useful knowledge and religious improvement' to the people of India."[43] Notwithstanding anxiety about how the Indians might conflate this objective with the promotion of Christianity, the establishment of the General Committee on Public Instruction in 1823 renewed the charge for educational intervention. The committee's mandate was to take "such measures as may appear expedient to adopt with a view to the better instruction of the people, to the introduction of useful knowledge including the sciences and arts of Europe and the improvement of their moral character."[44] T. B. Macaulay, president of the Committee on Public Instruction for the East India Company and a chief architect of Anglicist policy, insisted that it would be more valuable to sponsor British-style education—with both the administrative and the cultural connections that it would establish. In his oft-quoted "Minute" he posited that "a single shelf of a good European library was worth the whole native literature of India and Arabia."[45] The Anglicists triumphed in 1835 when Governor-General William Bentinck decided in their favor. Thereafter, the British promoted British education, hoping to train Indian civil servants and to cement allegiance to Britain at the same time.

The intensity of debates surrounding British educational policy in India should not obscure the fact that the difference between Orientalists and Anglicists was principally one of tactics;[46] they both agreed on the superiority of British education and believed that Western knowledge was a means of uplifting the moral character, and thus the civilizational grade, of India—"civilization" that was inseparable from the understanding and expression of religion. British educational policy was driven by a firm conviction in the superiority of Western "culture," science, and Christianity. Both the Orientalists' and the Anglicists' ultimate aim was to Westernize Indian education. British missionaries pressured the government to adopt a more aggressive policy of Christianization, although they recognized the tactical difficulties associated with overt proselytization. In the words of Rev. James Gray, religious backwardness was the heart of the problem in India, one that only British education, and ultimately Christianity, could solve:

> It has been often a subject of sharp contention between conflicting parties, whether as Christians we are or are not justified in conceding the grand point of religious instruction, to conciliate the prejudices of heathen natives. On one side, it has been argued by devout men, that christianity [sic] is the foundation-stone upon which all instruction should be based. Secondly, that learning unaccompanied by religion is useless, and more calculated to mislead than to improve mankind. . . . [I]n endeavouring to impart religious instruction to the natives in India, our efforts are not met by a child-like unoccupation of the mind; an uncultured, but weedless soil, awaiting only the labourer's hand to spring into fertility. No! deep are the prejudices to be contended against.[47]

Ultimately, Gray believed that Bible instruction, which was never explicitly outlawed, would have the desired effect: "It will follow in due course [from Bible study] that the monstrous absurdities of his father's creed will strike upon his enlightened mind with all that force of contrast excited by a knowledge of a purer religion, and that the faith he has learnt to despise, he will subsequently abandon. The weeds will be then eradicated; and his heart cleansed from the corruptions of a false belief, will, we humbly hope, be prepared to receive the good seed of Christ's most blessed word."[48] Gray was confident that the British understood their moral imperative as Christians when he wrote that "both wisdom and foresight are conspicuous in the plans adopted by Government for the education and ultimate conversion of the native youth of India."[49]

From the outset, there was a strong connection between British education and social and religious reform. In addition to the clear call for Christianization or, at the very least, the adoption of British culture as a remedy for "backwardness," the British pinpointed the status of women as a litmus test for civilization. British models of sociability and gender relations were promoted as "civilized" and connected to a greater morality. British missionaries and officials believed that the education of women would inject British ideas of morality, civilization, and progress into Indian society and ultimately counter "superstition" and "barbaric" practices such as sati and gender segregation. Women were essential targets of educational reform, not only as symptomatic of greater levels of "civilization," but also for their role as mothers and nurturers. Women held the key to religious life—either ensuring "backwardness" through the continued performance of superstitious practice or, conversely, by promoting a more enlightened and thus moral education of children at home.

Scottish missionary John Wilson believed that women's education was essential to the larger "civilizing" mission of religious reform. In a letter to a fellow missionary, he wrote, "I am more and more convinced that, in seeking for the moral renovation of India, we must make greater efforts than we have yet done to operate upon the female mind. In Christian countries it is, generally speaking, more on the side of religion than the male mind. In India it is the stronghold of superstition."[50]

Max Müller, among the most prominent European scholars of Indian religion and an advocate of comparative religious studies, concurred on the backwardness of Indian religion cum civilization and on the singular role of women as its bearers: "When the female population of India will have drawn out of its present state of degradation, a better education and a purer religion alone bringing home to it the sentiment of moral responsibility and self-respect, so soon will it learn that there is, in the true lot of the woman, something above the laws of caste, and curses of priests; that, it will be its influence which will have most force, on the one hand, to burst the artificial barriers of caste, and, on the other, to maintain in India, as elsewhere, the true caste of rank, of manners, of intellect, and of character."[51] Europeans frequently congratulated Parsis for being the first to "throw off the shackles of superstition" by which they meant the adoption of new forms of sociability along British lines. By the late nineteenth century, residents remarked that "in the houses of the higher classes, the furniture is elegant, the service conducted on the European style."[52] Parsi women are also credited with adopting European customs: "Of late the Parsi ladies of Bombay have betaken themselves to wool-work, and a variety of European amusements and tastes, to fill up their leisure hours . . . their women, certainly, are not now so confined to the house as was the custom formerly: they are even permitted to go abroad in open carriages, which was quite unusual so late as fifteen years ago [circa 1835]."[53] Wacha similarly notes that "the Parsi ladies of the city moved about freely both on foot and in carriages. The purdah was wholly lifted and since then the intermingling of males and females in Parsi and European society became universal."[54] Henry Moses in his *Sketches of India* (1850) was not alone in noting the stir it caused when Sir Jamsetjee Jeejeebhoy appeared in public with his wife on his arm, calling it the "first occasion on which a Parsee lady had ever been seen in public."[55]

Graduates of the European-style schools, especially the Elphinstone Institute, formed a close-knit cadre that provided the leaders of an emerging Parsi reform movement. They championed social and religious reform, focusing in particular on improving the status of women and on revisiting religious tradition. Reformers took up the "cause" of women's education as part of the larger reform effort. At this time, girls' schools were limited to the ones established by missionaries. Margaret Wilson, wife of Scottish missionary John Wilson, had set up three schools for girls as early as 1830 and had established three more shortly thereafter. According to Wilson, by 1836 more than 180 girls attended mission schools, and by 1849 the number had risen to more than 500.[56] In 1832 Margaret Wilson established the Bombay Ladies' School for Destitute Native Girls with 29 students, some of them Parsis.[57] Students of the British-style men's schools similarly believed in the moral imperative of women's education. In 1848 graduates, students, and teachers at the Elphinstone Institution formed the Students Literary and Scientific Society, which quickly turned its attention to issues of social reform. Under the leadership of Dadabhai Naoroji, the society initiated the first steps in the realm of women's education. In the words of a contemporary Parsi reformer:

> The young men who had been educated in Government schools and colleges viewed the question of female education in its proper lights. . . . [T]hey plainly saw that their own domestic life could not be rendered happy if their wives remained uneducated, nor could the Parsee community generally be said to have advanced in a moral or social point of view if their women remained in a semi-barbarous state. They rightly understood that, if the seeds of education were to be generally spread, they should first germinate with the gentler sex. The influence which a mother or sister exercises upon a child was rightly conceived, and the enthusiastic youths determined to do some service to their country and countrymen, by earnestly directing their attention to the cause of female education.[58]

As early as 1849, four Parsi girls' schools were established by the society with a total of 44 students.[59] The society also established and provided teachers for three Hindu girls' schools. By 1855 the Parsi community had established nine girls' schools with a total of 740 students (of which 475 were Parsis). By 1858 there were more than 1,200 Parsi girls in school, and by 1870 more than 1,000 Parsi girls had received a secondary education.[60] In the census of 1891, a full half of Parsi women were considered literate.[61]

From the outset, the goals of education focused on the development of "the whole character." Educational reform was clearly believed to generate social reform, and the formation of new moral individuals was paramount to this project. In the words of British professor Patton, an early champion of female education, "Chief attention will be given to the culture of the moral nature, under which is included the formation of habits of order, propriety, and cleanliness."[62] The curriculum in the girls' schools stressed the development of a new morality and the making of "modern" women through hygiene and "domestic industry" (sewing, embroidery). Instruction centered on fables, "songs of a moral nature," the *Moral Class Book*, as well as "moral tales taken chiefly from English books." The "habit of cleanliness, order, regularity and truth are regularly inculcated." In addition, vernacular languages, "natural history and the trades" were also taught.[63] An advocate of female education noted that "we trust . . . [that Parsee women] will not only become better wives and better mothers, but by their mental qualifications and advanced position exercise a great influence on the future *moral and social advancement of their race*."[64]

The strong moral component in "civilization" and "progress" was obvious. In the words of a reformer, men and women in the Parsi community "have fully succeeded in awakening in the minds of their countrymen the necessity of a general and rapid advancement in the path of knowledge and enlightenment, if they desire to be classed among the civilized nations of the earth."[65] This notion was widely accepted, as illustrated by the words of the Parsee Society that declared its main goal to be a conscious imitation of English manners—manners that clearly demonstrated the connections between gender and English "civilization." A statement made by the society read: "We want the English language, English manners, and English behaviour for our wives and daughters, and until these are supplied, it is but just that the present gulf between the Englishman and the Indian should remain as wide as ever."[66]

The Parsis embraced their own Europeanness as further proof of the difference between themselves and other Indian groups. In the words of Parsi reformer Dinshaw Edulji Wacha, "There was a wide gulf fixed between the two communities [the Hindus and Muslims] and the Europeans. Not so as regards the Parsis. Free from the trammels of caste and custom indigenous to the country of their domicile, they were able to mix freely in European society. They dined with them and took a share in their sports and entertainments."[67] In this vein, Parsis were the first to adopt cricket, establishing the Oriental Cricket Club in 1848 and the Zoroastrian Cricket Club in 1850. The English paper *Cricket Chat* published an account of the visit of the Parsi team to England—the first Indian team to do so— and of the political benefits to be reaped of shared cultural sensibilities: "A visit of a team of native Indian Cricketers (Parsis) to England is an event of no small significance, not only from the stand-point of cricket, but also from a political point of view. Anything which can tend to promote assimilation of tastes and habits between the English and native subjects of our Empress Queen cannot fail to conduce to the solidity of the British Empire. . . . [T]he Parsi fraternity is the most intelligent, as well as the most loyal, of the races scattered over our Indian possessions."[68] Notwithstanding Parsis' "partiality for Europeans," their "favorable

5. "The Parsee Representative Cricket Team at Bombay." *Graphic* (1893).

disposition to the British Government," and their adoption of British language, education, and cultural sensibilities, they remained essentially and irrevocably Indian in the eyes of the British.[69] Briggs articulates this point eloquently in his damning conclusion that "[Parsis] have studied the address and the courtesy of the European, without acquiring that fine sense of honour, and that genuine philanthropy, which mark the gentleman from the far west."[70]

2

The Protestant Challenge
to Zoroastrianism

I was somewhat convinced of my folly in worshipping the elements, which
is quite contrary to reason. . . . I afterwards read Dr. Wilson's lecture on the
Vendidad Sadi and became convinced of the fallacy of the Parsi religion.
— DHANJIBHAI NAUROJI, explaining why he converted
to Christianity, ca. 1835–39

Scholarly interest in Zoroastrianism, the developing field of linguistics, and
Christian missionary activity in India combined to form a powerful challenge to Zoroastrian religious tradition. Parsis were forced to reconsider their
practices and beliefs in light of new scholarly analyses of their religious texts
and practices. Parsi reformers, in seeking to "rationalize" their religion, were
deeply influenced by Western notions of religion and by the conviction that
rational, or "enlightened," religion was responsible for "progress" and "civilization"—tropes for social and political reform. Both Reformers and traditionalist Orthodox, while defending Zoroastrianism from missionary and scholarly
attacks, adopted many of their presuppositions concerning the nature and
function of religion in modern society. Despite the range of positions taken
by the Zoroastrian community—from reform to retrenchment—all were
deeply affected by the religious debates concerning the nature and function
of "true" religion. The Parsi reform movement resulted in a serious reconceptualization of Zoroastrianism in India. It also shaped the intellectual and
social context in which Parsis came to Iran and sponsored religious and social
reforms there.

Western Perceptions of Zoroastrianism

Western scholarly engagement in linguistics and ancient religions in the eighteenth and nineteenth centuries led to an interest in Zoroastrianism as one of the oldest world religions. Zoroastrianism, however, was not completely unknown before this time. From the outset, European travelers' accounts of religion in India made clear distinctions between Hindu practices and Zoroastrianism. According to Hinnells, "It was easier to see Zoroastrianism as being in harmony with the beliefs and principles of the British and their current theological concerns than it was those of Hinduism, especially in the latter's popular form. As a result each traveler tended to comment on the same features of Parsi religion, their monotheism, their lack of idols, their high moral standards and their attitude to fire. The Iranian origin of the community and *dokhmas* were also often commented on."[1]

The very earliest known account was written in 1616–19 by Edward Terry, a chaplain in the service of the East India Company. Terry recounted, "[The Parsis] believe that there is but one God, who made all things, and hath a sovereign power over all."[2] The author of the second known account, Rev. Henry Lord, also stressed Zoroastrianism as monotheistic and having a "Lawgiver" prophet similar to the Abrahamic tradition. He wrote, "Fire was delivered to Zertoost their Lawgiver from God Almighty, who pronounced it to bee his virtue and his excellencie, and that there was a lawe delivered for the worshippe of this fire, confirmed by so many Miracles, that therefore they should hold it holy, reverence and worshippe it as a part of God, who is of the same substance, and that they should love all things, that resemble it, or were like unto it, as the Sunne and Mone which proceeded from it, and are Gods."[3]

European scholarship (as opposed to travelers' accounts) on Zoroastrianism is generally dated to 1700 with the publication of the work of Oxford professor Thomas Hyde *De vetere religione Persarum*.[4] Hyde maintained that Zoroaster had brought monotheism, repeating the work of Abraham.[5] It was not until the middle of the eighteenth century, however, that portions of the Avesta were obtained and translated into European languages. Frenchman Anquetil Du Perron distinguished himself as the first European to meet with the Parsis of Surat, to study with Zoroastrian priests, and to obtain quantities of Avestan manuscripts.[6] As a result, accounts of Zoroastrianism changed from travelers' tales of "curiosities and wonders," or as a foil for denouncing Christian exceptionalism, to analyses that display an increased awareness of the sources and historicity of Zoroastrianism.[7]

As the Avesta became increasingly accessible to Western scholars and Zoroastrian priests, linguistic studies inaugurated debates concerning the dating of the Zoroastrian texts in the process of exploring the relationship between Iranian languages and Sanskrit.[8] This discussion threw into question the authenticity and even authorship of some Zoroastrian texts that had been held sacred in the past, but were now accused of being produced much later than Zoroaster's own time.[9]

Such textual analysis of Zoroastrian texts also led to a recognition of the historicity of the religion. Accounts such as the one by Grose and Mackintosh clearly distinguish between Zoroastrianism *as currently practiced* and Zoroastrianism *in its original form.* John Henry Grose, writing in 1750, asserted, "The two cardinal points on which his [Zoroaster's] religion entirely turns [are] The belief in one supream [*sic*] God, and of the Sun or element of fire being his first minister throughout all his works, as well as the symbol and eternal monitor of purity. The rest of his tenets were only subordinate to, or emanations from them."[10] Sir James Mackintosh, writing a generation later, described the Parsis as ancient Iranian monotheists: "The remains of those Persians who three and twenty centuries ago . . . destroyed the Temples of Idols, who were among the most ancient monotheists and iconoclasts of the world, still preserve their abhorrence of Idolatry, and shew it with peculiar force against those Idolatrous symbols which . . . are always peculiarly abhorrent from the moral sentiments of man unperverted and undegraded by superstition."[11] In a trend that would become firmer as the century wore on, Mackintosh associates monotheism with morality and idolatry with false religion, delegitimized by the use of the term *superstition.* Implicitly therefore, Parsis practiced a superior religion to their Hindu neighbors.

Over the course of the eighteenth and nineteenth centuries, scholars grew increasingly interested in Zoroastrianism as a critical stage in the evolution of religion. Scholarly questions concerning the nature and origin of religion proceeded to drive the study of Zoroastrianism. By the turn of the nineteenth century, accounts of Zoroastrianism evidence a pronounced emphasis on the close generative connection between religion and social change that was absent in earlier centuries. Monotheistic, moral religions were implicitly contrasted with ritualistic religions, the first promoting progress and the latter backwardness.

One of the most elaborate accounts that expressed these ideas was written by Sir William Erskine in 1818. Contrary to Grose, he emphasized the continuity of Zoroastrian religions practice: "No religion on earth, that of the Jews excepted, has continued from such remote times as that of the Parsis with so little apparent change of doctrine or ritual."[12] Erskine attested to Zoroastrianism as monotheistic, despite the existence of multiple "superior beings." He wrote, "In spite of this multiplication of superior beings, and though in the Liturgy of the Parsis all of these are occasionally addressed, they are never worshipped as deities, but only as the media through which praise is conveyed to the Supreme Being . . . the ancient Persians, like the modern Parsis, being strict Unitarians."[13]

However, despite its evident monotheism, Zoroastrianism was essentially ritualistic, which in Erskine's mind meant that it lacked a moral profundity. Erskine clearly understood ritual and ceremony as useless in their pretense of affecting the Divine and lacking consciousness of God. In his understanding, Zoroastrianism consisted of assisting the good in the "continued warfare between good and evil spirits."[14] Religious practice thus entailed the participation of man in this warfare. To this end, "Endless prayers must be repeated, as contained in a tedious liturgy, which prescribes the solemn words to be used not only on great and important occasions, but even on the most common and vulgar operations and functions of life. Numerous vain and frivolous ceremonies are prescribed . . . as the language of the *Zend-Avesta* is known to none of the vulgar, and to few of the priesthood, the stated prayers are mumbled over as contained in the ritual, with incredible velocity, and are considered rather as charms and incantations producing effects by their sound, than as in any degree fixing the mind on its object, or elevating it to the father of spirits."[15] Erskine believed that the result of such a ritualistic understanding of the nature and function of religion was the absence of religious morality. He opined, "Their religion, if we may judge from their practice, has but little connection with morals at all. It is a religion of ceremonies and of prayers; and the prayers being in an unknown language, and their meaning unknown to those who repeat them, cannot be supposed to have much influence on the conduct of life."[16]

Not surprisingly, in line with his condemnation of ritual, Erskine is dismissive of the Parsi priesthood and partially blames them for lack of moral content in the religion. Priests are described as "not in general learned, seldom understanding the meaning of the books they read, or the prayers they recite" and even "generally not only disliked, but despised" by the Parsis.[17] He noted that "whether from the ignorance of the priests and the little respect in which they are held, or from whatever other cause, [religion] seems to have very little influence of any kind except of a social and political nature, arising from the connexion [sic] of caste. . . . Parsis have little regard for their religion as such."[18] In short, Erskine conceived of Zoroastrian ritualism as absent of a morality that would inform "conduct of life." Rituals were thus in a sense meaningless.

Precisely *because* of such religious superficiality and consequent lack of moral commitment to religion, Erskine believed that Parsis could be "improved." He clearly distinguished Parsis from other religious groups in India, more closely identifying Parsis with Europeans. This classification entailed both racial and cultural affinity. He asserted that "in the midst of the deep coloured and effeminate Hindus and Mussulmans, [Parsis] still retain the fair complexion, the hardy constitution, and stubborn activity of more northern climates."[19] He was impressed with what he described as Parsi willingness to "imitate European culture" and as a result saw them as uniquely "improvable." Paradoxically, he believed that such progress was owing to the *form* of their religion: "The Parsis are, however, the most improveable caste in India. Religion and customs supposed to be connected with religion are the great obstacles to the improvement of the Orientals, whether Mussalmans [sic] or Hindus. From such restraints the Parsis are remarkably free, they are in every respect much like Europeans than any other class of natives in Southern Asia; and being less restrained by ancient and acknowledged law are more prepared to adopt any change of which they see the benefit."[20] Erskine's evaluation of Zoroastrianism evidences profound assumptions of Protestant superiority and the notion of morality and a central function of "true," rational religion. His ideas were influenced by natural religion and not surprisingly therefore denounced ritual and evidenced a profound anticlericalism. Erskine also understood certain *forms of religion* to be generative of social progress. He had no real impact on the Parsi community and their own perception of religion, however, since he was writing for a European audience and not involved with the Parsi community. Yet in the years that followed, similar understandings of religion by scholars of Zoroastrianism and Protestant missionaries actively seeking to convert Parsis would have a profound effect on the Parsi community and contribute to the beginnings of religious reform among the Parsis.

Wilson's War

The intensification of British involvement in Indian affairs led to the influx of Christian missionaries who attacked Zoroastrian traditions, practices, and beliefs. The East India Company had not permitted missionary activity in India during the seventeenth and eighteenth centuries. This policy changed in 1813 in part owing to pressure from the British public fanned by evangelists.[21] The first Christian missionaries arrived shortly thereafter and began actively proselytizing.[22] Official policy toward missionary activity, however, remained ambivalent throughout the century. Although governors of Bombay and other government officials often actively supported missionary work, the government refused to take an official policy toward Christian conversion—something that continued to irk missionaries. The British government, which took over governance of India from the East India Company in 1858, was actually more sympathetic to missionaries' goals than had been the East India Company, which actively pursued a policy of noninterference in religious affairs. Nonetheless, despite more interventionist support for Anglicization in many areas, missionaries continued to criticize the government for its "tolerance" toward "false" religions and for failing to officially promote Christianity.[23]

The most immediate and consequential challenge to Zoroastrianism was posed by Scottish missionary John Wilson. Wilson journeyed to India in 1829 for the purpose of converting Indians to Christianity. He was unabashed in this aim, admitting that "I have consequently challenged Hindoos, Parsees, and Mussulmans to the combat. . . . At present I am waging war."[24] Wilson's deep knowledge of Zoroastrian texts made him a formidable opponent, as did his proselytizing vigor. Unlike earlier scholarship that did not actively seek to change Zoroastrian faith or practice, Wilson's overt attacks on Zoroastrian theology and texts forced the Parsis to defend their faith.[25] He was thus nearly single-handedly responsible for inaugurating a dialogue within the Zoroastrian community concerning their religious tradition.

Wilson remained in India for forty-seven years. During this time he headed the Church of Scotland's mission; preached; taught school; traveled; established and edited a journal, the *Oriental Christian Spectator;* and authored numerous works on Hinduism, Islam, and especially Zoroastrianism.[26] He was a talented linguist, mastering Persian, Hebrew, Portuguese, Arabic, Sanskrit, Avestan, Marathi, Gujarati, Hindustani, and a number of other local languages.[27] Wilson, called "the most prominent public man in Western India" by his biographer, was on close terms with a series of governors of Bombay, especially Mountstuart Elphinstone (1819–27), Sir John Malcolm (1827–31), Sir Robert Grant (1835–39), and Lord Elphinstone (1855–60).[28] All of these men were supportive of Wilson's missionary work and sought his advice on educational and other matters. With the exception of Grant, they were all also, coincidentally, Scotsmen, as was another missionary and confidant of Wilson's: the famous Dr. Livingstone.[29]

In addition to his scholarly work on Zoroastrianism and his dialogues with Parsis in the press, Wilson regarded educational work as central to his missionary goals. In 1835 Wilson established a school close to the Parsi section of Bombay, the "General Assembly's Institution," in order to teach Christianity.[30] Over the years he did in fact succeed in converting a number of Zoroastrian students at the school—events that caused enormous uproar within the Zoroastrian community, as discussed below.

The effects of Wilson's offensive against Zoroastrianism, however, were much further reaching than the conversion of a handful of Parsi youths. His attacks were challenged, but undefeated, by the Zoroastrian community. Wilson's criticisms of Zoroastrian theology centered on four interrelated issues: monotheism, sin and salvation, ritual and prayer, and knowledge of the Divine. Although arguably more aggressive than many of his fellow missionaries, Wilson operated under assumptions concerning the nature of religion that were prevalent among missionaries and laypersons alike. Foremost among them was the conviction that polytheistic religions were by definition untrue and furthermore were more primitive than monotheistic religions. Polytheism was essentially a misunderstanding of the Divine. He was convinced that Zoroastrians were "true polytheists in the most rigid sense of the term."[31] He elaborated that "[the Parsi] religion is decidedly *polytheistic.* Not only does it set forth an erroneous object of supreme worship, and circumscribe the glory and the power of that object by an imaginary being of an opposite character; but it recognizes a vast, and almost uncountable, number of objects of religious worship and reverence."[32] Wilson was convinced that the Zoroastrians were dualists and dismissed their attempts to argue otherwise. A Zoroastrian priest, Dosabhoy Sohrabji, attempted to counter Wilson's characterization of Zoroastrianism as dualistic by arguing that "the evil principle" was in fact the personification of the evil qualities of man, not an independent object of worship. Wilson caustically dismissed his attempts with the quip that "an Ethiopian is not made white by washing."[33]

Wilson also knew enough about the extant Avestan literature to claim that the revered books were not in fact revelations from the Prophet Zoroaster, but rather later scholarly compositions. This point, he believed, called into question the entire basis of their faith: "The Parsis are entirely destitute of an authoritative rule of faith. The books which they esteem sacred are mere fragments of works which are now lost."[34] The Vendidad (a section of the Avesta) was not divine revelation, Wilson insisted, dismissing the text as "unreasonable," "illogical," "not in accord with science," and full of "absurd ceremonies."[35]

Wilson also expressed a common Protestant assumption about "true" religion, which was its orientation toward an individual's spiritual *relationship* with God, rather than with ritual as an *attempt to affect* the supernatural. He thus exhibited a strong antipathy toward ritual as "absurd" and ignorant of the fundamentally moral nature of man's relationship to the Divine. In one passage, Wilson's understanding of true religion takes shape: "The knowledge of the Supreme Being, it must be universally allowed, lies at the foundation of true religion. If the attributes of his nature, and the character of his providence, be misapprehended or inadequately realized, there can not possibly be produced that right state of contemplation, and thought, and feeling, and action, in reference to God, in which genuine practical religion consists."[36] Wilson thus fundamentally understood "true" religion as rational religion, which involved the shaping of individual consciousness through an awareness of the nature of the Divine. It is this understanding of God that he believed ultimately distinguished Protestantism from other faiths, particularly "false systems of religion" such as Zoroastrianism. Without an understanding of God, there can be no salvation from sin.[37]

Wilson's own religious convictions focused solidly on the issue of sin. In an entry in his "diary of religious experience" at age twenty, Wilson wrote, "I was very early under conviction of sin, and I trust that the Lord at an early period of my life took a saving dealing [sic] with my soul."[38] Wilson's principal criticism of Zoroastrianism was that it fundamentally misunderstood the nature of God and thus man's obligation to God. It did not, therefore, provide a route toward salvation.

In a response to a Parsi critic who argued that conversion was unnecessary since "at last all *roads* meet in one point (*Heaven*)," Wilson argued that this belief was mistaken: "[This view] supposes that all religions are alike true, and acceptable to God; and that they are all alike beneficial to men. Now this is far from being the case. . . . [I]f sinners be saved at all, their salvation must be through the grace of God."[39] The crux of the problem, according to Wilson and other missionaries, was that Zoroastrianism falsely promised salvation. Simply put, God's grace alone, not man's own actions, could provide salvation. This argument was most clearly articulated in an article he printed in the *Oriental Christian Spectator* signed by R. N.: "He that comes before God and says that he himself has wrought out an acceptable righteousness comes with a lie in his mouth. The righteousness of God's own son must alone be pleaded in the court above; and this is the only plea which God will regard. . . . [We must ask] 'Receive me, O God, on account of the righteousness of the Son.'"[40]

The question of ethics appears frequently in Wilson's debates with Zoroastrians. He insisted that Zoroastrianism was a false religion, that Zoroaster did not receive a divine mission and was only "an impostor" and that the Avesta was full of "errors and absurdities."[41] According to Wilson, the proof was obvious: "Would God every [*sic*] recommend the worship of inaminate [*sic*] objects? Would he ever give such trifling orders as are to be found in the Avesta? . . . [W]ould he ever teach that men could sin when they pleased, and remove that sin which they had committed by the work of their own hands, or by a few insignificant ceremonies? . . . [Thus] [t]he Avesta cannot claim God as its author."[42] Wilson understood true (read: Protestant) religion as creating moral consciousness that then naturally leads to social commitment and action.[43] The espousal of true versus false religion affects more than the salvation of individuals—it affects the moral level of society expressed as "civilization." Religion thus has a causal effect on the "progress" of society. Wilson articulated this premise in a sermon delivered on November 8, 1835, titled "The British Sovereignty In India." "And for what purpose," he asked, "has God conferred upon us the sovereignty of this great country? . . . I believe that all of you will not only admit, but readily declare, that it is for this country's weal that it hath been given to us." He then proclaimed that "the triumph of our holy faith" and the concomitant "destruction of the systems of error" would lead to India's salvation.[44] Wilson expressed belief in the direct link between the form of religion and the level of "progress and civilization" again years later in a public lecture in 1856 when he solemnly declared that the sovereignty of India had "been given to a Christian nation, to a protestant nation, and to the most protestant, most enlightened, most philanthropic, and most powerful nation for the deliverance of India."[45]

Other Voices in the Fray

Wilson's dismissal of Zoroastrianism as a dualistic religion did not go unchallenged in European scholarly circles. Foremost among the defenders of Zoroastrianism as a monotheistic religion was Martin Haug, professor of Sanskrit and comparative philology at the University of Poona.[46] The publication of his theories in 1897 inaugurated the predominance of the monotheistic interpretation of Zoroastrianism among the Western scholarly community that continues largely uncontested to this day. In so doing, he provided ammunition to the Zoroastrian community's own refutation of Wilson's attacks. At the same time, however, Haug reinforced many of Wilson's assumptions concerning "true" religion that were subsequently accepted by the Zoroastrian community.

As a philologist, Haug's primary interest was in the dating of Zoroastrian texts. He insisted that although many of the Zoroastrian religious texts were indeed of a later, and even suspect, provenance, the Gathas dated from the time of Zoroaster and thus constituted the original and true Zoroastrian religion.[47] Based on the teachings in the Gathas, Haug argued that Zoroaster was the first to establish monotheism in a polytheistic world. Haug equated Zoroaster's conception of the Supreme Being with that of Abrahamic faiths, calling it "perfectly identical with the notion of God which we find in the books of the Old Testament."[48] In fact, Zoroastrianism was the originator of many ideas later absorbed into Abrahamic tradition, including God as "the Creator of the earthly and spiritual life, the Lord of the whole universe, in whose hands are all the creatures. He is the light and source of light; he is the wisdom and intellect. . . . As the ruler of the whole universe, he not only rewards the good, but he is a punisher of the wicked at the same time." The origin of the concepts of heaven and hell and resurrection were also ascribed to Zoroastrianism.[49] Later Zoroastrian dualism resulted from imperfect understanding of Zoroaster's teachings and the personification of abstract ideas of good and evil. Later texts, such as the Vendidad, were in fact corruptions of true, original Zoroastrianism.[50]

Haug primarily differed from Wilson in his interest in Zoroastrianism. He was concerned with understanding it in its historical context and in trying to ascertain what Zoroaster's original religious message had been. He was not a missionary and consequently less concerned with issues of salvation than of understanding the evolution of man's religious experience. The Zoroastrian community in India embraced Haug's insistence on Zoroastrianism as essentially monotheistic and his belief in Zoroastrianism as the origin of many Abrahamic concepts. Haug's view of later Zoroastrian tradition as a corruption of pure monotheism, however, buttressed Wilson's challenge of Zoroastrian religious texts and contributed to a process of reconstruction and reevaluation of tradition itself—a process that would deeply divide the community.

The Conversion Controversy

Although Parsi conversion to Christianity was rare, several instances did occur. The controversies that erupted as a consequence illuminate Parsi understanding of both Christianity and Zoroastrianism at the time. There were two principal conversion incidents, both involving Zoroastrian boys attending Wilson's school.[51] The first conversion occurred in 1839 and involved three students: Dhanjibhai Nauroji, Hormusji Pestonji, and a third who is identified only as Framjee.[52]

In court testimony, Nauroji maintained that he had written a letter to Wilson describing his Christian faith and requesting Christian baptism. Nauroji explained that he had come to view Zoroastrianism as polytheistic and founded on spurious texts: "I was somewhat convinced of my folly in worshipping the elements which is quite contrary to reason. . . . I afterwards read Dr. Wilson's lecture on the Vandidad Sade, and became convinced of the fallacy of the Parsi religion."[53] In his autobiography, Nauroji explained that it was not only the question of polytheism but missionary insistence on the existence of only one true God that affected him so profoundly: "[Wilson] showed us what wild and superstitious things are contained in it. It was impossible to resist the conclusion that the Vendidad was not from God, and I lost faith in the Parsi religion. Not only so, but gradually I became convinced that as the dogmas of different religions are quite irreconcileable [sic] with one another, they cannot all have been given by God. As there is only one God, and He cannot have given contradictory teaching, the dogmas of true religion must be harmonious one with another; and He can only have given one religion to illumine our hearts."[54]

Wilson read his account and concluded that the boy "had, through divine grace, been truly enlightened by divine truth."[55] When word spread of the impending conversion, the Parsi community rallied against Wilson and his school. One of the boys, Framjee, was kidnapped by his family.[56] Nauroji's uncle accused Wilson of forcing the boy to convert and insisted that he was underage. Wilson, for his part, insisted that the boy was well beyond the age of maturity and that he remain at his residence in order to protect him from possible violence at the hands of his family and community. The case eventually went to court where Nauroji testified that he had effectively already abandoned Zoroastrianism: for the past ten months he had "never performed any of the public or private religious services peculiar to the Parsis."[57] Members of the Parsi Panchayat supported Nauroji's uncle and maintained that Wilson should respect the British policy of noninterference in religious matters—which was typically understood as a nonconversion agreement. Jamsetjee Jeejeebhoy, head of the Parsi Panchayat, offered Nauroji a high salary in his family's employ if he would renounce Christianity.[58] For the community, the question centered on whether missionary schools deliberately sought to convert students. Nauroji's uncle maintained that he had no idea that his nephew received "Christian" education—a claim that Wilson dismissed as clearly mendacious. The court found in favor of Nauroji's right to convert, which he did. Two days later the second Parsi boy was also baptized. Nauroji went on to study theology in Scotland in 1843, was ordained by the Free Presbytery Church of Edinburgh in 1846, and subsequently returned to India as a missionary.[59]

In order to forestall other conversions, some 2,115 Zoroastrians, Muslims, and Hindus signed a petition urging the British authorities to outlaw the conversion of minors. The British government refused, declaring itself officially neutral in the matter.[60] The Parsis consequently withdrew their children from Wilson's school, sending the numbers of children plunging from 500 to only 60–70, none of whom were Parsi. The Panchayat threatened to excommunicate anyone who enrolled their child in a school that required Bible reading. The fear of conversion also provided impetus for the establishment of Parsi-run British-style schools that did not teach Christianity. The overwhelming appeal of British education, however, led the numbers of students at Wilson's school to rebound to 300–400

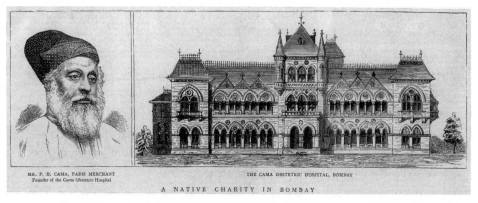

MR. P. H. CAMA, PARSI MERCHANT
Founder of the Cama Obstetric Hospital

THE CAMA OBSTETRIC HOSPITAL, BOMBAY

A NATIVE CHARITY IN BOMBAY

6. "A Native Charity in Bombay," *Graphic* (March 14, 1885).

by 1852. By 1864 the General Assembly's Institution had established as many as twenty-one schools with a total of 3,049 students.[61]

The second Parsi conversion controversy transpired some seventeen years after the first. Four students at the Elphinstone Institution addressed a letter dated June 14, 1856, to John Wilson and Rev. Adam White. In it they detailed their reasons for wishing to convert to Christianity. Their letter reveals the extent to which Protestant missionary ideas, and Western notions of religion more generally, had achieved fluency in the premier English-language school, the Elphinstone:

> We are fully convinced . . . that Parsiism is a *false* religion; and it consists of VAGUE and EXTRAVAGANT principles. It is the INVENTION of man; not the REV-ELATION of God. We have found out, after inquiring nearly two or three years after the TRUE RELIGION, that every comfort, joy, hope, success, and every good thing in this world, as well as in the world to come, are concentrated in the Lord Jesus. . . . [W]e are fully convinced of the TRUTH of CHRISTIANITY, we wish to become baptized, and to be admitted into the visible Church of Christ. . . . We are now in a position where SALVATION is at hand and very near to us. . . . Up to this time . . . we were so blind . . . we did not know the way of Righteousness and Truth. . . . We are much moved by the sorrows and sufferings which shall befall our parents by this public step of ours; but what can we do? Salvation we *must* have. . . . Nothing has led us to join the Christian Church but the pure hope and desire of the salvation of our souls.[62]

The letter reveals an understanding of religion reminiscent of the first convert—Nauroji. These boys were similarly swayed by arguments concerning the origin and authenticity of the Avesta, citing its "inventedness" (as opposed to having been revealed) as symptomatic of its falsity. It is also noteworthy that the students were primarily motivated by the promise of salvation, which they believed to be uniquely available through Christianity. Christianity thus, they believed, was *the only true religion*, rather than one path among others. This view was dominant among evangelical missionaries at the time, but differed from many scholarly and subsequent religious understandings.

The students were accorded protection at the Scottish mission house after they insisted that they feared for their safety. Wilson then began "a reasonable course of Christian probation" and instruction to make sure that they were genuinely prepared to convert. The students wrote letters to their families explaining their decision. The families exerted considerable pressure on the students and urged them to reconsider, promising them that they would not be punished. Three of the students subsequently recanted during their "probation" and returned to their families. The only student to stay the course was Behramji Kersasji, who, after three months of religious instruction at the mission house, was baptized by Rev. Adam White on June 16, 1856.[63]

Kersasji was asked a series of questions on the occasion of his baptism to confirm his commitment to evangelical Christianity. In response to the question "Do you not reject the ungodly opinion, that all religions are true; and do you believe that there is none other than the name under heaven given among men whereby we must be saved, but the name of Jesus Christ?" he replied, "I do."[64] Kersasji's religious education at the hands of Wilson is obvious from his subsequent personal statement issued on August 31, 1856. His statement reads as follows: "I feel that I am a great sinner, deserving the curse of God.... I trembled, because the sins which I have committed are countless, and cannot be pardoned for my own righteousness . . . and cannot be removed by my own efforts. . . . [T]he more I knew of the poor doctrines of Zoroaster, and fabrications of Mobeds and Dasturs, the more I was led to forsake my own religion wholly for the true one. I found that repentance, charity, giving alms, cannot give salvation or the remission of sins. I believe that [the practice of Zoroastrian] rites and ceremonies . . . were only adding to my sins. . . . [S]alvation appertains unto the Lord alone."[65]

Each of these conversion testimonies explicitly contrasts Protestantism with Zoroastrianism. The converts denounced Zoroastrianism as false on two grounds: first, because it was not a revealed religion and, second, because it was grounded in the performance of ritual. The assertion that Zoroastrianism was not a revealed religion rested on recent scholarly linguistic analysis of the Avestan texts that suggested that they postdated the Prophet Zoroaster. More interestingly, the question itself testifies to the acceptance, by both sides, of the centrality of texts and the primacy of revealed religion as indications of "truth." Both of these definitions rest on Protestant categorization of the characteristics of "true" religions. The converts dismissed the performance of ritual as misguided and insisted that faith, not formal ritual, was the key to salvation. Salvation thus was a function not of correct practices, but of individual religious consciousness— piety and faith.

These conversion stories also suggest subtle changes in the relationship of religion and identity. Conversion itself was described as a result of interior conscience. It was the product of interiorized experience of God. Religion was thus claimed as a matter of personal choice and individual consciousness and was divorced from corporate (sectarian) identity or loyalty to the state.[66] To the extent that religion was understood as a matter of personal commitment rather than sectarian identity, conversion necessitated public testimony of this interiorized change, rather than participation in sectarian ritual.

The Parsi Response: Refuting Wilson

In the 1840s a number of Parsis, some sponsored by the Panchayat, wrote works refuting Christianity and denouncing conversions as the results of misinformation propagated by Christian missionaries. The purpose of these essays was to respond to Wilson's denigration of Zoroastrianism and to prevent further desertions from the Parsi community. Parsi authors attempted to counter Wilson's attacks on the authenticity and validity of Zoroastrian texts, yet were forced to respond in his own terms—something that they found difficult to do. Several authors avoided theological discussions of Zoroastrianism or the scriptures themselves, confining themselves to protesting Christian missionary attacks and cultural pretensions.

The first of these refutations appeared in Gujarati in 1840 by the name *Talim-i Zurtoosht on Vundidad* (The Teachings of Zoroaster in the Vendidad). The author was a Parsi priest and well-known judge, Dosabhoy Sohrabji. The book was commissioned by the Panchayat and funded by Sir Jamsetjee Jeejeebhoy in order to respond to Wilson's attacks on the Vendidad.[67] It also attempts to instruct Parsi youth on their religion.[68] Wilson's lectures on the Zoroastrian text of the Vendidad, argued Sohrabji, misunderstood Zoroastrianism and misled the two youths who converted to Christianity.[69] Sohrabji maintained that the boys' actions were absurd: "Two immature Parsee boys . . . of tender age, left the religion of their birth, which enjoins worshipping one God, converted to Christianity and began worshipping three gods."[70] Wilson and the boys were accused of ignorance of Zoroastrianism, and British officer and Orientalist Major Rawlinson was cited as an authority on the authenticity of the Avesta.

Throughout his book Sohrabji's emphasis is on the absolute monotheistic nature of Zoroastrianism. If the boys had only asked a Zoroastrian priest, he lamented, they would surely have been disabused of the idea that Zoroastrianism was a polytheistic religion. Sohrabji explained the strict monotheism of Zoroastrianism and the importance of an allegorical understanding of some concepts: "Our religion is the religion of Mazda worshippers. You call us fire worshippers in order to defame us but we are believers in one God, the God who created the sky, the earth, the sun, the moon, the first, the water and creatures of all the world. We worship Him and do not know any other God but Him. Nor do we believe in other gods but Him. This one God does not have any partner or father or mother or wife or sons or anyone else. Anybody who believes in any God other than this one is an unworthy man fit for Hell."[71]

Sohrabji attacked Christianity on two fronts. Heavily citing Voltaire, he accused "the true nature of Christianity" of being inferior to Zoroastrianism, since the Christian doctrine of the Trinity excluded it from true monotheism. The frequent recourse to Voltaire allowed Sohrabji to denounce Christianity, not so much from a comparative theological perspective, as on the basis of European Enlightenment criticism.[72] Sohrabji also defended Zoroastrianism in terms evocative of Islamic discourse on monotheism and idolatry. Susan Maneck convincingly argues that Zoroastrian "orthodoxy," owing to intimate contact with Islam, had "long before come to express itself in terms acceptable to categories of Islamic monotheism."[73] Sohrabji's mention of the Bible and biblical prophets in comparison to the prophet Zoroaster implicitly places Zoroastrianism within the biblical tradition.

Three years later an article by journal editor Pestonji Maneckji appeared in the newly established bimonthly magazine *Rahnuma-i Zartushti* (The Way or Guide of Zoroastrians).[74] In an imaginary dialogue between a Parsi and a Christian, the Parsi denounced the Christian doctrines of the Trinity and of original sin as absurd and immoral. Maneckji went further than Sohrabji in drawing on Enlightenment ideas of religion to criticize Christianity. Citing Thomas Paine's *Age of Reason,* Maneckji insisted that Zoroastrianism, unlike Christianity, was rational, humanistic, and moral. Rhetorically, he asked, Did God vouchsafe to man a Revelation in order that it may not be understood? If that be the case, and if every doctrine dictated by the Almighty in His Will be unintelligible, Revelation is of no use whatsoever.[75] Zoroastrianism, he insisted, propounds a rational, even deist, understanding of God.

Maneckji later published a book titled *Discussion on Christian Religion as Contained in the Bible and Propounded by Christian Clergymen.* Written in English, *Discussion* reproduced many of his earlier arguments that had appeared in *Rahnuma-i Zartusht* and also in the Christian missionary journal *Native's Friend.* In it, he again decried Christianity as insufficiently monotheist and irrational, going so far as to label it "absurd." The purpose of his book, however, differed from the defenses of Zoroastrianism made thus far. In *Discussion,* Maneckji railed against Christian claims to superiority on the basis of cultural and political might. He insisted that Christianity should not be credited with Britain's imperialist triumph over India. He went further, rejecting the connection between religion and culture and, more specifically, religion and "civilization." In a key passage, Maneckji rejected Christian missionaries' "civilizing mission" and their belief that "there can be no civilization without Christianity." He was infuriated by the audacity of the missionaries and their misplaced claims to cultural superiority. He accused the missionaries of seeing Indians as "mere savages, immersed in the grossest barbarism, devoid of knowledge, *morality,* and *true religion* and professing rude and debasing *superstition.*"[76] Maneckji explained to his audience that he would not have engaged in religious controversy were it not for the missionaries' behavior. They were "excessively outrageous, clamourous, virulent and audacious in their attacks against the religious doctrines and sacred books of the Natives, especially of the Parsees." Maneckji felt obligated to "critically investigate the nature of the doctrines preached by the missionaries" and found them "neither holy nor divine, neither pure nor moral, but . . . absurd in the highest degree and derogatory to the character of the Supreme Ruler of the Universe."[77]

Both Sohrabji and Maneckji's refutations rest on common assumptions concerning the nature of religion. They also share a rejection of what they see as Christianity's claim to cultural and political superiority. The emphasis on monotheism dominates their discussions of Zoroastrianism. At this time, if not previously, monotheism was accepted as the reigning "orthodoxy" among Zoroastrians and was certainly reinforced as the sine qua non of valid religion in the eyes of Westerners. This insistence on monotheism, however, exists in some tension with their view of conversion. If there is but one god, presumably this god would be the same god as in the Abrahamic (and thus Christian, Jewish, and Muslim) traditions. Their texts indicate some ambivalence as to whether Zoroastrianism is part of the Abrahamic tradition. It is never claimed that Zoroaster was first in the line of the biblical prophets, yet the frequent biblical references and alignment with Islamic conceptions of monotheism and God's attributes suggest a connection that is never made explicit. Insofar as monotheism implies a universal religious truth, however, there is a claim made that Zoroastrianism, like the Abrahamic traditions, is part of a universal religious truth.

Sohrabji and Maneckji found Christian missionaries' attempts at proselytization gratuitous and deeply offensive. Their rebuttals suggest a very different conception of religion from the missionary emphasis on a universal truth in the form of Christianity. Rather, they present Zoroastrianism as deeply associated with communal identity—and a community defined primarily by birth, not by tenets of faith. Zoroastrian resistance to conversion was not solely directed *against Christianity,* but also directed against those individuals wishing to convert *to Zoroastrianism.* This position is more suggestive of an ethnic basis of their religion, rather than as a universalistic theological system. They defend Zoroastrianism less as a theology than as an unassailable identity. In the Indian context of the caste system and diversity of religions, it is not surprising that the Parsis (unlike their coreligionists in Iran) rejected conversion to or from their fold. It is for this reason also that they rejected the equation of religious validity with political or civilizational power. For these authors, religious particularism precludes an acceptance of the value of comparing religions—and the explicit evaluation and choice of religion that this acceptance implies.

Sohrabji's exclamation that Christians were "mad, pigheaded and breakers of the peace" is indicative of his view that proselytization threatened respect for community difference.[78]

The understanding of religion as identifiable with different peoples is evident in a later conversion story—a failed conversion. Dhanjibhai Nauroji, who had converted to Christianity under the influence of Wilson, was ordained in the Free Church Theological College in Edinburgh and returned to India to preach in 1847. A year later, he managed to convert a young Parsi, Nuserwanji Maneckji, who was a teacher in a Presbyterian school. However, only days after his baptism, Maneckji renounced Christianity and returned to the Zoroastrian fold.[79] Maneckji's sudden about-face was owing to the intervention of a number of leading Parsis. A Parsi teacher and Elphinstone Institute alumnus heard of the conversion and wrote to Naoroji Behramji, a fellow alum, asking for help convincing Maneckji to reconsider.[80] Maneckji's reasons for converting follow familiar patterns as earlier conversions. According to the accounts, Maneckji had "reasoned himself into the belief that as the Missionaries are immeasurably superior to the natives in general, and his parents in particular, in point of intellect and morality, in every branch of science and literature . . . so must be their religious system. He has had it also continually impressed on his mind that the Parsee religion contains many childish absurdities and superstitious observances, which forbid the idea of its emanating from a divine source."[81]

According to Behramji (the Elphinstone alumnus), Maneckji mistakenly equated Christianity with European knowledge and political prowess. Europe's greatness, both intellectually and politically, was not owing to its being Christian. Rather, the opposite was the case. The rise of Europe was owing to a process of "throwing off the shackles of the superstitions of the church . . . freedom of conscience and the authority of reason," not the other way around. Behramji noted that the heyday of Christianity in Europe was the Middle Ages, which were also Europe's Dark Ages. "The morality, the refined and polished manners, the customs, institutions, etc. of civilized Europeans" were the "effects of advancing knowledge and civilization."[82] Behramji thus accepted that religion had a causal effect on progress, but rejected the Christian notion that Christianity was the most evolved and enlightened. Rather, other religions have the capacity to likewise free themselves from the "shackles of the superstitions of the church" and similarly to generate civilization.

It is also important to note the recurring theme of "superstition" and irrationality in conversion stories. In each case these reasons were given as the impetus for conversion. They echo Wilson and other scholars' portrayal of Zoroastrian ritual—particularly devotions offered to multiple deities or elements—as backward and superstitious and thus incompatible with a true monotheistic understanding of the Divine. The converts were moved by these arguments and the emphasis on direct spiritual contact with one god, rather than ritual offerings of a more pluralistic nature. Would-be converts echo the Protestant emphasis on scripture as divinely inspired and thus insist on its essential understandability, which they term "rational," as opposed to a more ritualistic set of prescriptions, which are decried as "superstitious."

Maneckji's explanation of his decision to return to Zoroastrianism is equally revealing. He later stated that the best way to please God was by "continuing to profess the faith in which I was born, by worshipping one Supreme Being, and by practicing morality."[83] His reference to morality, monotheism, and religious identity as something into which one is born all illustrate the general perception at the time of the nature of true religion. On the one hand, he accepts the primacy of one God, yet on the other hand, he lays equal claim of Zoroastrianism to worship one God. The argument suggests that there were multiple paths to the same God and that Zoroastrianism was a valid path. As such, there was no need to convert. The notion that there were multiple paths to salvation, although deeply discredited by missionaries, was influenced by European deism and universalism and was professed by many scholars, as well as Zoroastrians at the time. This notion of religious pluralism also reinforced the idea of the centrality of the *form and practice* of a given religion, rather than the truth-value of only one religion.

Although deeply resentful of missionary attacks, the questionable authenticity of sources was not easily refuted. Some Parsis rallied behind the validity of their texts, insisting that they were authentic and worthy of reverence. Others, however, accepted many of the charges against them. One such internal dispute is recorded in the pages of the *Christian Oriental Spectator*. Parsi priest and translator of the Bundaheshn[84] Eduljee Dustoor Dorabjee insisted that it was a true book of religion. However, a Parsi opponent of Wilson's who wrote under the pseudonym "Goosequill" agreed with Wilson that this text should be rejected as "not one of our religious books." He decried it as so full of absurdities that "even a sucking child would not believe. How then shall we term such a book,

7. Parsi priest with umbrella. Phototype of postcard, Bombay, ca. 1919.

a book of religion?" In the Bundaheshn "there are hundreds of observations so contradictorily written as to be utterly at variance with all sense." He then cited several instances, including: "when the ass deposits water in the sea, the waters of the seven worlds become purified thereby," and "poison is rendered innoxious [sic] by hearing the buzzing of flies."[85] Goosequill thus accepted the premise that books should stand up to rational evaluation and in this respect agreed with Wilson that the authenticity and origin of Zoroastrian books must be revisited. To Wilson and Goosequill, the term *rational* connoted the ability of mankind to ascertain the "purpose" of the text. Goosequill was put in an awkward position, however, since the question of the authenticity and dating of the texts was a complicated issue. Once one of the sacred texts was rejected, all of the texts were put in jeopardy. Wilson dismissed all of the Zoroastrian texts as fraudulent. Illustrating the Protestant conviction of the revealed or divinely inspired nature of scriptures, he insisted that the Zoroastrians must "prove that your books came from heaven. And if not, as I believe, then you shouldn't put any confidence in them."[86] He explicitly linked the internal logic of the texts themselves with the validity of the religion: "Can you prove that Zoroastrianism has a divine origin? Every thing which they reveal must be worthy of God, and free from error of every kind. Now, instead of endeavouring to prove that Zoroaster had a divine commission, and that his doctrines were in every respect pure and holy, you admit that your own religion has defects and faults; and that it is your practice to reject that which is bad. You are consequently in a painful situation. Because your religion has faults, it is evident that it did not come from God."[87] The onus was placed on the Parsis to "prove" that their religion was true and to prove it based on the authenticity of their texts that was a function of internal logic, "understandability" as "rationalism," and Divine inspiration as outlined by Wilson. This enormous task would fall to subsequent generations, as discussed in the next chapter.

Long-Term Implications

Wilson, as a product of Scottish evangelical Protestantism, articulated many common Protestant assumptions concerning the nature of religion as a phenomenon. For instance, the anti-Catholic bias implied by anticlericalism and the denunciation of petitionary prayer and formalism were dominant in Wilson's critique of Zoroastrianism. Moreover, the stress on revelation and divine inspiration for scripture, the authority of scripture and text as opposed to "practiced" religion, and the centrality of the moral individual and concomitant moral responsibility toward society were all evident in his dialogues with the Parsis and were largely shared in the Protestant, and thus missionary and scholarly, world.[88] These characteristics of "true" religions were adopted and remained influential criteria as Parsi reformers took up the challenge of reexamining their own traditions, beliefs, and practices.

Wilson and his fellow missionaries had an enormous impact on the Parsis in India, completely disproportionate to their very marginal successes in enticing conversion. Wilson's "war" with the Parsis inaugurated a half century of serious theological dialogue both between himself and the Parsis and, ultimately, within the Parsi community itself. Wilson's attacks on Zoroastrian practices and beliefs threatened not only Zoroastrian theology, scriptural authenticity, and tradition, but also the foundation of community identity as expressed in the two conversion crises. The Zoroastrian community could not afford to avoid confrontation. But what is important here is not just that Wilson initiated serious dialogue on Zoroastrianism, but that he largely dictated the *terms of debate,* the *categories of understanding,* and the *method of analysis* that these dialogues were forced to adopt. In other words, although Wilson was refuted, his presuppositions, definitions, and categorizations surrounding the nature and function of "true" religion in society were largely adopted.

Although Parsis rejected Christian claims to define "civilization," their refutations nevertheless indicate an acceptance of a causal relationship between "moral" religion and "civilization." The refutations of Wilson and other Christian missionaries, along with the conversion stories that prompted them, all equate moral religions with "rational" religion, privilege a spiritual understanding of God over ritual performances, and agree on the unassailable superiority of monotheism. However, it was not so much a question of preferring one religion over another as one *form* of religion over others. This partiality had several implications.

First, the idea that there were multiple paths of salvation based on multiple "true" forms of religion meant that there also existed multiple avenues to achieving civilization and progress. If more than one religion were thus "true" (depending on a religion's *form* and practice, not its essential *validity*), then Zoroastrianism, like Christianity, could be revised in form, providing an avenue toward progress and "civilization." This "multiple paths" notion implicitly denied

European claims to exclusive access to modernity or that Westernization was a prerequisite for "progress." Instead, it posited that modernity was achievable through different religious mediums, although concurring on the forms that any given religion needed to assume. Modernity, as "civilization and progress," therefore was in a sense universal, not essential to Europe or Christianity.

Second, achieving "progress" necessitated that Zoroastrianism assume certain forms or characteristics, which included monotheism, interiorized piety, lack of formalism and ritual, and the notion of individual moral responsibility toward society. This understanding of the relationship between "rational" religion, modernity, and individual consciousness spurred a rethinking of religious tradition. The next generation of Parsis would embrace "moral religion" and its relationship to "civilization" as reasons for religious reform.'

3

The Parsi Response

Rational Religion and the Rethinking of Tradition

> Mere chattering without understanding of mind, followed by heart and soul,
> is not prayer, it is a joke and a mock.
>
> —BAHMANJI FRAMJI BILLIMORIA, *A Warning Word*
> *to Parsees* (1900)

The impetus behind the Parsi religious reform movement derived from both the missionary debates as well as the effects of British schooling on a new generation of Parsis. Reform thus resulted from external theological attacks on existing beliefs and practices that necessitated defense and response. It also had an internal impetus in the form of new cultural and social values instilled by the new Western-style schools. Not surprisingly, the form that religious reform adopted reflected the ongoing religious debates and was believed to be firmly connected to larger goals of "civilization" and "progress." These two contexts indelibly shaped the contours of the reform movement. Many Zoroastrians agreed on the need for change, but not on the extent or the form that this change should take. While most agreed that they needed a priesthood that was capable of responding in kind to the missionary challenges, others took a much wider and more substantive view of the question of modern religion.

The Beginnings of Reform

New theories surrounding the dating of the Zoroastrian religious texts challenged many of the assumptions and traditions held dear by the Zoroastrian community. Scholars, on the basis of strong linguistic evidence, agreed that the Gathas were the only part of the Avesta that dated from the time of Zoroaster.

The rest of the text was of a later provenance and thus certainly not authored by Zoroaster himself. The implications of this new linguistic "discovery" were tremendous. If, as most scholars now believed, only the Gathas were written by Zoroaster, then the subsequent writings were products of later times and did not represent Zoroaster's own teaching. Scholars concluded on the basis of this linguistic evidence that Zoroastrianism as a religion had undergone significant changes in the post-Zoroaster period—changes that were frequently at variance with Zoroaster's message.

The view that religion has a history and thus is contextually determined represented a very different understanding of religious tradition than that of the hallowed practice of truth. If religious traditions were contextual and changing, then the "authenticity" and truth-value of tradition itself was thrown into question. The recognition of historicity prompted the reconsideration not only of various specific traditions but of tradition itself. Parsi reformers, following Western scholarship, now understood Zoroastrianism as an unfolding historical process. They thus identified "true" and "authentic" Zoroastrianism with Zoroaster only (and thus the Gathas only), dismissing later texts and the traditions associated with them as spurious, false, and deviations of "true" Zoroastrianism.

This understanding meant of course that Zoroastrianism as currently practiced was not "true" Zoroastrianism. Parsis explained deviation as historical accretions, distinguishing them from what they claimed was "essential" and "authentic" Zoroastrian practice. In other words, those practices they deemed inauthentic were rejected as Hindu customs that had gradually infiltrated Parsi practice. Community leaders, as well as various Zoroastrian religious figures, moved to "purify" the tradition from historical accretions that had occurred both as a result of the passage of time and as a result of contact with other (in this case primarily Hindu but also Muslim) traditions. As early as 1819 but especially after 1823, the Panchayat took the lead in identifying "backward" practices as Hindu, including child marriages, polygamy, participation in Hindu festivals, excessive expenditures for weddings and other events, and the overindulgence of priests. A contemporary Parsi historian of the Panchayat describes these practices as "stupid," "unseemly," "savage," and "flesh-creeping" and noted that they were "of purely Hindu origin" and "entirely at variance with the spirit of the Zoroastrian religion."[1] Reformers employed their own self-whittled yardsticks in this process of evaluating traditions and practices.

In 1852 reformers coalesced around the Religious Reform Association (Rahmuma'i Mazdiasna), which formulated a clear set of objectives for change in religious belief and practice. The central mission was to reevaluate Zoroastrian beliefs and practices using current scholarship and social values as a yardstick. Reformers thus sought to identify which aspects of their tradition were conducive to modern society and religion and which inimical. It was no coincidence that reformers' commitment to new social values and notions of "progress" became the measure of the authenticity and thus validity of religious practices. Whichever practices and beliefs were deemed inconsistent with their values were conveniently labeled as "foreign" and attacked as superstitions. Not coincidentally, the practices that were identified as foreign accretions were the ones that had been clearly singled out by the British as "backward" and "primitive." British reformers had long railed against child marriages, sati, polygamy, and, betraying their largely Protestant predilections, priestly privileges.[2] Parsi reformers justified religious reform as a "return" to original, authentic practice and prophetic intent even as they adopted contemporary British social values as their own measure of authenticity. Many in the Zoroastrian community, despite the labeling of polygamy and child marriage as "Hindu," were reluctant to forsake them, although they did relinquish them before many other groups did—a fact widely touted as symptomatic of Zoroastrian "civilization" as compared to other Indian communities.

Reformers were determined to identify the "original" or "essential" Zoroastrianism and to return to it. Such a return necessitated an identification of both what was "essential" and what had resulted from specific historical contexts and spurious later texts. The identification of "essential" Zoroastrianism was deeply influenced by Western notions of religion. Not surprisingly, reformers determined original Zoroastrianism to be very much in line with current notions of "true" religion. They identified "original" Zoroastrianism as monotheistic, deeply ethical, and nearly devoid of ritual. They also emphasized Zoroastrianism's contributions and similarities to later Abrahamic traditions. Reformers were also influenced by their social reform agenda and notions of what constituted modern civilization and "progress." Accordingly, they claimed that "original" Zoroastrianism promoted women's rights and was rational, anticlerical, and a progenitor of modern science and hygiene.

Reformers broke with their orthodox brethren especially over the issue of the Avestan language and its use in prayer. Citing lack of familiarity with Avestan, both by the priesthood and by the laity, reformers refused to recite prayers in Avestan and demanded a translation of canon prayer into the local language of Gujarati as well as English. Their position was symptomatic of their view that modern, rational religions do not require a mediator between God and the individual. Reformers, in many ways echoing Wilson, emphasized the individual's spiritual connection and understanding of the Divine. Since they believed that the function of prayer was to relate to God, they denigrated prayer that was formulaic and thus devoid of any spiritual connection.

Criticism of ritual practices and Avestan prayers directly challenged the religious status of the Zoroastrian priesthood. Reformers argued that the priesthood was uneducated and ignorant, and even unnecessary. The translation of religious texts into vernacular languages and their emphasis on a direct, spiritual relationship between God and believer made the ritualistic role of priests as mediators anachronistic. In the vituperative words of a reformer, "Ignorant and unlearned as these priests are, they do not and cannot command the respect of the laity. The latter are more enlightened and educated than the former, and hence the position of the so-called spiritual guides has fallen into contempt."[3] Reformers thus blamed the priesthood for what they saw as the inaccuracy of Zoroastrian practices. They also changed their understanding and expectations of the function of the priesthood. Rather than performing sacred liturgical rituals, reformers now believed that priests should serve as "spiritual guides" to the community—a function deeply influenced by Protestant ideas of believers' relationship to God mediated only through scriptures, not clerics, as well as the primacy of spirituality over formulaic ritual.

For orthodox Zoroastrians unwilling to dismiss long-standing traditions, reformers' abandonment of Avestan in prayer was tantamount to a renunciation of the religion itself. They believed that Avestan was a holy language and that prayers in Avestan had an effect on the Divine. They defended the priests' mediating roles as the guardians of the Avestan language and the performers of rituals that alone could affect the Divine.[4] Priests were envisioned not as spiritual guides for individual understanding of God, but rather as practiced performers of sacred rites.

One of the principal chasms between Reformers and the Orthodox was and would remain the efficacy of rituals. Orthodox and reform-minded laity, however, did largely concur on the intellectual poverty of the Zoroastrian priesthood. There was a general consensus that the priests were unable to respond to Christian challenges to Zoroastrianism or to serve as intellectual leaders of the community. Reformers and Orthodox alike were willing to compromise on the issue of heredity, and the tradition of only allowing sons of priests to enter the priesthood was gradually abandoned, permitting those boys interested in pursuing a religious career to do so. The absence of a strong group of educated priests, however, certainly allowed the impetus for reform of the religion to fall to the laity. Quoting a Reformer, "Inquiring and intelligent youths from among the laity, are also now engaged in the study of their religious books; and considering the present state of Parsee society, it is probable that through their instrumentality more good will be effected than from the exertions of the priesthood."[5]

Religious reform thus also involved the reeducation of the priesthood. New exigencies required the mastery of new intellectual methods as well as "spiritual" guidance. A number of new seminaries were established to train Zoroastrian priests in Bombay such as the Mulla Feroze Madressa in 1854. As opposed to traditional training solely in memorization of Avestan prayers, priests were trained in European philology, languages, and comparative religion, as well as contemporary Zoroastrian studies. The founders of the new seminaries believed that "they should be in a position not only to recite prayers, but to present an intellectual exegesis of the holy scriptures and a sophisticated explanation of the essence of religion and religious matters also acceptable to educated believers."[6] The role of priests thus changed from primarily a liturgical one to one of an intellectual capable of discoursing in the most up-to-date international religious studies arena. The relatively small number of priests who graduated from such training were prepared to participate in the debates surrounding Zoroastrian tradition and took up positions in both the Orthodox and the Reformist camps.[7]

The difference between the Reformist and Orthodox positions had significant ramifications for their respective conceptions of God and man's relationship to the Divine. These differences were most vehemently expressed in the disagreement over the efficacy of ritual. Both camps, however, engaged in serious revision of Zoroastrian tradition in light of Western scholarly research and Protestant missionary perspectives on the nature and function of religion in the modern world. A closer examination of several representative texts provides a much fuller illustration of their respective positions and their new understandings of Zoroastrianism in light of contemporary religious studies.

Reformist Zoroastrianism

Dosabhoy Framjee, a leading exponent of the Reformist position, published a comprehensive work on Zoroastrian history, religion, and tradition in 1858 titled *Parsees: Their History, Manners, Customs, and Religion.*[8] Ostensibly, he wrote the book in order to "acquaint" the British public with the Zoroastrians (Parsis) in India so that they could develop greater understanding and mutual support. In fact, the book is an attempt to demonstrate that Zoroastrianism is a modern (a.k.a. rational) religion, akin to Christianity, and that as a consequence, the Parsis are natural allies of the British in their commitment to progress and civilization. Framjee's arguments are a prime example of early Reformist ideas.

First, he suggested that not only was Zoroastrianism a monotheistic faith, but that it was *the origin* of monotheism and later influenced Abrahamic religions. He therefore claimed that not only were Zoroastrianism and Christianity *currently* compatible, but their very *essences* were similar. Zoroastrianism "inculcate[s] those sublime doctrines and sound precepts of morality which command the respect of every civilized nation on earth."[9] Framjee made these claims not based on any presentation of theological material, but solely on his own characterization of these two religions, together with comprehensive quotations from European travelers attesting to its monotheism.

Framjee identified Zoroastrianism as a "progressive" religion by describing it as "a simple form of theism" and Zoroastrians as "pure Deists."[10] In essence, it is a moral philosophy, he argues, and should be understood allegorically. Any emphasis on ritual is simply a result of misunderstanding that led to superstitions and reifications of theoretical concepts. Quoting European traveler Forbes's *Oriental Memoirs,* Framjee explained that "superstition and fable have, through a lapse of ages, corrupted the stream of the religious system which in its source was pure and sublime."[11] Although he continued to accept the existence of miracles (a position contrary to later, stricter, Reformist views of religion), he did emphasize that the value of prayer was to the psyche of the worshiper, not as the Orthodox understood it, to affect the Divine and the physical and spiritual worlds. In line with other Reformists, Framjee renounced ritual, positioning salvation as a function of social commitment and behavior, rather than the correct performance of prescribed ritual and prayer. This deeply Protestant construction of religious ethics focuses on the spiritual relationship of man to the Divine through knowledge and the effects on individual character that result.

Framjee concluded that original Zoroastrianism was true, pure, and spiritual and that contemporary Zoroastrian beliefs and practices must be purged of superstition and a mistaken orientation toward ritual. In addition, Zoroastrians must rid their religion of non-Zoroastrian beliefs and practices that had gradually seeped in owing to the influence of other religions. He explained that "it was natural that the Parsees should have contracted, as time passed on, many of the practices of their neighbors. The first Parsees in India had of necessity to follow certain of the Hindoo practices, in order to secure the protection, assistance, and goodwill of the Hindoo princes." The problem, he expounded, was that "Parsees fell into the error that these borrowed practices were sanctioned by their own religion."[12] Zoroastrianism thus need not be revised, simply *rediscovered* through purification.

Framjee was at pains to distance Zoroastrianism from other "Oriental" religions in his attempt to align it with Christianity. The claim of commonality with Christianity enabled him to posit that religious commonality produced "civilizational" commonality. Framjee claimed that Zoroastrians were racially and intellectually the most civilized of Oriental nations and, as such, natural allies of the British. He directly linked the nature of Zoroastrian religion with the Parsis' ability to achieve social and political progress. The Parsis, he claimed, "have few prejudices to stand in the way of their advancement. They are neither trammeled by the miserable institution of caste, nor does their religion lie like a stumbling block to arrest their onward progress."[13] "Year by year," he wrote, Parsis "are becoming more Europeanized, not only in their manners and customs, but in their thoughts and feelings."[14]

Civilization, as expressed by a commitment to contemporary social values, was also clearly demonstrated by the status of Parsi women: "In their domestic relations, they are almost European; women with them are something more than the degraded playthings which they are with other Eastern nations. . . . [T]he Parsee's wife is his companion, and his children are his friends."[15] Framjee concluded his work with a tip of the hat to the British: "Our task is now accomplished, and if the present work has succeeded in familiarizing Europeans with a race who are

8. Parsi tower of silence outside of Bombay, India, ca. 1906 postcard.

seeking to become, in one sense, Europeans themselves, the aim and end of the writer will have been realized."[16]

Religion and "Civilization"

Three additional important Reformist tracts written around the turn of the century illustrate the parameters and commonalities of Parsi Reformist ideas: Bahmanji Framji Billimoria's *Warning Word to Parsees* (1900), Ervad Sheriarji Dadabhai Bharucha's *Brief Sketch of the Zoroastrian Religion and Customs* (1903), and S. A. Kapadia's *Teachings of Zoroaster and the Philosophy of the Parsi Religion* (1908).[17] Like Framjee, Billimoria, Bharucha, and Kapadia were all associated with reformist institutions and were familiar with Western scholarship on Zoroastrianism. They echoed and elaborated on many of the themes articulated by Framjee. Billimoria held ardently to the veracity of the Gathas alone of all Parsi texts and insisted on a return to the "pure" religion of Zoroaster. In keeping with Reformist views of the historical corruption of Zoroaster's teachings, he maintained that "true" Zoroastrianism was the original monotheism and superior to all other religions. Bharucha and Kapadia, like Framjee, were convinced of the intimate connection between the form of religion and the ability to generate "civilization" and "progress." Their principal intellectual objective was to liken Zoroastrianism to Christianity and thus to demonstrate that Zoroastrians were "civilized" like the (Christian) British. They illustrated the deeply causal relationship between religion and society typical of Reformist Zoroastrians. It is noteworthy that all three of these first-generation Parsi Reformists addressed their works on "true" Zoroastrianism not only to their own community, but to a British audience as well.

Billimoria's *Warning Word to Parsees* is specifically addressed to the Parsi community and styled as an admonition against keeping faith with a "perverted" religion—one that is not "true" Zoroastrianism. He also addressed a copy of his treatise to "The Librarian, British Museum" and acknowledged his debt to European scholars for bringing the "true" Zoroastrianism of the Gathas to light: "Even at the cost of being called a flatterer, I must say, and it is well-known, that before the learned savants of Europe took up the study of Zoroastrianism, the Parsee and his priest were as ignorant of their true faith, as preached by their prophet in his Gathas and of the corruptions admitted therein in the later Avesta books, as newly born babes. Sincere and heartfelt thanks are due to such European Scholars as have brought the truth of the Zoroastrian religion to the knowledge of the Parsees."[18]

Billimoria virulently attacked Parsi priests, not simply as defenders of tradition, or as ignorant of Avestan language, or even for their inability to counter Western criticism—the charges typically leveled against Parsi priests. *A Warning* is more scathing in its claim that priests were deliberately responsible for sneaking "perverse" dogmas and "corrupt" practices into Zoroastrianism and thus undercutting Zoroaster's rejection of these ideas. Zoroastrianism as preached by Zoroaster and as embodied in the Gathas is a spiritual, monotheistic religion "without angels and other deities joined to [God]."[19]

After Zoroaster's death, "false faiths and creeds have been introduced . . . side by side with pure Zarathustrianism these false faiths have crept in and made thy pure faith a degraded one."[20] The responsibility for this degradation of Zoroaster's message lies on the shoulders of the priests: "What hell bound sinner brought these and other vile dogmas into the pure faith of thy Zarathustra [sic]? See well; it is thy priest of yore who preacheth it, teacheth it to thee, calls upon thee to believe in it and practise the vile doctrine, thine priest of yore curseth them."[21] Billimoria challenged Parsis to "see for thyself how angels and other creatures have been joined to thy Lord, praised and worshipped with Him."[22] He called *nirang* (consecrated bull's urine) the "filthy piss of filthy beasts" and abjured its use.[23] Speaking directly to each Parsi, he called on them to reject all texts with the exception of the Gathas. "Is thy present day faith, O Parsa, the faith that thy prophet brought to thee from God? No, certainly it is not; much alien has crept into it and has corrupted it, nay even perverted it. Wouldst thou know this truth for thyself? Then read and study the Gathas of thy prophet . . . and not those interpolated later on."[24] He continued, "Back with vile dogmas and viler doctrines and all filthy importations of older faith, back with them all again to the darkness whence they rose. Forward with thee and thine to the pure faith. . . . in its original purity."[25]

Billimoria's "pure" Zoroastrianism emerges as a spiritual, ethical, and monotheist faith, one whose ethics revolves around knowledge of God. He called on each individual to "teach thyself and true knowledge will shed the beams of Light Eternal on thee, for true knowledge brings true belief the rest is only false belief."[26] Ethics, in Billimoria's rendering, focuses not on correct "performance" of ritual or the recitation of set Avestan prayers, but rather on a much more individualized spirituality. Real prayer involves intent and consciousness, not simply outward forms. Billimoria urged Parsis to "purify thine prayers, take them only from that *sacred spring* thy Gathas, the prayers of thine prophet, the *will* and *wish* of Ahurmazd thy God."[27] He made a particular point of rejecting prayer as performance, insisting on the necessity of knowledge and love as prerequisites for "real" prayer. He admonished Parsis to "chatter not thy prayers like a monkey nor patter it off like a parrot, without heart or mind in it; but make it understood by the mind, felt by the heart, loved by thine very soul. . . . [U]nderstand how thou praisest thy God. . . . [U]nderstand what you sayest to Him."[28] Knowledge is at the center of prayer: "Mere chattering without understanding of mind, followed by heart and soul, is not prayer, it is a joke and a mock. . . . Thine prayers should be pure and sincere coming from the heart and mind and not from a chattering tongue."[29]

At the end of *A Warning* it is clear that Billimoria was in dialogue with Christian claims to superiority. Contrary to Christian pretensions, "true"

Zoroastrianism is superior to any other faith, he argued. Zoroastrianism is the origin of monotheism and is a universal religion of mankind. Here he directly challenged Christian missionary claims that Christianity was the most evolved religion and thus uniquely suited to become the universal religion of mankind. Billimoria provided his audience with shields to defend themselves against proselytization: "When men and missionaries of other faiths and creeds come to thee and say to thee 'come ye unto us and our faith, for therein is salvation,' then answer thou aloud to them 'Liars and knaves, salvation comes of God only, of His *Holiness* and *good mind,* of His *Devotion,* His *Piety* and *Bounty,* of practised virtues and moralities, of good acts and deeds done in this life; not of any particular creed or faith, not of any human creature born of a woman.'"[30] Billimoria then proceeded to arm his community with weapons to claim superiority over other faiths: "Remember, O Parsa, thine faith was the first faith on Earth, thine prophet the first on Earth; thou the first to know the Eternal Creator of All."[31] For these reasons, Zoroastrianism is superior to other faiths and enjoys more claims to universality than Christianity: "Thine God the Universal Lord, not the God of a faith or a race; Thine prophet the father of all prophets, thine religion the mother of all religions; thine Gathas, the preaching of thy prophet, his *ideas* and *conceptions* are the root, branch and foundation of all subsequent religions."[32]

Bharucha, a fellow at the University of Bombay and custodian of the Mulla Feroze Madressa Library, was commissioned by the Reformist *Rahnumai Mazdayasnan Sabha* to write his essay in order to present it at the World's Parliament of Religions held in conjunction with the World Exposition in Chicago in 1893.[33] His audience was thus twofold—first, the international audience of missionaries and religious scholars at the Parliament of Religions and, second, the Parsi community in Bombay. Bharucha echoed the refrain of Gathic purity so central to Billimoria, insisting that the true essence of Zoroastrianism must be extracted solely from the Gathas and that the rest of the tradition must be historicized.[34] "The Gathas show very clearly that Spitama Zarathushtra preached and inculcated a pure monotheistic creed based on the quintessence of morality"; "many . . . passages occur in the Gathas which go a long way to prove that Zoroaster proclaimed pure Theism to the world long before other prophets of other nations appeared."[35] Bharucha painted Zoroastrianism as the first, if not original, monotheistic religion. Any current deviations were a result of divergence from Gathic Zoroastrianism: "In the ancient Iranian world, Zoroaster alone seems to be the first to have taught pure, unmixed monotheism which, owing to the later deteriorating accretions, came to be reduced into what may be called a kind of polytheism."[36] Bharucha, like Billimoria, downplayed the prevalent ritualism, instead emphasizing individual spiritualism: "Generally *every one prays individually by himself,* but on several important occasions public worship by the whole congregation is also performed."[37]

True Zoroastrianism promotes individual ethical behavior in society. Bharucha described Zoroastrianism as "moral," "utilitarian," "practical," "rational," "ethical," and "humane." Such "progressive" values as "loyalty to sovereign," "industry and diligence," "chastity," "self-reliance," "charity," "promotion of education," and "cleanliness" figure prominently among his list of Zoroastrian ethics.[38] Echoing Framjee, Bharucha blamed "backward" practices such as child marriage on the adoption of Hindu customs. Zoroastrianism, by contrast, promotes "sanitary and hygienic notions which are a striking reflex of the teachings of modern science."[39] In effect, Bharucha argued that "backward" beliefs and customs inimical to "civilized" values were not quintessentially Zoroastrianism and as such easily jettisoned.[40]

Kapadia's *Teachings of Zoroaster and the Philosophy of the Parsi Religion* was dedicated to Her Royal Highness the Princess of Wales and portrayed Zoroastrianism in a very similar light as did Framjee, Billimoria, and Bharucha. Themes of Gathic purity and the subsequent historical degeneration, or "fall," are repeated. Kapadia reiterated Reformist depictions of Zoroastrian essence as spiritual and ethical, downplaying ritualism and formalism. In a now familiar refrain, Kapadia disassociated Parsis from Hindus. He was more determined in his efforts than Framjee and Bharucha, however, and asserted that the principal difference between them was a function of the contrast between monotheism and polytheism. Zoroastrianism, with its "pristine purity of Ahura worship," was contrasted with "the great evil" of polytheism.[41]

Kapadia explicitly discussed the evolution of religions and the importance of certain *forms* of religious thought and practice as more conducive to "progress" than others. He argued that the "great Christian nation of England" produced the British Empire. Linking religion with civilization, he argued that Zoroastrianism in its pure form (implicitly when it most closely resembled "progressive" Protestantism of the British Empire) produced the greatest empire of the day.[42] In Kapadia's rendering, "true" religion enables political power and, ultimately, domination over other, lesser, civilizations. The connection between religion and progress is reiterated in Kapadia's conclusion, where he asserted that as a result of the "teachings of Zoroaster," Parsi households live in "peace and happiness," are "loyal and peace-abiding subjects of the British Crown," and serve as an example of a "benevolent community to the people of the world."[43] "It is very rare to find a Parsi of a criminal instinct," Kapadia asserted, "because Parsis have acquired the conception of God and nature."[44]

Origins and the Claim to Modernity

Reformist texts such as the ones discussed above employ arguments that reveal the authors' understanding of the connections between religion and civilization, as well as their views of the relationship between modernity and the West. The assertion that "pure" (Gathic) Zoroastrianism enjoys similar (rational) qualities as Protestantism is central to claims for religious reform, as well as to Reformist arguments that such a revived, or "cleansed," religion would engender "progress" and "civilization." The authors, however, go further than arguing for similarities with Christianity. They frequently assert claims of "origins." In other words, Zoroastrianism was the original progenitor of monotheism. This claim is founded on more than a desire to jettison religious traditions believed to be inimical to contemporary social values and return to the clean slate of the Gathas. The authors' claims of *origins* implicitly involve the relationship between the West and modernity.

Claiming origins means that religious reform actually entails a *return* rather than a departure. This point has several related implications. First, in its essence, Zoroastrianism has the desired characteristics. Returning to them would thus be a regeneration of existing, albeit dormant, qualities, rather than the adoption of foreign qualities. It is in this sense that the argument for "authenticity" has such profound resonance, since if something is "authentic," it is indigenous and essential rather than being foreign and thus external. Second, this statement then implies that "authentic" or essential characteristics do not need to be engendered. If Zoroastrianism did not inherently have these desirable qualities, it would necessitate *adopting* foreign qualities. It is in a sense an argument about causality. Claiming origins is a claim of possible engendering, rather than adoption. This point has profound implications for reformist views of modernity.

The claim to origins is simultaneously a claim to the universality of modernity and the denial of uniquely Western claims to having engendered it. Rather than necessitating imitation of the West, or adoption of Western institutions, Reformists are in essence claiming that modernity is accessible, produceable by Zoroastrians as well. While affirming the causal connection between the form and function of religion and the level of progress and civilization of a country, Reformists argued that this form of religion was not uniquely Christian. Rather, Zoroastrianism, like Christianity, had access to these forms that promoted "civilization." Great Britain was an example, not a model to be imitated. If religion were purged of nonoriginal, nonessential, that is, untrue, practices and understandings, then it would also generate similar salutatory effects on society.

The consciousness of the constructed nature of tradition enabled reformers to "uncover" the essence of religion. Reformers insisted that they were uncovering, or *recovering*, original ideas, when really they were themselves constructing it anew. One of the problems with Reformist arguments is their inconsistent use of historicism. They insisted on the recognition of context as a way of recovering essence, yet in fact their arguments rested on the denial of *their own context* as shaping their notions of the essential. What is interesting but ultimately false

9. Parsis worshiping before the new moon, with Church Gate railway station in the background, Bombay, India, postcard. #516, negative no. V27426T, from Keystone "Tour of the World," 1930s.

about their reasoning is the claim to be able to discern essence, when really the process was more one of labeling what was undesirable from what was believed to be conducive to "progress and civilization." That "progress and civilization" rest not only on religion *as practiced* but also on religion *as conceived* is significant. It is evidence of the change in conception of the nature of religion as a human phenomenon itself and its deep connection to individual and society.

"Modern" Orthodox Zoroastrianism

The Orthodox reformulation of Zoroastrian tradition began somewhat later than the Reformist abandonment of tradition as historically corrupted in favor of an "original" spiritual essence. It is possible that it was a more complicated task to revise and reevaluate traditions than it was to reject them. Certainly, the Orthodox position required a sophisticated understanding of traditional religious texts and commentaries, as well as mastery of the Avestan language, that the Reformist challenge did not. In any event, the Orthodox position, like that of the Reformists, owed a great debt to the new seminaries that were established in the mid-nineteenth century as well as to European philological and religious studies.

In 1867 an orthodox Zoroastrian priest, Dastur Erachji Sohrabji Meherjirana, wrote a Zoroastrian catechism in Gujarati (*Rehbar-e Din-e Zarthushti*).[45] He explained his motivation in the introduction, stating that Zoroastrians needed instruction on correct religious practice: "The commandments of our religion are not known to all because they are written in a variety of books many of which are in different languages. For this reason many of us do not know exactly what is proper or improper in regard to our holy religion. Zoroastrians often go astray because of their ignorance."[46] Erachji is clearly responding to "ignorance" of "proper" "commandments" of the Zoroastrian religion that interestingly he attributes to the variety of texts and languages of the sources. This condition, however, is not new. What is apparent at this point in the mid-nineteenth century is twofold. First, individual Zoroastrians seek to read the texts themselves (and thus need linguistic access). Second, Zoroastrian individuals are implicitly claiming the right to *understand* and thus to *interpret* and practice the religion themselves, rather than following the existing set of traditions.

Erachji's conception of religion centers on the role of ritual in man's relationship with the Divine. He clearly defines *correct religion as correct practice of religious commandments.* Salvation thus results from correct religious *performance,* rather than belief in, or knowledge of, the nature of God, as formulated by the Reformists. For Erachji, knowledge of the Divine is an acceptance of the relationship of the material and spiritual realms. Ethics thus consists of proper nurturing of the Divine interaction in the material world through a conscious participation in the furthering of good versus evil. The tripartite avowal of "good thoughts, good words, good deeds" signifies ethical behavior that both results from and causes the maintenance of the proper relationship to and between the material and spiritual realms. Prayer and other ritual behavior are the principal and most efficacious means of achieving this goal. Salvation largely depends upon man's attempt to counter evil by correct ritual behavior. Individual Zoroastrians must consciously and accurately follow the "proscribed way" of ritual and prayer as it is the fundamental commandment of religion.[47]

Ritual is thus an essential, not tangential, element of Zoroastrianism, according to Erachji. His catechism frequently mentions the *effects* of rituals on the Divine: prayers are described as literally, not figuratively, "health giving," and they "keep away evil" and "protect our body."[48] Ritual utterances in the Avestan language, *manthras,* have power to affect the Divine, as do the various liturgies required by both laymen and priests. Erachji is adamant about the importance of offering prayers only in Avestan, directly challenging the Reformist position that prayers ought to be offered in a language understandable by the layperson.[49] Although he nowhere insists on retaining the traditional hereditary nature of the priesthood, he does emphasize the necessity of priests for the performance of certain liturgies—the ones requiring extensive knowledge of Avestan language, ritual, and lengthy purification ceremonies central to their efficacy. Furthermore, the priests guide the community in correct observance, as did Zoroaster: "It is the dastur [priest] who succeeds Zoroaster and shows [the way of] the religion. The guiding role of the prophet should not be absent; thus there is need for dasturs."[50]

The catechism as a whole is a powerful reassertion of the necessity of ritual, and although he does not state this point explicitly, Erachji clearly rejects the Reformist position that seeks to ignore the effect of ritual on the Divine. Despite this fundamental, indeed irreconcilable, difference between Erachji's orthodox and the Reformist positions, Erachji too evidences the nineteenth-century reform context. His text, while Orthodox in the sense that it defends traditional Zoroastrian beliefs and practices, is nonetheless affected by the

Christian challenge to Zoroastrianism and clearly a product of nineteenth-century debates on the nature of religion and the role of the individual. This fact is illustrated in three ways.

First, there is the question surrounding Erachji's treatment of Zoroastrianism as monotheistic. Despite his acceptance of the traditional corpus of texts (most of which were rejected by the Reformists) as authentic and thus authoritative, there is a marked absence of dualistic understandings of the religion in his catechism. Monotheism reigns supreme, yet also unchallenged in the *Rehbar:* "God Himself is Creator; no one except Him; God alone cares for an nourishes all."[51] As pointed out by the editors, "Much of the Pahlavi [traditionally accepted] literature cannot be interpreted as teaching a simple monotheism. . . . [I]t affirms a dualism: evil in combat with a superior God of Wisdom, Ohrmazd."[52] The editors suggest that Erachji's own monotheistic approach may "reflect what has always been the heart of the living Zoroastrian concern." However, they also posit that "the monotheistic tone . . . may be a reaction to the influence of Christian missions among the Parsis."[53] I would argue that Erachji's emphasis on monotheism and the absence of any discussion of dualism lends credence to the second of these hypotheses. Regardless of how dualism-monotheism was traditionally understood, the clear dominance of monotheism suggests an acceptance of the view introduced by the Protestant Christian missionaries, that dualistic religions are primitive and false.

It is Erachji's *use of texts,* however, that most clearly demonstrates the changed religious context of nineteenth-century India. His textual citations, seeking to prove and provide evidence of his interpretation, are evidence of a change in the way he understood the relationship of religion to individuals. Rather than simply listing correct observances and asserting that they are correct *because they are part of tradition,* Erachji instead provides textual citations as proof, as demonstrable evidence of rational explanations of the function of traditions—locating their justification in their *function* and *meaning,* rather than tradition per se. This consciousness of social context and function along with argumentation based on evidence is by definition a *rationalist* rationale that is clearly divergent from *traditionalist* explanations of events or practices.

Erachji's "rational" context is even more apparent when one considers his reasons for writing the catechism. The very fact that he is providing an explanation of the rationale behind Zoroastrianism—a rationale explained to an audience of laypersons—suggests the influence of nineteenth-century religious discussions concerning the nature of religion and the preeminence of the individual worshiper as well as the locus of discussions among the laity, as opposed to the priests. An exploration of the nature of his argument, and the audience he addresses, illustrates this point.

Erachji's argument based on citations of historical texts (as proof) and rationale based on purpose of religion, the nature of man, God, and their relationship is not a traditionalist argument and first emerges in the nineteenth century when tradition and traditions were reexamined and reevaluated from a contextual standpoint. Moreover, in the past, even the priestly class was not familiar with such rationale, as opposed to memorizing texts and rituals. The Zoroastrian community did not have seminaries at any level, as did the Muslim community where every child learned the basic beliefs and religiously requisite practices. Among Zoroastrians, these beliefs and practices were taught only at home, and there was a much wider gulf between laity and the priesthood, especially since entrance to the priesthood was exclusively hereditary.

In Erachji's case, his audience is the laity. And he is clearly committed to convincing his audience, not simply asserting the value and efficacy of traditional religious practice. He therefore evidences no compulsion, but is instead in the position of attempting to explain and thereby convince his audience to choose to follow traditions. His recognition of Zoroastrianism as not correctly followed also suggests that in addition to a falling off of practice in general, there may have been a general dearth in traditional practice owing to the decline of the priesthood, in numbers as well as authority. Certainly, Parsi community members in the twentieth century would complain of just this problem. Erachji wrote the catechism for laity to understand and practice religion. This purpose indicates an attempt to protect and safeguard traditions, not an assumption of automatic practice based on priestly authority. Yet it also betrays the need to justify religion, to provide a rational explanation to the laity. This need is tantamount to an acknowledgment of the right of each individual to understand the intent of practice and dogma—in other words, *to discern God's intent*. In so doing, it also acknowledges the authority of individuals to interpret, for themselves, religious practice and belief and to engage with God's intent in individualized, spiritual, and meaningful ways. In this manner, religion thus becomes an individualized piety. It is no coincidence that the catechism was composed in the local language of Gujarati so as to reach as wide an audience as possible.

Conclusion

The Zoroastrian community in India underwent significant changes over the course of the nineteenth century. Foremost among these changes were the growth of merchant community leadership and the emergence of a reform movement that connected religion with a social reform agenda articulated along British lines. The authority and community leadership enjoyed by the middle- and upper-class merchants served the community well since they were skilled at organization and management and had generous financial resources at their disposal. It also undoubtedly lent a certain pragmatic and British-oriented tenor to their reform projects that not surprisingly centered on the development of educational, religious, and community institutions.

In addition to defining community interests, merchant leadership was remarkable for its depth and breadth. The comparative paucity of the priesthood, intellectually, financially, institutionally, and socially, relative to the merchants is noteworthy, particularly when considering that the reevaluation of religious tradition (whether reformist or orthodox) took place largely outside of the religious establishment. Whereas in the Islamic case, the reevaluation of tradition occurred *both* from within and from without the religious establishment, the Zoroastrian priesthood was never in a position to dominate the discussion, let alone dictate its parameters or claim ultimate religious authority. In the Parsi context, Zoroastrian priests certainly *participated* in religious debates, but always as individual scholars, rather than representatives of a powerful interest group with institutional backing.

It is illustrative of the clergy's weakness in this regard that even on the question of morality and religious duty, the laity dominated public space. In one striking example, a public lecture was delivered by Sorabjee Jamsetjee on March 27, 1856, in the town hall of Bombay. According to Framjee, the lecture "was entirely of a moral character, dealing with the responsibility of man to God, the importance of life in relation to eternity, the necessity of preparation for death, and the final judgment which awaits every individual of the human race. It appropriately and strikingly illustrated the primary and essential duties of man to himself, to his fellows, and to his Maker, its whole aim being to induce every member of the community to live soberly, righteously, and godly." Not surprisingly, Framjee equated this lecture with Protestant Christian notions, remarking that "with a very few alterations it might have done for the Christian pulpit." He also noted the threat that this lecture posed to the authority of the Zoroastrian priests: "The Mobeds will see from it that they must either soon amend their teaching or have their services dispensed with altogether."[54]

The reevaluation of Zoroastrian religious tradition was initiated, if not spawned, by the context of British imperialism and Parsi merchant leadership. The two principal positions, Reformist and Orthodox, were characterized by their understandings of Zoroastrian religious texts and their respective attitudes toward Tradition itself. Reformers, accepting only the Gathas, reasoned that original Zoroastrianism was not ritualistic and thus that its strong tradition of ritualism was in fact a historical departure from true Zoroastrianism. They were antagonistic not only to specific traditions (as ultimately false) but also to the emergence and solidification of tradition itself as merely the sum of incorrect practices. Asserting the need to return to a pure, original Zoroastrianism, Reformists were in line with both evolutionary scholarly studies of religion and Protestant convictions concerning the nature and function of "rational" religion. Reformists claimed Zoroastrianism as a rational religion by insisting on its essential spirituality and its location as the original monotheistic faith in line with the Abrahamic tradition. This spirituality they associated with deist notions of religion and with the intimate and moral relationship of the individual vis-à-vis God.

The question of the authenticity of religious texts was also important for the Orthodox, although they were unwilling to abandon tradition altogether as a consequence of the historicization of texts. Rather than rejecting tradition as always and necessarily a product of changing historical context, Orthodox Zoroastrians maintained the validity of tradition while seeking to readjust some of the particular traditions. They therefore used a new yardstick to measure the validity of traditions. This yardstick included the concepts of utility and function (and later science and hygiene) and as such was new. This position allowed for the realignment of traditions, and their careful relocation through selective abandonment, revision, or reinterpretation, while retaining the validity of tradition per se. The question of tradition would remain the cornerstone of divisions within the Zoroastrian community in India. In the period between 1900 and 1940, the emergence of Parsi scholars of religious studies would further elaborate on these understandings of "true" religion.

Western Religious Studies Scholarship

Historicism and Evolutionism

> I have long felt that it was high time . . . to place the study of the ancient
> religions of the world on a more real and sound, more truly historical basis.
> —MAX MÜLLER, *The Sacred Books of the East* (1879)

Religious studies as a "scientific" discipline originated in Europe in the nineteenth century. Max Müller, Albert Réville, E. Tylor, Émile Durkheim, and George Fraser were just some of the most prominent of the scholars who grappled with and, in so doing, shaped the discipline of religious studies. The prevalent ideas and premises of "modern" religion that were developed influenced not only Western scholars, missionaries, and the general public, but also Parsi scholars of Zoroastrianism. Western scholarship on Zoroastrianism was read by Parsi priests and lay students of Zoroastrianism alike. Those Parsi students who studied abroad with Western scholars were of course even more profoundly influenced by the ideas in the discipline of religious studies. They were trained in the prevalent assumptions and methodology and themselves contributed to the field by applying these assumptions and methods to their own scholarship of Zoroastrianism.

Western religious studies scholarship directly and fundamentally impacted the discourse on modern Zoroastrianism in two ways. First, the notions of religion that were developed in academia widely overlapped with Protestant missionary views of religion. The scholars and missionaries who engaged with the Parsi community in India were imbued with certain beliefs concerning the nature of religion. Second, the reconsideration of Zoroastrian tradition from within the Parsi community cannot be divested of the intellectual impact of the wider field of Zoroastrian scholarship. The intellectual dominance of religious studies scholarship fundamentally shaped the reconstruction of Zoroastrianism—both by Western and by Parsi scholars—and for this reason it is essential to determine the parameters of religious studies thought in this period. The prevalent religious studies theories were based on evolutionism, historicism, and the use of linguistics as the principal tools of intellectual archaeology. These premises, in turn, directly shaped not only the approach to the study of religion, but also the consensus surrounding the form and function of "modern" religion. It is in this period that religion becomes firmly rationalized. Internal, individual piety and morality were the cornerstones of new understandings of citizenship.

Friedrich Max Müller

Of all the giants in the field of religious studies, Max Müller (1823–1900) deserves the place of honor. A native of Germany, Müller studied in Berlin, Paris, and Oxford before assuming a teaching position at Oxford University in 1854. He studied Greek, Latin, Arabic, Persian, and Sanskrit and was a founder of Indian studies as well as the discipline of comparative religion. He assumed the first professorship of comparative theology at Oxford University from 1858 to 1875. At the request of Lord Salisbury, chancellor of Oxford University and secretary of state for India, he edited the classic series *The Sacred Books of the East* (1879–1910), a fifty-volume work of translations of major religious texts (including Zoroastrianism). He authored numerous scholarly and popular works on Indian religions and comparative religious theory. Müller was a recognized expert on Indian culture and religion, and his opinion was sought by both the likes of the East India Company and the Hindu religious reform movement, the Bramho Samaj.[1] Müller, a member of Oxford's Christ Church since 1851, remained a committed Lutheran throughout his lifetime.[2] He cut a controversial figure in more traditional religious circles and was accused both of subverting Christianity as well as of promoting it. Müller was a significant if not *the* premier scholar of religion at the time and enjoyed wide-ranging influence on the shape of religious studies.[3]

Müller was interested in the changing nature of humankind's religious experience and conceptualization of religion. His concern was with the nature of religion as a human phenomenon, rather than with religion as a specific tradition.

For this reason, he believed strongly in comparative religious studies. Citing Goethe's famous adage, "He who knows one language, knows none," Müller insisted that the same held true for religion.[4] His emphasis was on the universal phenomenon of religion: "Religion distinguishes man from animal. We do not mean any special religion, but we mean a mental faculty . . . [which] enables man to apprehend the Infinite under varying disguises. Without that faculty, no religion, not even the lowest worship of idols and fetishes, would be possible; and if we will but listen attentively, we can hear in all religions a groaning of the spirit, a struggle to conceive the inconceivable, to utter the unutterable, a longing after the Infinite, a love of God."[5] The intellectual project of religious studies was therefore to understand religion as a universal phenomenon differently manifested over time.

Müller believed strongly, as did most in his generation, that evolution applied equally to biology and religion. The goal of religious studies scholarship, thus, was to ascertain the evolution of religion over time and to identify different forms of religion as stages along this path. The story of religious change was the story of the evolutionary growth of the human mind. Religious studies was concerned with charting this progress from primitive to civilized, as manifested in different forms of religion.

According to Müller himself, his major contribution was postulating the science of language and the science of religion. He theorized language as an archaeological tool that manifested the intellectual doxa of the age. The history of the evolution of man's ideas was embedded, linguistically, in the evolution of language and could thus be excavated. As he put it himself, "If then we want to study the history of the human mind in its earliest phases, where can we hope to find a more authentic, more accurate, more complete documents than in the annals of language."[6] The objective therefore was "to watch the growth of the human mind as reflected in the petrifications [sic] of language."[7] Comparison between religions was essential. As he explained in the preface to *The Sacred Books of the East,* "I have long felt that it was high time . . . to place the study of the ancient religions of the world on a more real and sound, more truly historical basis."[8] Indeed, the purpose of this voluminous undertaking was precisely to make available religious texts for the purpose of both "scholarlike" and "comparative study." Müller made major contributions to the methodology of religious studies, as applied linguistics.

The notion of the evolution of human religion had several critical implications. First, the nature of religion was conceived of very differently from theological-based arguments of truth or falsehood. The question changed from an evaluation of dogmatic *truth* or lack thereof, to an investigation into the relative *progress* of a religion, or lack thereof. Second, in Müller's idea of religion, each religious tradition has an original, authentic core. Over time, tradition itself changes, is modified, advances, and sometimes regresses. There is thus evolution *between* different religions as well as *within* a single religion. The study of any given religion therefore is an essay in the historicism of tradition. Tradition itself is conceptualized as contextual and historically dependent. The project is therefore an excavation of the tradition, the charting of its changes in historical time, in an attempt to ascertain the "essence" or original authentic nature of the religion.

Third, ideas of civilization and progress were inescapably and causally tied to the notion of evolution of human religion. Some religions were more primitive, others more civilized. Since religions were understood as manifestations of consciousness, the relative evolution of this consciousness was responsible for the relative "progress" and civilization of the religion. The two were inextricable. Christianity was believed to be the highest form of religion, the most evolved. Thus Christians were explicitly the most "civilized." Although Müller insisted that Christianity was not the sole *true* religion, he was at pains to point out that it was the most *evolved*. Christianity was viewed as the most evolved of *human religious consciousness*. Christianity thus was in a sense posited as a universal religion, accessible and relevant to all humankind, and certainly imagined as the end result of human religious consciousness. As different, less evolved peoples became more civilized, therefore, they would naturally turn to Christianity. This notion of the universalism of Christianity, while emerging from the evolutionary theories of religious studies, resonated deeply within theological and missionary circles, serving as justification for proselytization.

According to Müller's categorizations, religion moved from the visible to the invisible, from the literal to the abstract, from an emphasis on ritual to greater levels of spirituality, and from conceptions of God as an idol or nature to God as Himself.[9] These characteristics served to classify religions along the evolutionary path from primitive to civilized, with Christianity as the pinnacle of evolution. Zoroastrianism, according to Müller, was not fully monotheistic, and so it ranked below other monotheistic religions.

Müller's ideas were shared by many. Notions of evolutionism and historicism were the hallmarks of the new understanding of religion and were echoed throughout the scholarly community. They marked an important departure from theological-based arguments of truth such as the ones promoted by John Wilson, yet paradoxically found no less a firm ground for theorizing Christian superiority.

Albert Réville

The parameters of the field of religious studies are also illustrated by another giant in the field, Albert Réville (1826–1906). Together with Müller, Réville founded comparative religion as an academic discipline. A distinguished Protestant theologian, Réville spent decades as the pastor of the Reformed Church in Rotterdam before accepting the first chair of comparative history of religions at the Collège de France in Paris in 1880. He was a renowned public speaker and author of the four-volume work *Histoire des réligions,* published in 1881. Réville shared Müller's basic methodology and conceptual premises, yet went further in developing the relationship between religion and "civilization."

Réville echoed Müller's concern with the nature of religion. Postulating it as a shared human phenomenon, the important issue was charting the evolution of mankind's religious experience. Scholars must have a "historical notion of religion in itself" and look for "common cause of its various manifestations."[10] Like Müller, Réville argued for the abandonment of focus on the truth-value of religions. *Truth* was not a meaningful term anymore, now that all religions were understood as part of "the religious development of humanity."[11] The objective was to "disengage [religion's] essence and central idea in such a manner that we shall be able to recognize it under all the forms which it may assume in history."[12] For this reason Réville, like Müller, championed comparative religious studies: "Sur le terrain surtout de l'histoire réligieuse, je pretends qu'aucune recherche de détail ne peut se passer de la comparaison" (Especially in the field of religious history, I assert that no detailed research can avoid the use of comparison).[13]

Réville, perhaps more than Müller, was interested in the evolutionary development of religious morality. He believed that religious development could be charted as the progress of moral conscience: "In proportion as we rise in the religious scale [of evolution], the relation between religion and morality comes into operation."[14] Réville also drew important connections between histori-cism, progress, and morality. Tradition, Réville argued, should be understood as the embodiment of authority. As an original religion becomes distanced from its "essence" over time, tradition is constructed in order to preserve authority by positing its connection to this "essence." Priesthoods emerge in less evolved religions as the "depositories of tradition." They preserve religious authority by emphasizing continuity. "Tradition has authority in virtue of its antiquity, or, better, of its apparent eternity."[15]

The absence of a consciousness of historical context requires the mainte-nance of tradition. Once we understand that religions are all contextual, then traditions become historicized and the monopoly of the priesthood is challenged. Advanced, more evolved religions do not need tradition, since they are conscious of historical context. This very consciousness enables the release of morality from the confines of ritual and tradition, and thus its essentialization and spiritualiza-tion. So whereas more primitive religions manifest a theological commitment to tradition, more evolved religions "move as boldly and freely in the field of inquiry as any other branch of knowledge."[16] Science and religion are not incompatible, Réville argued, but science is hostile to religions that lack the consciousness of the historicism of tradition, since they thus lack the facility of critical analysis that is a prerequisite for science. (Protestant) Christianity allows for science, and even contributes to the ability to engage in scientific inquiry, something that less evolved religions cannot and do not.

The connection between civilization and religion is explicit. "Religion has always been prejudicial to civilization when it has cherished a spirit of supersti-tious routine, which places itself obstinately in the way of all scientific progress, of all social reforms, of all the freedom claimed by the human spirit."[17] Evolved reli-gions are thus generative of civilization, of social progress and science. Because of their commitment to tradition as truth, less evolved religions retard civilization and progress.

Religion and the Production of Knowledge

The emergence of the discipline of comparative religion was intimately tied to the production of knowledge about the nature and function of religion.[18] Cat-egorization and comparison shaped the definition of religion and privileged

Western presuppositions. Müller argued that comparative religion reflected recognition of the "truth" or validity of each religious system and an appreciation of the historical context of difference. But it also comprised a much more sinister objective. Müller's and Réville's insistence on comparison also shaped the religions themselves through the forcing of categories of "comparability." In other words, in order to compare religions, they must be *comparable*. Rather than evaluating religions on their own terms, the project of comparison actually forced all religions into categories created according to deeply Protestant assumptions and models. The authority of scripture, the primacy of monotheism, the privileging of nonpetitionary prayer and spirituality, and the conviction of religions as promoting moral self-cultivation were all deeply held Protestant convictions—convictions that were unconsciously held and thus unrecognized for their role in shaping categories of religious belief and practice.[19] As a result, *comparability* was forced, at best shaping and at worst distorting other systems of thought and practice.

The production of knowledge through the creation of categories of comparability was epitomized by Müller's grand project of editing *The Sacred Books of the East*. His selections for inclusion in this series went a long way toward establishing the cannon of "authoritative texts" and "scripture" of non-Western religions.[20] In so doing, Müller appropriated the right to decide which elements were "comparable" and which not, which texts were essential to their traditions and which not. Müller's publication of the Rg-Veda was critical for the emergence of Hindu reform movements that sought a reinterpretation of sacred texts and the consequent rejection of historical traditions and practices.[21] Prior to this time, there had been no central text or authoritative reference, but rather a variety of stories that were orally transmitted.[22]

This Victorian production of knowledge was deeply involved in shaping Western understanding of the "Orient." It was, moreover, intimately related to Western claims to have originated modernity and the associated validation of colonialism. What should be underlined is the reflexive nature of this process. Although undoubtedly comparative religion dominated the international intellectual orthodoxy on the subject, it has been insufficiently appreciated how much non-Western religious systems themselves contributed to this process. In other words, without denying the deep impact of Western categories of knowledge, these very categories were created *as a result* of Western contact with the

10. Postage stamp of Friedrick Max Müller from the "India Personalities" series, issued July 15, 1974.

non-West. The fact that they were used to justify, if not encourage, colonialism should only alert us to the implications of the Western creation of West-Rest dichotomies in this period and the myths that sustained them.

Réville and Müller, as primary creators of the discipline of comparative religion, illustrate the principal presuppositions of the age. They were accompanied by a growing host of other, primarily Protestant, scholars with similar interests. Émile Durkheim (1858–1917), Ernest Renan (1823–92), and Sir James George Fraser (1854–1941) were just some of the most famous among those individuals who believed religion to be the subject of scientific study and, ultimately, proof of Western and Protestant Christian superiority. They worked on uncovering the history of religious evolution, explored the nature of religion itself, and tried to reconstruct, like religious archaeologists, the earliest forms of religious life. Evolutionism, historicism, and their relationship to tradition were central tenets of nineteenth-century religious studies thought. Yet these ideas were not the monopoly of theoreticians. The same ideas were shared by scholars of Zoroastrianism as well as Protestant ministers active in the Zoroastrian community. Often the same individual wore both hats, since most scholars had profound Christian convictions and were advocates for Christianity. This next section explores scholarship on Zoroastrianism carried out by leading scholars in the field in the West: John Henry Barrows, James Hope Moulton, and A. V. Williams Jackson.

Barrows and the World Parliament of Religions

John Henry Barrows (1847–1902), deemed "one of the foremost preachers of his time," was pastor of Chicago's First Presbyterian Church (1881–96) and fifth president of Oberlin College (1899–1902).[23] He gained worldwide recognition for his role as president of the World's Parliament of Religions held in Chicago in conjunction with the Columbian Exposition of 1893. He subsequently edited the conference proceedings and traveled for two years in India and Asia, where he delivered a series of lectures. He also authored a number of books, including *Christianity, the World Religion* (1897) and *The Christian Conquest of Asia* (1899). Barrows's ideas represent the prevalent concepts of religion that spanned academic, congregational, and missionary milieus in the United States and abroad.

The World's Parliament of Religions was an unprecedented gathering of representatives from the world's religious traditions. As set forth in its mission statement, the goals of the parliament were to "unite all religion against irreligion," to establish "their common aim and common grounds of union," and to help secure "the coming unity of mankind, in the service of God and man."[24] The parliament's agenda, thus, was very much a function of the objectives of the liberal movement in Protestantism, namely, "to adjust to modernity and to infuse it with its spirit, and [the conviction] that history was moving toward the establishment of the Kingdom of God on earth."[25]

The parliament was conceived as an arena for the exploration of the commonalities of different religions, as a necessary stage on the evolutionary path toward the triumph of Protestant Christianity as the universal religion of mankind. The much-touted interfaith dialogue was thus an exercise in religious proselytization.

Protestantism was lauded as the most civilized and evolved religion, capable of serving all of mankind, whereas other, "less evolved," religions were showcased as specimens, subject to investigation and evolutionary categorization.[26] As Barrows proudly claimed, the parliament "was a great Christian demonstration with a non-Christian section which added color and picturesque effect.... [N]o Christian struck his colors nor allowed himself to be compromised by the presence of men of other faiths."[27]

Comparative religious studies, first established by Müller and Réville, was embraced as a means of evangelization. Mutual understanding was understood as a tool for the achievement of eventual Christianization. As articulated by a later commentator, "Every missionary school should be a college of comparative religion.... [T]he first requisite to successful missionary work is a knowledge of the truths and beauties of the existing religion, that they may be used as a *point d'appui* for the special arguments and claims of that with which it is desired to replace it."[28] Commenting on the parliament, Professor Thayer of Harvard University enthusiastically declared that "only by a comparison can superiority be discovered."[29] The Zoroastrian representative at the parliament, Jivanji Jamshedji Modi, presented Zoroastrianism in line with the reigning ideas of evolutionism and historicism.[30] At the outset of his paper, Modi quoted Max Müller as saying that "there is a religion behind all religions." He emphasized Zoroastrianism's commonalities with Christianity, such as notions of heaven and hell, an emphasis on morality, and confirmation ceremonies. He insisted that Zoroastrianism was monotheistic (despite the ongoing controversy surrounding this point in Zoroastrian studies circles), described Zoroastrian rituals as largely symbolic and equated ritual purity laws with "sanitary science"—taking care to cite the Christian proverb "Cleanliness is godliness." Modi portrayed Zoroastrianism as a moral, spiritual religion, supportive of constitutional government, women's rights, "charity and brotherhood," and religious tolerance. He presented Zoroastrianism, in direct contrast to Islam, as generative of civilization and progress and cited as evidence its support of women's legal and educational rights.[31]

A subsequent, more intensive expression of Barrows's ideas occurred in India in 1895–97. During this period, Barrows presented a number of lectures in Bombay on the subject of the evolution of religious belief that was later published as *Christianity, the World-Religion*.[32] In these lectures, Barrows makes an explicitly causal connection between evolutionism and the universalism of Protestant

Christianity. His arguments clearly illustrate the prevalent intellectual orthodoxy concerning "modern" religion and its characteristics.

Barrows privileges monotheism, spirituality, and morality as distinguishing characteristics of Christianity. The notion of Christ as a savior who fills an individual's "intellectual and moral needs" is contrasted with religious formalism, ritual, and particularism. According to Barrows, it is these qualities of Christianity that generate social progress and civilization. It is primarily the spiritual nature of man's understanding of the Divine, in Barrows's conception, that creates progress: "Christian religion, which has been concerned chiefly with the individual spirit, is directing its energies as well to the social progress of mankind."[33] Significantly, progress is articulated in both political and social terms. Politically, Christianity "prepares men . . . for liberty,"[34] and socially, [Christ] "illustrates the spirit of self-sacrifice. . . . He gives a new honor to womanhood and to childhood. His instruction is meant to regenerate the household, and to remold society."[35] Barrows's primary interest is in convincing his audience that "Christianity is fitted to become the world religion."[36]

Although Barrows differs from Müller and Réville in his application of notions of evolutionism, he shares with them the defining characteristics of modern religions. There is a powerful consensus that spiritual religions are superior to ritualistic religions, monotheisms superior to polytheisms, and that these criteria are themselves generative of social progress and "civilization." Missionaries sought to use these criteria to justify their efforts at conversion; scholars were more interested in determining the path of evolution. Both, however, concurred on the causal relationship of religion to modern "progress" and on the characteristics of the most evolved religions.

Moulton: Christian Universalism

James Hope Moulton, author of *Early Zoroastrianism* and *The Treasure of the Magi: A Study of Modern Zoroastrianism,* was professor of Hellenistic Greek and Indo-European philology at Manchester University in England. He was also a committed Wesleyan Methodist minister. It was in both capacities that he traveled to India in 1915–17. In his capacity as a scholar, Moulton befriended Maneckji Nusserwanji Dhalla, a US-educated scholar of Zoroastrianism and high priest of the Karachi Parsis, making use of his extensive library. In his capacity as a missionary, Moulton gave a series of lectures to the Parsis in Bombay that were later published in both English and Gujarati.[37]

Moulton's ideas pivoted on his conviction that the Gathas represented the true message of Zoroaster and that all subsequent Zoroastrian tradition was a corruption of this truth. He insisted that Zoroastrianism should return to its Gathic form and that Zoroaster's message would ultimately lead to an acceptance of Protestantism. Building on Haug's theory that the Gathas were in fact written by Zoroaster, Moulton firmly believed that the "simple monotheism" of Zoroaster was not only identifiable, but retrievable.

Moulton maintained that this Gathic Zoroastrianism was true religion and that what he called "Later Avestan" was a divergence and corruption of this truth. John Wilson, he said, was too absolute in his condemnation of Zoroastrianism as a false religion; had he read the Gathas, he would have recognized the kernel of truth there.[38] As practiced, Zoroastrianism is false. Yet the essence of the faith is retrievable. According to Moulton, "This pure and simple faith is set forth in the Gathas, or Hymns, which form the central part of the Avesta. The Later Avesta, in verse and prose, shows at every point that it must be separated by some centuries from the Gathas, from which it differs in language, and still more in thought. It seems clear that the old worship returned when Zarathushtra was gone."[39] In the Gathas, Zoroaster preached a "fastidious monotheism"[40] with a "purely spiritual heaven," where there was "no feasting, and no Houris."[41] The Gathas "wholly ignore the Fravashis"—belief in which led to dualism. In the Gathas, there was "very little emphasis upon external or ceremonial religion" and "no priestly caste therefore is in view."[42]

This true religion was corrupted soon after Zoroaster's death by the Magi, a priestly caste that carried out a "very drastic modification" of Zoroaster's message, reincorporating the very ideas that Zoroaster had sought to eliminate.[43] "It was only necessary to subordinate [the main cults of the old nature-worship] to the supreme deity—to call them angels instead of gods . . . and everything might go on as before."[44] This reversion was led by the priesthood. "The Magi were responsible . . . for the great development of Ritual. Just as the Brahmans extended the simple Aryan ritual to the enormous complexity it attains in India, so did the Magi in Iran. The stamp of a priestly caste is all over the whole system."[45] A further corruption was the "revival of the old habit of using spells." Ultimately, pure Zoroastrianism was corrupted. "As the Gathic dialect became

ALPHABETS

GRANDAN.   des GAURES, ou Ancien PERSAN.

rdre,Figure.	Nom.	Ord.	Figure.	Nom.	Ord.	Figure.	Nom.	Nom.	Figure.	Nom.	Figure.
1	ă.	18		kha.	35		dha.	ueh.		houeh.	
2	â.	19		ga.	36		na.	oueh.		i.	
3	ĭ.	20		gha.	37		pa.	deh.		ah.	
4	î.	21		nga.	38		pha.	scheh.		queh.	
5	ou.	22		tcha.	39		ba.	teh.		gheh.	
6	oŭ.	23		tchha.	40		bha.	rch.		hheh.	
7	roŭ.	24		ja.	41		ma.	feh.		kich.	
8	roŭ.	25		jha.	42		ya.	kheh.		scheh.	
								kha.		enkeh.	
								yeh.		teh.	

11. "Caractères et Alphabets de Langues mortes et vivantes." Lithograph by Grandan, 1784.

archaic and finally unintelligible, the Gathas took on a character their authors little dreamed of. . . . [T]he words in a dead language acquired a special sanctity, and the manthra, by which Zarathushtra meant a word of prophetic inspiration, degenerated into an incantation."[46] According to Moulton, "The end of it all has been of course to make the priest the one indispensable intermediary between god and His worshippers."[47] This religious revival, thus, included the return to ritual and the incorporation of old nature-worship deities into the religion, perverting the monotheism and spirituality preached by Zoroaster.

Moulton's theory of religious corruption relies on the historicism of tradition and linguistic tools of excavation. However, his conviction concerning the truth of Zoroaster as embedded in the Gathas relies on Moulton's beliefs of the nature of true religions. Had the Gathas preached a different religion, Moulton would not have identified them as "true." It is the message *itself,* therefore, that marks it as "true." Truth resides in monotheism and spiritualism. Moulton opined that Zoroastrianism in many ways suffered from the same symptoms of orthodox Christianity in its corruption of the prophet's message. "The radical difference between the orthodox Christian and the orthodox Zoroastrian point of view is that the former considers the case of Jesus to be unique, whereas the latter considers that of Zarathushtra to be so."[48]

In both cases, much of the blame rests on the shoulders of the priests. The teaching of Jesus, like the teaching of Zoroaster, was deeply spiritual and promoted intimacy between believers and God. "Apart from prayer, which as he taught it was no part of external religion at all, but a simple and spontaneous out-pouring of the heart to God, he left no directions concerning worship. God expects no precise and elaborate rules to stiffen our communion with Him. . . . He to whom our thoughts speak far more loudly than our words assuredly cares nothing for that in which the heart is not concerned."[49] A similar development occurred as religions developed traditions and departed from the message of their prophets. "Like ourselves, you began with hardly any ritual at all. It is always so with Prophets: they are never prone to bind the free communion of men with God in fetters imposed by priests."[50] True religion lay in the original spiritual preaching of God's intent by Zoroaster. "No prophet ever invented ceremonial."[51]

Monotheism and spiritualism are essential qualities of "true" religions because they facilitate the individual believer's knowledge of God. Moulton, in line with religious studies conceptions of the Divine, believed that literalism and ritualism obscured the nature of God. He objected to ritual for two reasons. First, because it substituted performance for meaning. The example provided concerns the Zoroastrian *manthras.* Rather than understanding their meaning, they have degenerated into formulas that pretend to affect the Divine. They are decried as "magic" and superstition since their intent and function have been lost to performance. Second, rituals substituted an ethical consciousness for a literal performance of prescribed ritual. Outward performance should never be a substitute for a consciousness of man's obligations toward God. The key to true religion, thus, is an understanding of God, which leads to a consciousness of ethical obligation. Moulton believed that formalism served to distance an individual from God, insofar as it served as a substitute for meaning and consciousness.

Moulton, although sympathetic with the Zoroastrian religious reform movement, was critical of its lack of progress. On the one hand, he believed that Reformists were correct in their struggle against ritual, formalism, and tradition. He concurred that rituals outlined in the Vendidad should be abandoned, calling them "driveling nonsense" and "silly rubbish."[52] "The Vendidad is the very acme of absurdity [in respect to ceremonial]."[53] Yet he was quick to admit that basing reform on the Gathas was a challenge, since "in spite of all that has been done in the last two generations to clear up their meaning, it cannot be said that the Parsis even now have any familiarity with the Hymns which in theory stand at the centre of their religion. Even if accurately translated, they are highly elusive; and the shallow easiness of the Later *Avesta* assures it of an unchallenged supremacy in practice."[54] In many ways, reform was still in its infancy, since there was still an emphasis on rote learning, priests were sorely uneducated, and ritualistic practices still dominated: "Nearly all of the religious observance of every Parsi lies wholly outside the Gathas and their outlook."[55]

Moulton also cautioned the community against some of the unintended consequences of reform. The problem, as he saw it, was that the reformers, while subjecting traditional practices to rational evaluation, had failed to develop meaningful substitutes. He warned reformers that they had been unable to fill a "spiritual craving."[56] He asked, "Have you a great and worthy substitute ready for all the outworn rubbish that you wish to throw into the bonfire? If you have not, I warn you in the name of all history that your 'reform' will accomplish nothing, however justified you may be in your zeal against things which Zarathushtra never knew and of which you are sure he would never have approved."[57]

Moulton advised the community to follow a twofold strategy; first, to "bring the Parsis back to the Gathas" and, second, to integrate meaningful sermons into existing ceremonies, rather than eliminate them without anything substantive taking their place. He firmly believed that an acceptance of Gathic Zoroastrianism would eventually lead to an acceptance of Protestantism. Indeed, Moulton believed that Zoroaster's teachings prepared the way for Christianity. "The Teaching of Zarathushtra is truly on the way to Him."[58] However, "like the Jews, though with more excuse, [the Zoroastrians] missed their Saviour when He came, and languidly they look for another who may come some day."[59] Although Gathic Zoroastrianism is "true," it is not complete like Christianity.

Christian superiority rests on its emphasis on knowledge of God—something lacking in Zoroastrianism. "Every religion stands or falls by what it can teach about God. Its standard of conduct—and this is the ultimate end of all religions—will always depend on its conception of God."[60] Jesus Christ is more immediate and accessible to believers than is Zoroaster and so enables a greater intimacy with the Divine. Zoroaster is far away, whereas Jesus "is a Real Presence abiding with us in home and street and office and school."[61]

In this way, Christianity generates social commitment through consciousness of God. Unlike Zoroastrianism, Christianity had developed notions of divine love, the "cultivation of self-renunciation," and the "call to sacrifice."[62] "Zarathushtra was assuredly led by God in the Way, and he had a great, a splendid vision of Truth. But of the Life he had only a very partial knowledge, for Life is in the Love of God, and that Love was not revealed to him."[63] There is nothing "untrue or unworthy" in Zoroastrianism; it just had not been developed as far as Christianity. According to Moulton, "We have to convince [the Parsi] that . . . without weakening his conviction that God spoke to Zarathushtra he may accept the further revelation that grace and truth came through Jesus Christ."[64]

Moulton consciously compared himself with John Wilson. In many respects, they were comparable. Certainly, Moulton was no less fervent in his desire to convert Zoroastrians to Protestantism. Like Wilson, he was a scholar and a missionary, and his arguments grew out of his scholarly studies, as well as his Christian convictions. And like Wilson, his faith in Christian superiority and his extensive knowledge of Zoroastrian tradition lent an added persuasion to his arguments. They both engaged in direct conversation with the Parsi community, as scholars and as missionaries. In many important ways, however, Moulton differed from Wilson—differences that were symptomatic of the intellectual premises of their generations.

The influence of comparative religious studies as a social science is obvious in Moulton's work. Religious studies no longer involved the assertion of the truth of Christianity and the falsity of other religions. Religion was understood as a universal phenomenon. The objective was to ascertain the "essential," true religious core of each religious tradition, as an archaeological project of scraping away the accumulation of tradition. Like Müller, Moulton was confident of his ability to determine this true essence. He described a trajectory of religious divergence and decay as manifested in increasing formalism and priestly prerogative that is reminiscent of Réville. Interestingly, although a champion of historicism of tradition in order to excavate the "true" essence of religion, Moulton is not conscious of his own context, or biases. His hubris is shared by his scholarly generation, which believed that they could ascertain "truth" as a scientific project according to universal rules and that these rules clearly identified monotheism and spirituality as central features of "modern" and thus "true" religions.

As a missionary, Moulton differed little from Barrows in his insistence that Christianity promotes understanding of God and in turn generates a social consciousness of which other religions are incapable. Their emphasis is thus not Wilson's notion of religion as a spur to "civilization." Yet the insistence on Christianity's promotion of social progress and individual responsibility is not, in fact, dissimilar.

Williams Jackson: The Scholarly World of Zoroastrian Studies

A.V. Williams Jackson (1862–1937) was the preeminent scholar of Zoroastrianism in the United States in the early twentieth century—a century that witnessed the integration and internationalization of the field of Zoroastrian studies. Educated at Columbia University and in Halle, Germany, Jackson taught Indo-Iranian studies at Columbia University from 1886 to 1935. He trained both American and Parsi scholars of Zoroastrianism and contributed significantly to this field.[65] He also traveled for extensive periods of time in Iran and India (1901–18) for research among Zoroastrian communities and to engage in discussion with his Parsi counterparts. His many honors display his worldwide recognition—most notable among them a two-term presidency of the American Oriental Society, honorary membership in the Royal Asiatic Society and the French Société Asiatique, as well as his decoration of the Iranian Lion and Sun and an honorary degree from the Dar al-Fonun university in Tehran.[66]

Jackson illustrated the changing nature of religious studies scholarship in his era. Although a Protestant, he was not, like Barrows or Moulton, either a preacher or a missionary, instead restricting his enterprise to academic scholarship. Jackson concurred with many of the premises concerning the evolution of religions and the consequent characteristics of evolved religion and certainly privileged Christianity. He was much less dogmatic about the superiority of Christianity, however, and neither sought Zoroastrian conversion nor emphasized the connection between religion and civilization in a moral sense. Rather, Jackson evidenced notions of nationalism and racism in his works on Zoroastrianism—attitudes that no doubt made him welcome in Reza Shah's Iran.[67]

Jackson took a paradoxical view of Zoroastrianism on a number of issues. He emphasized both its essential duality and its "numerous points of resemblance to Judaism and Christianity."[68] At the same time that he recognized that religions, like "every other living organism" change,[69] he noted that Zoroaster's "pristine ideals" were restored under the Sassanians[70] and that Parsis in contemporary India have remained true to their original faith apart from "some changes here and there."[71] Jackson essentialized Zoroastrianism, downplaying historical change and divergence. He did adhere to the consensus that the Gathas was written by Zoroaster, but departed from many of his predecessors and Parsis themselves who rejected all later texts, by emphasizing the religious continuity of the later Avestan works. He did not, therefore, dismiss what Moulton termed "Later Avestan" Zoroastrianism as a corruption of "true" Zoroastrianism.

Similarly, Jackson did not decry ritualism as inimical to spirituality, although he was critical of ritualism when he believed that it obscured an otherwise "noble" ethical code.[72] Jackson described Zoroastrianism as a moral religion akin to Judaism and Christianity, one in which "almost every article of our own duty toward God and duty toward our neighbor" was present.[73] His frequent, almost parallel connection of Zoroastrianism to Christianity, including the idea that "the Gabriel of the Faith" revealed God's word to Zoroaster, supports the idea of Zoroastrianism as a precursor to Christianity.[74] He wrote, "Outside of the Jewish and Christian scriptures it would be hard to find a higher standard of morality, a nobler code of ethics, than that embodied in the teachings of the great prophet of Ancient Iran."[75]

Interestingly, Jackson identified religious reform among the Parsis in India as inclining the religion more firmly toward monotheism. He equated this tendency with progress, writing that the Parsis are "largely inclined to follow European leads in all that makes for progress."[76] This position is inharmonious with his claim that Parsis have remained true to their original faith and that the religion has seen only "some changes here and there," especially since he attributed dualism to Zoroaster himself.[77] Unlike Moulton, Barrows, and the more theoretically minded religious studies scholars earlier in the century, Jackson was not interested in evolutionism or the historicism of tradition. He was more intent on compiling information surrounding various stories, legends, and practices than he was on excavating "true, original" Zoroastrianism from its historical debris.[78]

Jackson evinced a notion of racism in his characterization of Zoroastrianism (a term he uses infrequently) as "the Persian religion," or "the national religion of Iran," which is described as an "Aryan nation." In a similar vein, Zoroaster is termed "the prophet of Iran."[79] It is not surprising that in the age of nationalism and racial theories he does so, but it does indicate theoretical distance from the universalistic understandings of religion propounded by Müller, Réville, and others of their generation.

Parsi Religious Reform
in the Second Generation

The Recovery of "True" Religion

Religion is not Tradition.

—MANECKJI NUSSERVANJI DHALLA (1875–1956)

This chapter concerns itself with the second generation of Parsi religious scholars and the discourse surrounding religion roughly between the years 1900 and 1940. This generation was characterized by a number of features that set it apart from the earliest Zoroastrian reformers discussed previously. This new generation of Zoroastrian intellectuals was a product of earlier reforms and the new education system that had resulted. They were educated along British lines in India, and often additionally in Europe or the United States. This group was conversant not only in Reformist ideas, but also in Western religious studies and Zoroastrian scholarship. They thus were formed by, and fully participated in, the discipline of religious studies and applied this methodology to their own work on Zoroastrianism. Their works were not simply a response to missionary attacks, but also systematic scholarly endeavors. Participants in this era's discourse on religion included lay scholars and Parsi priests, Reformists and Orthodox. Both groups were engaged in similar discussions and participated in the increasingly international field of Zoroastrian studies, publishing books together with Parsi and Western colleagues.

The Second Generation of Parsi Reformers

This second generation includes a range of voices—some Reformist, others seeking to defend more traditional practices and identifying themselves as Orthodox.

In all cases they grappled with contemporary theories of religion and sought to reconcile these theoretical assumptions with a continued commitment to the relevance and meaningfulness of Zoroastrianism. Orthodox and Reformists consciously engaged in reconstructing and rationalizing Zoroastrianism. Although they differed forcefully over points of ritual and tradition, they also concurred on many fundamental notions of religious evolutionism, historicism, and the primacy of individual piety. It is as important to underscore their similarities as it is to explore their differences. It is their similarities that indicate the consensus surrounding what were essential components and features of rational religion and which features were no longer intellectually defensible. Their differences illustrate the spectrum of beliefs surrounding the application of this consensus to the specific Zoroastrian religious tradition in India. This generation of religious scholarship witnessed the fruition of the form and function of modern Zoroastrianism that continues to define the spectrum of thought on the question of tradition and the practice of Zoroastrianism to the present day.

The second intellectual generation of Parsi reformers emerged as a product of earlier reform initiatives. It was characterized by intellectual sophistication gained from the incorporation of Western analytical tools of religious studies into the curriculum of the *madressas* and other institutions. Study abroad and dialogue among scholars led to a genuine internationalization of the field of Zoroastrian studies that was reflected in Parsi and Western scholarship alike. The second generation of reformers was deeply imprinted with new understandings of the nature and function of religion that had emerged in Europe over the course of the nineteenth century. Reformers, both laity and priests, were profoundly affected by the changing parameters and assumptions of religious studies. New conceptions of religion were reflected in reformers' understandings of their own religious tradition, as well as in their intellectual objectives.

The first generation of reformers had criticized the Zoroastrian priesthood as uneducated, both in Zoroastrian tradition and languages as well as in Western analytical tools and concepts. It had been one of their primary objectives to establish schools to remedy this educational void, so that the priesthood could more ably defend Zoroastrianism from Christian attacks. A number of *madressas* were established that taught Avestan languages and used Western philological techniques. Among the most important were the Mulla Feroze Madressa and library (established in 1854), the Sir Jamshedji Jeejeebhoy Zarthoshti Madressa (1863), the Tata Madressa (1884), and the Cama Athornan Institute (1922). In addition to new schools that combined Avestan studies with new Western analytical tools, reformers established discussion and research groups to further intellectual understanding of their religion. The Rahnuma Sabha (Reform Society), initially established in 1851, emphasized outreach to the Parsi community through ongoing sponsorship of public lectures. Several new groups were also formed that contributed to educating the public as well as providing forums for intellectual discussion. These groups included the Zarthoshti Din-ni Karnari Mandli (Society for Researches in Zoroastrian Religion) in 1864, the Gujarati Dnyan Prasarak Mandli (Society for the Diffusion of Knowledge) in 1870, the Gatha Society of Bombay in 1902, and the K. R. Cama Oriental Institute in 1916.

The internationalization of the scholarly arena indelibly marked the second generation of Reformists. They were trained in the tools and concepts of the field and contributed to the vibrant dialogue in Zoroastrian scholarship. Leading scholars collaborated with their European and American colleagues in research, as well as book publications. They distinguished themselves with the reception of multiple honors in India, as well as honorary degrees from Western universities. The second generation witnessed the intellectual initiative of reform pass from merchant leaders to scholars of Zoroastrianism. This sea change also implied a greater emphasis on theology and traditions, texts, and concepts that the first generation of reformers was less fluent in. The lay merchants, who had monopolized authority in community and religious reform in the preceding generation, were ousted from this position owing to the new, more demanding educational requirements for participation in religious dialogue. As a consequence of these new educational initiatives, several priests rose to prominence as scholars of Zoroastrianism. Although the priesthood as a whole never regained its monopoly on the interpretation of Zoroastrianism that it had enjoyed in the past, several of the most prominent reformers in the period 1900–1941 were priests. Trained in Avestan texts and languages as well as Western analytical tools of religious studies, they were active participants in Zoroastrian studies internationally and significant shapers of modern Zoroastrianism.

This era also saw the triumph of Reformist notions of the role and function of priests. The priestly ideal emerged not only as a learned scholar in both Western and Zoroastrian tradition, but also as a spiritual guide for the community.

This ascendancy demonstrates the Reformist emphasis on the primacy of the individual spiritual connection to God over that of performers of hallowed ritual. This new ideal is clearly manifested in the introduction to a Festschrift dedicated to Dastur Hoshang, where the editor lauds him for his guidance: "He rightly perceived that the high-priest's work does not end with the performance of ceremonials, but that it is his duty to improve the moral tone of the community whose leader he is in all religious matters."[1]

The most notable characteristic of the second generation of reformers was their intellectual context. New theories concerning the nature of religion as developed in the West fundamentally altered the parameters of the discussion concerning Zoroastrianism and distinguished the second from the first generation of Zoroastrian reformers. The first generation emerged in the context of Christian and European scholars' attacks on Zoroastrianism. Christian missionaries denounced Zoroastrianism as "false," and European scholars refuted the revealed nature of the Avesta. As a consequence of these challenges, the debates on Zoroastrianism centered on whether it was a "true" or a "false" religion. "True" religions were distinguished by their monotheism, rationalism, and the promotion of "progress" through the creation of moral individuals. Reformers' refutation of these attacks consciously and unconsciously adopted these same intellectual parameters and definitions of "true" religion. Reformers insisted, endlessly, that Zoroastrianism was a monotheistic religion. They also emphasized its moral nature, likening it to Christianity. The denunciation of "superstitions" that figures so prominently in the initial reform agenda was really a process of distancing Zoroastrianism from ritual behavior. Rituals prescribed in the Avesta were denounced by Western scholars and missionaries alike as "absurd," "irrational," and "full of superstitions," which connoted a lack of moral content. In order to prove that Zoroastrianism was not a cause of backwardness, reformers sought to establish its compatibility with new notions of sociopolitical progress, such as science, hygiene, and women's rights—the markers of "progress" at the time.

Reformer's frequent claim that Zoroastrianism was the crucible of Abrahamic ideas, including monotheism itself, was fundamentally defensive. By claiming Zoroastrianism as the origin of key components of "true" religions, reformers could insist that any changes to the religion did not actually constitute imitation or change, but rather were a return to "essential" fundamentals and inherent attributes. Reformers spent much time noting how many ways Zoroastrianism resembled other Abrahamic religions, especially Christianity, since a stress on commonalities also supported claims of sharing "truth." It is for this reason that first-generation reformers frequently insisted that Zoroastrianism was a "simple" theism. Paradoxically, reformers seized upon the European scholars' denunciation of the Avesta as an opportunity to claim the "truth" of the Gathas, which were more easily reconcilable with the characteristics of "true" religions: monotheism, lack of ritual, and ethics as internalized morality. It was to these criticisms, thus, that the entire debate surrounding Zoroastrianism in belief in practice addressed itself in the first generation.

The second generation operated in a very different intellectual and religious context. New concepts of the nature of religion permeated understandings of Zoroastrianism and consequently affected the reconstruction of beliefs and practices. "True" religion for the first generation was dependent on its approximation of "true" Abrahamic religions. True religion for the second generation signified something very different. It referred to the original "essence" of the religion that could be identified, excavated, and restored. The second generation's reform project was to determine, reclaim, and promulgate the "original" "true" religion by extricating it from later accretions.

Critiquing a Christian Paradigm:
Dhanjishah Meherjibhai Madan

The repeated attempts to claim rationality and thus "enlightenment" for Zoroastrianism typically rested on arguments concerning origins and universality, compatibility with science, and the promotion of social progress. Zoroastrian scholars never conceded Christian superiority to Zoroastrianism. One scholar in particular challenged Christianity on its own terms. Although scholars of this second generation frequently maintained the importance of knowledge of God, none emphasized man's inherent capacity for rationality as much as Madan. In his essay "Revelation Considered as a Source of Religious Knowledge," Madan posited that rational thought, not revelation, was the source of knowledge of the Divine.[2]

Madan denounced Christian claims to superiority based on revelation. According to Madan, the superiority of Christianity rested on claims that

"Christian revelation is the manifestation of a divine life in the world . . . [which finally] condenses itself in the presence and person of the Lord Jesus Christ, the perfect Revelation of God."[3] Madan questioned the privileging of revelation: "Indeed for some reason or another—I do not know why—it is considered perhaps the greatest merit in a religion that it should be a revealed religion."[4] This claim was false. Rather, he argued, individuals know God through their own rational intellect, independent of revelation: "The knowledge of the teaching of and about God is acquired by holding a mental disquisition, by raising doubts and answering those doubts, by raising objections and answering them."[5]

Madan thereby rejected the Christian template of divine prophet and revelation, insisting rather that Zoroaster's real nobility lay precisely in his humanity. Zoroaster "does nothing which has any supernatural or preternatural ring about it. His measures are human; his resources are human; but so great is his work that though a man, he shines out quite above the level of his contemporaries."[6] Madan then challenged Christianity to prove its worth according to rational criteria rather than resting on "the claims of . . . pretended revelation" or "miracles."[7]

Madan's argument is unusual and unique for its paradigmatic challenge to Christianity. Madan argued that the value of religion lies not in whether it was revealed, but in its essential and thus inherent qualities. Zoroastrianism's survival is proof of its excellence: "The survival upto [sic] the present day is due only and solely to the dominion which it has been able to exercise on the minds of men by the excellence of its teachings, the *universality of its principles,* and the *rational tone of its doctrines."[8] Madan takes an interesting position concerning historicism as the history of human understanding of the Divine, yet is careful not to claim human monopoly on agency: "While I assert that religion is the creation of man, I do not forget that man is a creature of God."[9]

Although he identified himself as "an orthodox follower of the faith,"[10] Madan's arguments are more radical in their privileging of man's agency, and historical contextuality, than many of the Reformists'. He emphasized rationality and thus the ultimate *understandability* of religion. Likewise, he privileged knowledge of God over divinely ordained ritual as the ultimate aim of "revelation." His claim to orthodoxy was as much an indication of the vibrancy of the Orthodox position as it was an indication of how much orthodoxy itself had appropriated new methods and assumptions concerning the nature of religion.

Extracting the Moral Kernel of Zoroastrianism:
Jivanji Jamshedji Modi

Sir Jivanji Jamshedji Modi (1854–1933) heralded from a priestly family and was a student of the famous Zoroastrian reformer and European-educated scholar Kharshedji Rustamji Cama. Educated at the University of Bombay, he received the honorary title of *Shams ul-Ulama* and was a scholar of international repute.[11] Modi had a foot in both the Reformist and the Orthodox camps. He was a Freemason, had a long association with Cama's society for the promotion of religion (the Zarthoshti Din-ni Karnari Mandli), yet also served as secretary of the more orthodox Parsi Panchayat for thirty years.

Besides numerous academic works on Zoroastrian religion and customs, Modi penned two works for the explicit purpose of teaching Zoroastrianism. *A Catechism of the Zoroastrian Religion* (1911) and *Moral Extracts from Zoroastrian Books for the Use of Teachers in Schools* (1914) were both designed to be used in schools, to explain to Zoroastrian children "the principles of their faith" and to assist teachers in "giving moral instruction." The catechism was actually published several years earlier in 1907 in the local Gujarati language, but in the foreword Modi explained that he decided to produce an English translation because "there are many [children], whose parents would wish them to read the principles of their Faith in English."[12] *Moral Extracts* began as a collection of translations of Zoroastrian religious texts commissioned by the government of Bombay. The British government intended to cull moral lessons from all Indian religions for use in schools. In the words of the editor, R. E. Enthoven, "by including extracts from all great Indian religious works, Brahmanistic, Jain, Buddhist, Musalman, and Zoroastrian, alike, should be fully representative and incidentally illustrate the fundamental agreement, with regard to most questions of ethics, that prevails."[13] These two works together, written in English, create a functional and practical canon of Zoroastrian beliefs and practices along with carefully selected textual sources from the Avesta. These works reconstruct Zoroastrian belief and practice based on allegorical textual interpretation. They clearly manifest Modi's commitment to rationalism, religious universalism, and the individualization of piety. He also stresses individual consciousness of God as a path to ethical social behavior and citizenship.

The *Catechism* expresses Modi's deist conception of religion. God is called the "great Architect" of the world's natural laws. "We see, in all Nature, uniform and constant Principles, harmonious invariable Laws, regular undeviating Order. All these show that there must be in Existence an All-wise Lord as the Originator and Maintainer of all."[14] Accordingly, Modi simplified the "Articles of Faith" to include only three: belief in the existence of God, belief in the immortality of the soul and afterlife, and human responsibility for thoughts, words, and actions that echoes the threefold ethical foundation of Zoroastrianism: good thoughts, good words, good deeds.[15] Zoroastrianism is also highly rationalized, God's intent is imminently discernible, and the existence of religion as a phenomenon is explained in terms of its utility to mankind. Religion is useful, as it provides law and a reason for ethical behavior in this world.[16]

The existence of an afterlife and the notion of God's judgment come almost as a guarantee of justice, since Modi's real emphasis is on this-worldly ethics. Modi emphasized Zoroastrianism as promoting "virtuous conduct" as a function of consciousness of God: "All good thoughts, all good words, all good actions are the result of knowledge."[17] Ultimately, God's intent in discernible: "We should continually open our minds for the observation and reflection of God's Nature and for the proper understanding of His Laws."[18] The principal reward for ethical behavior is "the satisfaction of our inner self. The satisfaction of the Self within us is the greatest of rewards. . . . [O]ur conscience speaks from with in us: 'Bravo! We have done our duty.' This, to our mind, is the greatest reward."[19] Modi clearly posits the interiorization of morality based on consciousness of God's intent.

The *Catechism* and the *Moral Extracts* never mention ritual or the performance of religion as anything more prescribed (or circumscribed) than good thoughts, good words, and good deeds. The primacy of good thoughts testifies to Modi's stress on individualized piety and conscience. In the *Catechism* he wrote that "if our thoughts are good, everything else will turn out good. If our thoughts are righteous, then the words giving utterance to these thoughts would necessarily be righteous and hence the deeds also would be righteous."[20] Prayers, rather than being incantations that have an effect on the balance of good and evil, are construed as functions of individual piety: "A good, pure-hearted, well-intended prayer is a protection for a man."[21] Modi also downplayed any mediation in man's relationship with God and rejected the notion of salvation as a function of intercession. "Every man is his own saviour. His deeds alone will bring out his salvation. A man is the architect of his own fortune. He is his own savior."[22]

Consequently, piety is manifest as the conscious acceptance of responsibility to carry out good work and progress. The location of the sacred is the individual. In the *Moral Extracts* Modi wrote of the perpetual interior struggle engaged in by every individual "of improving himself, bettering himself from day to day."[23] In Modi's thought, good work takes on a very Christian meaning as serving to facilitate self-improvement. Zoroaster was the perfect example of doing so, since he "elevated Work to the position of Worship."[24] The Avestan emphasis on agriculture, Modi explained, should be understood allegorically: "We should understand it in the sense that it is man's duty to engage himself in some sort of work. Work is a kind of worship."[25]

Individual progress also manifested itself in social progress since individuals were enjoined to social participation and active philanthropy.[26] Accordingly, "every person should discharge his duty (1) towards Ahura-Mazda, (2) towards the outside world and (3) towards himself."[27] Civic duty was a manifestation of piety. Modi cited a translation of the Denkart by Dastur Dr. Peshotan B. Sanjana at some length on the nature of citizenship and its intimate connection to "true" religion. Sanjana's translation reads: "Be it known that, the life of citizens consists in (civil) government (being) connected with religion and religion (being) connected with (civil) government. . . . [T]he highest greatness to religion is from (civil) Government. . . . A Government is related to the good religion owing to there being a complete connection with the good religion as from this, the proposition, that Government is identical with religion and that religion is the Government of citizens, is clearly apparent."[28]

Modi also elaborated on religion's contribution to citizenship. In addition to engendering social and civic responsibility, Modi's religious universalism implies equality of citizenship across religious lines. He wrote that religious difference should be understood as entailing different *historical* experience and that in essence, all religions were paths to the same god.[29] Universality implied equality, tolerance, "brotherhood," and, ultimately, cooperation.[30] In both the *Catechism* and the *Moral Extracts,* Modi emphasized the importance of religious commonality and its role in promoting citizenship: "We should entertain love and fellow-feeling for all. Ahura-Mazda is the Father of us all."[31] Elsewhere he wrote that "we should live in harmony and peace with all, not only with our own co-religionists."[32] His rationale also included a utilitarian calculation: "Our first duty (towards the outside world) is, that we should do unto them as we would that they should do unto us."[33] Cooperation was a logical product of social responsibility and, ultimately, God's intent: "We must make the best possible use of our intellectual and moral powers and thus act for the highest good of all round about us. Ahura Mazda, the Father of us all would be pleased thereby."[34]

In Defense of Tradition: Dastur Darab Sanjana

Sanjana (1857–1931) was a renowned scholar of Zoroastrian studies and in 1898 succeeded his father as the high priest of Bombay. Born in Bombay and educated at Elphinstone and the Sir J. J. Zarthoshti Madressa, Sanjana later enjoyed prominent positions as a fellow at both the University of Bombay and the Sir J. J. Zarthoshti Madressa and was a member of several learned societies. He was awarded the title of *Shams ul-Ulema* by the government of India in 1899 and received an honorary degree from the University of Marburg in 1920. His scholarly reputation as well as his preeminence in the Parsi community as high priest positioned him as the leading exponent of the Parsi Orthodox position in India. Parsi orthodoxy in this period still differed significantly from the Reformist position, particularly on the questions of the nature of tradition and the function of ritual. Yet Orthodox Zoroastrianism had also changed profoundly from its articulation in the early nineteenth century. In line with Reformists, Orthodox Parsis too were deeply affected by changing conceptions of religion as a human phenomenon in historical context.

The relationship of the Gathas to other parts of the scriptures is tangled up in the history of Zoroastrianism. Sanjana had a complex and ultimately troubled relationship with Zoroastrian tradition, which he defended as authentic, despite recognizing its fallibility. His position on the relationship between scriptures, tradition, and the Prophet Zoroaster identifies him as distinctly Orthodox. Sanjana believed that Zoroaster received revelation from God that he then expressed in his teachings and, above all, in his own exemplary life. Zoroaster's followers practiced Zoroastrianism and together compiled the Gathas. According to Sanjana, there are two categories of Zoroastrian scriptures that constitute the Zend-Avesta. The Avesta is composed of "revealed truths, dogmas, doctrines and precepts,"[35] and the Zend represents "our tradition by which we mean the transmission of those revealed truths or doctrines with commentaries."[36] Like Reformists, Sanjana considered the Gathas to be the essential core of Zoroastrianism, what he called a "pure and simple code of ethics and religion, the real and essential Zoroastrianism which fell from the lips of Zoroaster and his immediate disciples"[37] and was "entirely free from all subsequent modifications or interpolations."[38] Yet unlike Reformists who limited "authentic texts" to the Gathas that they claim were written by Zoroaster himself, Sanjana argued that other texts, despite having been penned by later practitioners of Zoroastrianism, faithfully adhered to the essence of the religion and thus must also be considered "authentic" Zoroastrian scriptures: "We have our original Scriptures that we call the Avesta and we have the Zoroastrian Tradition which we call the Zend written mostly in the Pahlavi and the Pazend languages. The Zend upholds the canon of the Avesta and affirms its genuineness."[39]

Sanjana's argument is predicated on the assumption of the accuracy and necessity of tradition. He maintained that there *was* a known practice and teaching of Zoroaster that remained intact after his lifetime, and, concomitantly, that this teaching was accurately followed by his disciples, over time constituting Zoroastrian "tradition." There is a remarkable similarity here with the Islamic claim of the existence of a prophetic *sunna* that was faithfully adhered to over time. Paradoxically, Sanjana accepted the premise of historicism. He admitted that "a few of the primitive truths taught by Zoroaster and his disciples were in later periods corrupted in their transmission."[40] He continued, "It cannot be denied that some of the original doctrines are handed down to us, intermingled and alloyed with non-Zoroastrian beliefs and superstitions."[41] For example, Sanjana described the Bundahishn as "a book mostly containing a confused mass of matters, imaginary, mythyological and legendary" and the *Vigir-gard-e Dinik* [sic] as a mass of "mutilated texts . . . of an unimportant and unreliable author."[42] Yet these admissions of historical error did not lead Sanjana to amend his central claim to continuity. He maintained that "the important Books of the Zend-Avesta have not till now undergone any alteration in their essential parts. Their integral ideas or truths retain their original character and consistency."[43] He referred to a "trend of uniformity which runs through all their thought and feeling" that gives them "clear unity of thought and purpose."[44] Sanjana insisted that Zoroastrian tradition accurately conveyed Zoroaster's teachings: "Development there certainly has been but no conspicuous break with the past."[45] Yet this view placed him in an unbearably contradictory position. Sanjana admitted that Zoroastrianism has not always been followed faithfully, that not all the scriptures are "authentic" or true to Zoroastrianism's core "essence," yet he still insisted that tradition can be trusted. He does not elaborate on how to distinguish between the spurious and the valid, simply insisting that "All distorted and eccentric reasonings as also inferenees [*sic*] which do not harmonise with the spirit of the religion and its integral doctrines, must be discarded as heretic stuff."[46] This contradiction is all the more powerful, given Sanjana's conviction that tradition was *necessary* for understanding the "essential truth" of Zoroastrianism: "*We are bound to believe tradition as a necessary aid to the understanding of the original works. The Avesta and the Zend both should be considered as the outcome of the same one Faith. The Avesta alone cannot be our sole guiding book. It often requires exposition, and for ascertaining many vital points, and for solving many abstruse and important questions we need the help of the Zend, our tradition."[47] Simply put, "*The religion of the past can never be rightly understood except in the light of the tradition of that religion.*"[48]

Sanjana's argument for the centrality of tradition is largely irreconcilable with his acceptance of historicism—the central premise of the Reformist position. The tension between these two positions emerged from his commitment to the *practical* importance of tradition for the survival of Zoroastrianism and the Zoroastrian community. This tension becomes clear in his refutation of the Reformists. The problem with the Reformist position, he believed, is that after ridding the moral essence of Zoroastrianism of all tradition and traditions (decried as accretions and historically impermanent deviations), and privileging individual piety as consciousness of God's intent over ritual performance, very little that is distinctly Zoroastrian remains behind. The Reformist emphasis on spirituality and religious universalism results in the boiling down of *God's intent* to ethical behavior, which leaves behind an empty shell. Sanjana believed that this erosion of Zoroastrian particularism was dangerous, warning that it would result in "racial suicide."[49] Sanjana stressed the urgency of retaining religious faith and practice that are specifically Zoroastrian, rather than sliding into a deist conception of God that effectively disintegrates into particularism. He urged his community to retain a "definite God with definite perfection, in a definite revelation of His will, in definite obligations and duties; for only then can we practice definite virtues and lead a truly pious life," for "definiteness in all these points is a necessary condition for practical action."[50] For this reason, Sanjana opposed Reformists as well as "rationalism, skepticism, materialism, sensualism . . . [t]heosophy . . . Freemasonry . . . specious dogmas and doctrines of Christianity," all of which sowed divisions within the Zoroastrian community.[51] "It is a sin to divide a race against itself."[52]

Sanjana, like Reformists, maintained that one should stay with the religion of one's birth. But in Sanjana's conception, it was not because all religions are paths to the same end, but because Zoroastrianism was superior to all other religions. He therefore claimed universalism for Zoroastrianism, but a very different universalism of the Reformists where it connoted commonality of intent with other religions, such that difference was merely a function of historical tradition, rather than essence. Sanjana claimed a different essence for Zoroastrianism—a superior truth—that allowed him to promote the retention of specifically Zoroastrian belief and practice as rationally advantageous, rather than a matter of historical circumstance. Sanjana's references to Zoroastrianism as a universal religion of mankind are manifest. He noted that God sent Zoroastrianism "not only in the country of Iran, but in the whole world, and among all races (of mankind)."[53] He also repeatedly cited the Dinkard as asserting the superiority of Zoroastrianism: "[It] is the unique, the perfect and true Religion revealed by the unique and true Prophet Zarathushtra."[54] Zoroaster is described as "the greatest Law-giver, the greatest Teacher, the greatest of prophets, the unique Prophet who revealed perfectly the Mind and the Will of Ahura-Mazda."[55] He asserted that Zoroastrianism was not only comparable to Christianity, or an early precursor, but that it was a more perfect monotheism and has never been surpassed. "As the author of a complete and unique Revelation, Zoroaster stands above all other prophets with the various dogmas and doctrines which they preached at different epochs."[56] In many ways, Sanjana's claims to universality echo those statements of earlier Christian missionaries who believed Christianity to be the end result of religious evolution. Like Madan, discussed above, Sanjana denounced Christianity as insufficiently monotheist, irrational, and in opposition to the laws of nature (owing to belief in miracles). "The true Religion of humanity owes its fundamental principles to Zoroaster and to him alone."[57] As such, "it is intended to be a universal Religion, leaguing humanity in one spiritual bond."[58]

Sanjana's position on Zoroastrian tradition is consistent with his embrace of ritual practice. On the one hand, he believed that ritual was essential for community cohesion and identity. Yet on the other hand, Sanjana maintained an instrumental, utilitarian, and largely rationalized view of ritual. Like Reformists, he emphasized the spiritual nature of Zoroastrianism. "The Zarathushtrian religion can justly be said to have given birth to pure and simple monotheism. The Gathas which are . . . the soul of our Scriptures, inculcate the purest and the most spiritual views of God."[59] Real knowledge of God is the way to spirituality and ethics. Ritual serves as a prompt, an outward expression of an inner essence. Prayer "is the elevation of the soul or the mind to God."[60] Prayer recitation "invigorates the mind with prudential instructions and gives it incitement to work for that holy rectitude and for that blessed state which is acceptable to God and most desirable for man."[61] Prayer, then, is not what orthodox Zoroastrians less than a century before believed were *manthras,* or incantations, which could ward off evil, protect the speaker, or otherwise affect the supernatural—an end in and of themselves. Rather, Sanjana, much more in line with Reformists, allowed that prayer was a *means* to achieve greater spiritual awareness, a *training of the conscious individual moral character.*[62] For example, in reference to the prayers that accompany the ritual tying and retying of the *sadre* and *kusti,* Sanjana wrote that "they become to him a continual aid in keeping vividly before his mind pure and noble thoughts and to repel, dismiss and protest against, with indignation and reproach, all evil thoughts . . . and by this continual aid, the mind learns to run easily into the channel of purity."[63] Prayers and rituals are the *external manifestations*—the "clothing," if you will—of *internal knowledge of God* and spirituality: "On the one side, there are beliefs and convictions belonging to the individual; on the other hand, there are legends, rites, ceremonies and formulae in which those beliefs and convictions are *clothed* and made visible. . . . [O]ur rites and ceremonies, when properly observed, stimulate our *imagination,* exalt our *intelligence* and affect the *will* so as to strengthen us for that *moral struggle and spiritual battle* which we have to fight in this world."[64] Note what is being affected here: "imagination," "intelligence," and "will"—all elements of an internalized moral and spiritual struggle.

Significantly, prayer also had a profoundly practical dimension, creating community cohesion and religious identity: "It is the conviction of wiser men that all attempts at a purely philosophical spiritual religion, discarding outward and imaginative expression, are unnatural and doomed to failure."[65] This view differs radically from earlier orthodox belief in the efficacy of rituals—in their ability to affect the Divine in the supernatural struggle between good and evil. In this sense, Sanjana's vision of ritual is rationalized and instrumental; ritual is not essential to belief and practice of "true" religion, but simply a useful aid to belief and to community coherence.

12. Parsi priest offering prayers, phototype of postcard, ca. 1910.

Ethics is understood as the outward manifestation of the understanding of God's "intent," rather than the performance of prescribed rituals. Piety is expressed in every act, rather than limited to rituals. "Zarathushtrianism is right living after a divine model. . . . [T]he sum of all Zoroastrian doctrines is that man should grow in godlineness."[66] God's intent is also for the pious individual to behave ethically in society: Zoroaster "promulgated a code of ethics for the guidance of the human race, the fundamental principles of which were universal charity and friendship and peace of mankind."[67] Spirituality alone is insufficient to regulate individual behavior in society; piety requires some form, some cohesion in the form of ceremony and "rites." Accordingly, "the Avestan religion is a philosophical spiritual religion, thou not without ritual."[68] Although Sanjana, like Reformists, looked beyond rituals themselves to God's intent, he nevertheless believed in their social utility.

Sanjana spent a good deal of time identifying causes of "racial suicide" and social problems in the Parsi community caused by loss of "character." He believed strongly that the purpose of religion was to form pious individuals who behave ethically in society. As a religious leader himself, he was concerned with community coherence and identification. Despite many intellectual commonalities with Reformists, his Orthodox position derived principally from practical concerns. Sanjana believed that Reformist universalism and spirituality lead to the dismissal of Zoroastrian tradition and particularism, which then emptied Zoroastrianism of ritual behavior, "specificity," and, ultimately, community cohesion. As a religious leader, he was concerned with promoting community survival through religious identity and practice: "One of the effective means for keeping a community welded in harmony and union is to insist on it a scrupulous observance of all that its religion enjoins."[69] The alternative is internal division, fraction, and, eventually, dissolution. This threat, he believed, was the challenge confronting his Parsi community. "Our Parsis, setting aside their time-honoured ancestral beliefs and practices, have adopted a tendency towards divergence in religious matters."[70] Individuals should not "make of religion what he/she wants" or "work out his own conviction as it pleases him," but rather "they must be in conformity with truth and not in accordance with his individual temperament or whim."[71] Despite Sanjana's inability to articulate how "truth" is determined, and by whom, his plea is heartfelt.

Life as the Consciousness of Ethics: B. A. Engineer

Zoroastrian scholars were deeply imprinted by the presuppositions inherent in the discipline of comparative religion. None perhaps employed Müller's arguments as explicitly in the service of promoting Zoroastrian Reformist views as did B. A. Engineer. In line with Müller's notion of evolution, Engineer, in her article "Advancement of Religion," adamantly argued that morality was a function of only the most evolved religions and that original Gathic Zoroastrianism should take its rightful place among these.[72] Engineer appropriated Müller's argument whole-sale, even in defining religion as "an insight into or a perception of the infinite."[73] She likewise argued that morality was an expression of advanced, abstract, and individualized understanding of the Divine, whereas performance-based religions were more primitive and indicative of a lack of real consciousness of the Divine.

In the evolutionary stage of "element-worship" (one stage below monothe-ism), "the mental caliber of the people . . . is such that the idea of the religious with most of them centers in the performance of ceremonies and the recital of prayers. Remove these props and religion has no meaning with them. . . . [A]ll the noble ideas connected with religion being inadvertently neglected and compar-atively scantly attention being spared for highly ethical principles."[74] Engineer posited that evolution "enabled [the human mind] to grasp higher notions, and to preserve the religious sentiment without the aid of religious rites and ceremo-nies . . . and, simultaneously, to act the religious in life . . . to act one's part in life entirely in accordance with the genuine spirit of the religion."[75]

Engineer's argument is interesting for its emphasis on religious ethics at its most evolved as implying individual consciousness of the purpose (or "spirit") of religion, with a paradoxical abandonment of performance. Essentially, perfor-mance becomes the consciously ethical living of life rather than acts that are spe-cifically dedicated, and thus implicitly limited, to "religious" worship. Engineer thus fully maintained that true worship was living one's life ethically, rather than specific ritual performance. In order to move Zoroastrianism forward on its evo-lutionary journey, Engineer urged that it be reformed and propagated. The prob-lem, she insisted, was that people were following "the comparatively degenerated notions of the later writings" rather than sticking to the "high level of thoughts expounded in the Gathas."[76] She continued, "The advancement of religion for the Zoroastrians would thus consist of restoring religion from its present degener-ated state back to its original, unblemished condition."[77]

From Orthodoxy to Reformism:
Maneckji Nusserwanji Dhalla

The most comprehensive articulation of this second-generation Reformist position belongs to Maneckji Nusserwanji Dhalla (1875–1956). His *History of*

Zoroastrianism and many other works embody Reformist Zoroastrianism and its reconstruction as a "rational" religion. Dhalla grew up in an Orthodox priestly family in Surat. His predilection for religious studies brought him to Bombay, where he attracted the attention of teachers at the Athornan Madressa. In 1905, with funding from Cama and J. J. Modi, Dhalla traveled to Columbia University to continue his Zoroastrian studies with Professor Jackson. As a result of his integration into the Western religious studies field, Dhalla underwent what he later termed a radical "metamorphosis." He abandoned "Orthodox" Zoroastrianism and emerged as the most prominent Reformist of his generation. In his memoirs, Dhalla attributes his radical transformation to the scientific study of religion: "Now that I had been enlightened by scientific study, and now that I had come to know and gain so much, I no longer adhered to old ideas. My thinking, my outlook, my ideals and my philosophy of life changed. . . . I was now eager to become the thinker of new thoughts, the student of new ideas and the propogator of new concepts. In 1905 I had set foot on American soil as an orthodox. Now in 1909 I was leaving the shores of the New World as a reformist."[78] Upon his return in 1909 Dhalla accepted the position of high priest of the Zoroastrian community in Karachi—a position that he held for forty-five years until shortly before his death in 1956. Dhalla received an honorary degree from Columbia in 1929 and continued collaboration with the international scholarly community, traveling several more times to the United States. Dhalla was awarded the title of *Shams ul-Ulama* by the British government in 1935—the fourth Parsi scholar to receive this honor.

Dhalla was deeply committed to the exercise of what he termed the "scientific" method in his analysis of Zoroastrianism. He attributed scientific method to European scholars who had introduced comparative philology and historical perspective as tools of religious investigation. These new tools "opened a new era of critical study" and ushered in "the scientific method of interpreting sacred books." Before this time, original Avestan texts were "largely unintelligible," much Avestan grammar was unknown, and Parsis had "never approached their own sacred books with a historical perspective."[79] Dhalla was adept at employing these tools of "scientific method" and was profoundly influenced by the ideas of Haug, Moulton, Müller, and others. His own scholarship resonates deeply with religious studies theory. Unlike his doctoral professor, Jackson, Dhalla relied heavily on concepts of evolutionism and historicism for his own reconstruction of Zoroastrian theology and tradition.

Echoing Müller, Dhalla understood religions as different manifestations of human evolution. The stage of evolution of a religion was a function of the level of consciousness of the Divine. Consciousness thus moved from the primitive to the advanced, the literal to the abstract, and was generative of different forms of religious practice. Understanding religions as universal phenomena changed the discussion from one of whether a given religion was "true" or "false" in a theological sense of providing access to salvation to one of ascertaining where a religion lay on the continuum of human development. Religion, as an integral part of society, evolved along with it. Likening social development to a tree, Dhalla wrote that "as a sapling in time grows into a tall, strong tree . . . even so does a society and its religious, moral, mental, social and economic institutions and movements grow gradually from childhood to adulthood, from immaturity to maturity and from barbarism to civilization."[80]

Dhalla understood historicism to be the solvent of tradition. Tradition, as the construction of authority that then becomes fixed and static, was believed to obscure the original, "essential" religious truth. "Traditions are born of events, circumstances and common-sense," Dhalla insisted, and "traditions terminate with the change of times, circumstances and with enlightenment. But traditions die hard. Tradition-addicts do not wish to see the end of them."[81] Historicism, or the contextualization of tradition, thus enabled the accretions and distortions of tradition to be dissolved, revealing the original kernel. Dhalla, like Müller and Moulton as well as Sanjana, was firmly convinced that there was a core of Zoroastrianism that was "true" and immutable. Historicism, as the recognition of context, enabled the excavation of tradition and thus the archaeological recovery of the original religion. Dhalla employed evolutionism and historicism to identify and rescue "true" Zoroastrianism from tradition. His scholarship was a reconstruction of Zoroastrianism in line with theories of religious evolution. Following closely Moulton's argument on the historical stages of Zoroastrianism, Dhalla maintained that the Gathas reflected the original ideas of Zoroaster and that all subsequent texts were products of later deviation and degeneration. He claimed that the essence of Zoroastrianism was embedded in the Gathas: "In the pre-Gathic religion the trend of religious thought struggles from the complex to the simple, from concrete to abstract, and is yet the farthest removed from the ideas stage. Zoroastrianism, on the other hand, as preached in the Gathas is the very embodiment of the simple and the abstract. It is the realization of the ideal. It is the form to which the coming generations have to conform. Deviation from it means a fall, a degeneration of the religious life."[82] Zoroaster was a reformer, inaugurating a new stage in human consciousness of the Divine. Dhalla described Zoroaster's attempts to move religion away from ritualism and polytheism towards a spiritual consciousness of God: "Their priests had laid great emphasis on outward observances and carried rules for rituals to meticulous casuistry. Their gods were fond of sacrificial offerings of animals and birds. Religion, preached Zarathushtra, did not consist in a scrupulous observance of outward forms, but was based mainly upon the heart. A broken heart and a contrite spirit were the choicest sacrifices that the faithful could offer to their creator. Burning tears of a penitent heart were better than a cupful of oblations. The aim and object and end of the religion that Mazda had commissioned him to teach was righteous conduct."[83]

Zoroaster's consciousness of the Divine was a result of his ability to experience what Dhalla terms "enlightenment." "Zarathushtra's creative mind evolved the highest conception of godhead, whom he named Ahura Mazda or the Wise Lord."[84] Emphasizing spiritual communion with God, Dhalla believed that "Mazda [God] spoke through [Zoroaster's] mind and he was enlightened."[85] It is significant that Dhalla emphasized communion with God as resulting in *knowledge*. He also claimed that Zoroaster's conception of the Divine was at the highest stage of evolution: "Zarathushtra acquaints mankind for the first time in the history of religions with the concept of the godhead that is most incomparable in sublimity and unprecedented in the grandeur of nobility. He is higher than the highest being worshipped by mankind before his day."[86] Truth is this spiritual knowledge of God, or knowledge of the "essence of divinity." In a departure from Zoroastrian tradition, Dhalla depicted Zoroaster not as the receiver of revelation, or as a first disciple of a monotheistic god, but as Divine himself. Zoroaster was a prophet like other, Abrahamic, prophets: "Prophets are gods in the flesh, and Zarathushtra, the prophet of Iran, was such a man-god."[87] In this way Dhalla argued that Zoroaster was *capable* of "enlightenment" through communion. Because of the nature of prophets as divine, they are able to understand perfect divine knowledge and not be bound by the shackles of mankind's religious evolution. Dhalla also emphasized *knowledge* as the central element in man's relationship to the Divine. In contradistinction to Zoroastrian tradition that emphasizes the formulas and performances prescribed by God to Zoroaster,

Dhalla described this "message" as knowledge. Zoroaster is portrayed in ways distinctly reminiscent of Jesus.

As a result of his "enlightenment," Zoroaster rejected religion as it was currently practiced. Dhalla articulated the antithesis of "true" religion as understood and promoted by Zoroaster: "[Zoroaster] sees with horror temples reeking with the blood of sacrificial animals. He finds that barren formalism, sanctimonious scrupulosity, meticulous ablutions, superstitious fear, and display of external holiness pass for religion."[88] This passage clearly illuminates Dhalla's own conception of the nature of true religion. First, "true" religion originates from knowledge of the nature of God. Second, this knowledge enables the individual to internalize meaning and live an ethical, righteous life. The performance of rituals that is not based on understanding of God is depicted as "external holiness" and "superstition." It is knowledge of God that leads to a consciousness of the *purpose* of ethical behavior that characterizes true religion. For Dhalla, ethics must be a function of knowledge, not simply the performance of specified acts. He reiterated his position on ritual in his account of his own personal transformation from someone who "believed that the greater the number of ceremonies performed, the larger would be the quota of happiness showered upon me," to his later renunciation of "traditional religion."[89] A central component of this transformation involved the relationship of religion to ritual. "Ceremony is merely the outer shell whereas religion is the kernel."[90] Yet this is not to say that ceremony is irrelevant. Dhalla conceded, as did other Reformists, that "ceremonials were an essential part of religion."[91] Yet it is their utility, their role as a prompt to individual piety, that gives them value. "Ceremonies are a unique, efficacious and inestimable means of kindling the flame of love in the heart of a devotee and to enthuse him with devotion and faith to sacrifice his body, mind and spirit to his Creator."[92] Ultimately, Ahura Mazda measures the religiousness or irreligiousness of a person according to his noble or ignoble life and by his character alone.[93]

Zoroaster's death marked the end of "true" Zoroastrianism. "After the prophets depart their disciples turn everyone into blind followers of the faith. Religiosity replaces religion. The intoxication of religion makes a man delirious. Socio-religious customs take the place of pure, ethical and devotional faith and turn it into tradition-ridden religion as a result of which men quibble and quarrel constantly."[94] After Zoroaster died, the community witnessed a "counterreformation" and the resumption of earlier forms of religious consciousness and practice:

"A great religious syncretism then took place, with the result that the successors of the prophet were obliged to accommodate the Indo-Iranian divinities in the divine household of Ahura Mazda . . . with the return of the pre-Zoroastrian divinities also came the ancient rituals and sacrifices, offerings and libations. The beliefs and practices of the old faith were engrafted on the religion. . . . Zoroastrianism became a blend of the two, that is, the Indo-Iranian religion and Zarathushtra's religion of reform. And so it remains up to the present day."[95]

Dhalla claimed that Zoroastrian tradition reflected this synchronism and thus embodied *both* Zoroaster's religion as well as earlier and later traditions based on less evolved conceptions of God. Tradition thus must be deconstructed in order to unearth the original essence. Dhalla displayed a comprehensive understanding of tradition and its relationship to context. He viewed tradition as the sum of practices given authority by their claim to authenticity and immutability and understood as "orthodoxy." Dhalla also understood tradition *as a rationale for belief.* He devoted an entire chapter of *The History of Zoroastrianism* to explaining the nature and function of tradition. Dhalla began by asserting a distinction *in kind* between religious and "secular" knowledge: "Religions rest on divine revelation. This revealed knowledge is static. Secular knowledge progresses with time and, by continuous research and discovery in the realm of the physics of nature and the laws of life, creates new knowledge."[96] Religious *tradition* incorporated earlier understandings of science, but as scientific knowledge advanced, people began to doubt religion's claim to scientific truth. Religious knowledge is not incompatible with science, but should not be bound by any limitations of scientific knowledge. Yet many people are reluctant to challenge accepted tradition, even if it is no longer scientifically valid. This reluctance to accept rationalist explanations, owing to a commitment to tradition, Dhalla terms "orthodoxy." "Orthodoxy is obstinacy to forget anything old and learn anything new. Orthodoxy has always and everywhere professed that the doctrines, dogmas, rituals, and the established views of life that a people has inherited are fixed and right."[97] Calling the orthodox "tradition-addicts," Dhalla attacked them for their reluctance toward change. He wrote that "traditions are born of events, circumstances and common-sense. Traditions terminate with the change of times, circumstances and with enlightenment. But traditions die hard. Tradition-addicts do not wish to see the end of them."[98] Truth cannot be contained by the limitations of tradition. It must be uncovered by rationalism, historicism, and "scientific method." Context must

13. Maneckji Nusservanji Dhalla (in white), standing with A. V. Williams Jackson, H. Y. Clews, and Djelal Munifbey at Columbia University (figure at far left is unknown). Reproduction of photograph, early 1900s.

thus be decoupled from revealed religious "essence," since it, unlike any historical context, is eternal and immutable.

Like other Reformists, and in direct opposition to Sanjana's Orthodox position, Dhalla sought to fundamentally alter Zoroastrian belief and practice. Reform entailed the recovery of religious "essence" from tradition. Scientific method will uncover the "truth" contained in the Gathas. In line with the nature of religious essence as knowledge of God that results in conscious ethical behavior, prayer and ritual must be refashioned. Prayer, as distinct from ritual practice, should be understood as resulting from spiritual consciousness. "Devotion is the first requisite. Mere mutterings of a few formulas with the lips, while the heart does not pulsate with devotional fervour, are no prayer."[99] Rather, Dhalla argued that "prayer is the heavenward soaring of the soul on wordy wings."[100] Traditional, "orthodox" Zoroastrianism mistakenly believes in rituals' ability to affect the Divine. Yet this view is a fundamental misunderstanding of divine purpose. The practice of "true" religion depends on *consciousness,* not *performance* in and of itself. "Ritual is not religion; but it is a powerful aid to religious life. It feeds the emotional nature of man which plays the most prominent part in religious life. It inspires devotional fervour and purity of thoughts."[101]

Dhalla advocated such reform, yet was clearly cognizant of some of the practical consequences of dismantling tradition and making consciousness requisite for efficacy of prayer. The unmasking of tradition and the delegitimization of priests, while in one sense inevitable and necessary, also caused the community to become estranged from religious practice. The challenge was to discard tradition without discarding religious belief altogether. Dhalla recounted the effects of Reformist ideas on the authority of the priesthood, as the efficacy of ritual itself was challenged:

> The priest hitherto had acted as an intercessor between the layman and Ormazd, and through elaborate ritual had undertaken to gain for him divine help, being duly paid to recite penitential prayers for the expiation of the sins of the living, and to sacrifice for the purchase of paradise for the dead. The youth of the new school argued that there was no more need of the Mobad's [sic] mediation between him and his Heavenly Father. He demanded that the priest should act as a moral preceptor, a spiritual ministrant to his soul. This, in those times, the priest could not do. He could not widen his religious outlook and adapt himself to the demand of the younger generation. The youth now grew up without religious instruction and gradually gravitated towards indifferentism. The apathy, callousness, and disregard towards religion on the part of the educated youth waxed stronger day by day, and culminated in an atmosphere of agnosticism that withered the beliefs in which they were brought up. Agnosticism became the threatening evil of the day.[102]

It was not only the priests' ignorance and commitment to orthodoxy, however, that threatened their position. Dhalla agreed with the scholarly consensus concerning the intrusion of foreign priests, the magi, into Zoroastrian tradition. Like other Reformists, he also stressed individual relationship to God, rather than priestly intermediation.

Dhalla was not alone. One of the sharpest criticisms of the Reformist position by the Orthodox, as most fully articulated by Sanjana, was the lessening of religious commitment that inevitably resulted.[103] Others were also cognizant of the tightrope that they walked between recovering "true" religion and dismantling faith altogether.[104] One of the most vehement critics of the Reformist threat was Ardaser Sorabjee N. Wadia. "Sometime" professor of English and history at Elphinstone College, Wadia was deeply critical of the Reformists who engaged in "metaphysical subtleties and philological disputes" that left the community confused and spiritually bereft.[105] As discussed above, Dastur Sanjana was also concerned with divisiveness in the community caused by Reformist denunciation of tradition and ritual and believed that it was tantamount to "racial suicide." J. J. Modi took a moderate position, advocating cautious change. He understood the intellectual and theological rationale for reform, yet also appreciated the needs of the Parsi community. Modi recognized that "original good simple ideas of purity . . . are, at times, carried to tiresome extremes [that] tend to obscure the original good object."[106] Yet reform could be taken too far. Reiterating the words of French religious scholar Ernest Renan, Modi warned that "I fear that the work of the twentieth century will consist in taking out of the waste paper basket a multitude of the excellent ideas which the nineteenth century has heedlessly thrown into it."[107]

Juggling theological imperatives with the needs of the community would remain a thorny issue for Reformists—particularly since they advocated a new conception of religion grounded not in identifiable practice but rather in an intellectualized, internalized consciousness. Reformists and Orthodox sought to make religion a more conscious spiritual relationship between individuals and God. Yet such a reconceptualization of living a religious life depended on moving away from ritual as representative of a simplistic understanding of God. The internalization of piety led to the de-emphasis of ritual performance.

Reformist and Orthodox Positions, Revisited

Orthodox and Reformist positions differed fundamentally on the nature of tradition, the degree to which ritual was superfluous, and related questions of religious universalism, as I will discuss shortly. But first I want to underscore how closely both Orthodox and Reformist Parsis converged on fundamental assumptions concerning the nature and function of religion in society. Both Reformist and Orthodox scholars in this generation took for granted that religion was a universal human phenomenon that played itself out in historical time; that faith consisted of knowledge of God, which contributed to the individual's spiritual life; and that true piety informed all actions in life and created ethical individuals who were conscious of social responsibility as a divine mandate. In this section, I will be comparing the ideas of Sanjana and Dhalla, as representatives of the Orthodox and Reformist positions, respectively.

Reformists proffered an internalized and rationalized religion, denouncing ritual as superstition and tradition as created. Sanjana, articulating a highly Orthodox position, took a similar view: ritual is rationalized, religion is defined as man's spiritual yearning, and the individual's spiritual relationship with God, based on knowledge and, ultimately, God's intent, is privileged. This centrality of the individual, and the individual's relationship with God, is in keeping with Sanjana's emphasis on the nature of God. In a manner strikingly similar to Protestantism, Sanjana described God as a "loving Father," "a Father who is ever watchful over His creatures, loving them with tender love and drawing them lovingly into communication with Him. Such is the conception of God which Zoroastrianism presents to us."[108] Zoroaster too embodies qualities that are distinctly individualized, rationalized, and internalized. Sanjana described Zoroaster as prophet and lawgiver and emphasized the purpose of religion as salvation, rather than participation in a supernatural contest between good and evil. Zoroaster "unfolds before our intellect a new consciousness of God, a new perception of our soul and spiritual nature, new ideas of perfection and progress, new convictions of Immortality and a new Heaven with its unending felicity and reward for the righteous."[109] Similarly, Zoroaster models individual spirituality and piety as expressed in social consciousness: Zoroaster "continually engaged himself in developing and perfecting his character . . . until he acquired [from Ahura-Mazda] that supreme spiritual light."[110] Zoroaster "furnishes us the convincing proof that the highest spiritual life is in natural alliance with the greatest active service to man."[111] The Avesta teaches us that "our happiness does not lie in the well-being of our solitary self but in that of the whole community to which we belong."[112] Individual spirituality expresses itself in the level of civilization: "If spiritual faith or religion has been found nationally beneficial and essential to such enlightened and advanced nations as the English . . . it ought to be equally so to our Zoroastrian Community."[113]

Orthodox and Reformist scholars were also united in the conviction of a causal link between individual piety, on the one hand, and "civilization" and "progress," on the other. Orthodox and Reformists concurred in defining "civilization" according to the yardstick of rationalism, modern science, women's rights, and citizenship. From the beginning of the reform movement, Reformists had posited a causal connection between rational religion and the attainment of civilization and social progress. Sanjana insisted that Zoroastrianism was equally as modern and equally progressive as Christianity, since it had promoted, if not originated, ideas of modern science, hygiene, and respect for women. He quoted Gladstone opining that the status of women was the best test of the level of civilization: "When we are seeking to ascertain the measure of that conception which any given race has formed of our nature, there is, perhaps, no single test so effective as the position it assigns to women."[114] In an article on the historical role of women in ancient Zoroastrianism, Sanjana reaffirmed this connection. Yet he simultaneously rejected Western claims that Christianity was "the origin of many of the purest elements of our civilization." He argued that "the common opinion of English writers on the history of civilization and morals, that the civilized nations of the East were, before the advent of Christianity into this world, quite unfamiliar with the highest and noblest ideas regarding woman which are embodied in the New Testament," was simply false.[115] Au contraire. Sanjana called such a view a result of "the ignorance of English philosophers of Zoroaster's ideal of women in the Parsee Scriptures." Even "a cursory glance at the most ancient ideas regarding woman" illustrates clearly that "Zoroastrianism had taught [them] to mankind many centuries before the Christian doctrines came into existence."[116] In fact, Sanjana maintained that Zoroastrianism *originated* progressive ideas toward women and thus should claim its rightful place as "civilized." He explained, "It has been my object to show the extent to which Zoroastrian men had, in very olden times, cherished respect for women, and the position they assigned to them in social, moral and religious relations—a position if not nobler, at least as noble as that accorded to them by the most civilized nations known in the history of the world."[117] Sanjana elaborated on women's equality in faith and piety, choice in marriage, and education in Zoroastrianism. He even proposed that Zoroastrianism promoted gender equality: "In the Avesta both sexes appear constantly as possessing equal rights; there is no difference as to their respective importance."[118] The Gathas "contain a higher and purer idea of marriage . . . and regard it as an intimate union founded on love and piety."[119]

Dhalla agreed that women's status must be revisited in light of contemporary values, yet refrained from claiming that modern women's rights could be traced back to ancient Iran. In particular, he condemned polygamy and refuted the view that women were religiously polluting during their menstrual periods. Traditions should be amended in light of contemporary values, he insisted. Dhalla disparaged those individuals in the Zoroastrian community who, as "tradition-addicts," could not see that the seclusion of women was a residual carryover from primitive man's irrational fear of blood—a practice since abandoned by all communities "in the advanced world" with the exception of the Parsis and some Hindus. Dhalla denounced this tradition as "completely invalid under scientific and sagacious scrutiny."[120] He asked derisively, "What quality of man's glory is it that is not in the least soiled by the glance or the touch of the most wicked, corrupted and debased male, but is made unclean by the customary monthly flow of a noble, honourable and honest lady?"[121]

Dhalla's understanding of the relationship of religion to civilization was more sophisticated than the insistence on Zoroastrian origins of modern social values, women's rights, science, and hygiene. It hinged on his conviction pertaining to human evolution. Adhering faithfully to ideas of religious evolution, Dhalla identified the path to "civilization" as one of religious enlightenment. Critical thought and individualism were the conduits not only to personal salvation, but, ultimately, to religious universalism. In his autobiography, Dhalla elaborated: "God made man a part of society, but He wished and willed that, living in society and serving it, man may develop his individuality—his personality which reveals man in his completeness. That a human being may enjoy freedom of thought and freedom of conscience in this world and build up his character and, after death, as a result of that fine character and his own good deads [sic], win the liberation of his soul."[122] The liberation of the individual from the shackles of tradition had two important consequences. The first resulted from the connection of individualism to secularism and, ultimately, democracy. Dhalla explained that "just as despotism imprisoned individuality in its claws for thousands of years all over the world, tyrannical religious dogma bound it with chains. From the beginning of the sixteenth century human civilization changed from Medievalism to Modernism. . . . England, France and the United States of America revolted against autocracy and replaced royalty with democratic rule. . . . [T]hey divorced the Church from the State . . . and made man's religious life independent."[123]

The second consequence of the liberation of the individual was the ultimate enlightenment of mankind and, with it, religious unity. According to Dhalla, as the individual "renounce[s] customs; he will break the chains of illusion. Then only will the religious conflicts between man and man be resolved and one Religion will be born of various religions."[124] He went on to explain how the recognition of shared religious essence, or divine intent, across religions would underscore the historical contingency of religious difference and thus unify mankind:

> Tradition is not religion. The religion of truth which is the quintessence of all religions is a unifying force and leads mankind on to the ideals of love and devotion. Conventions that float on the surface of religions, under the pretext of maintaining the solidarity of each community, only raise barriers between the various faiths of the world and, in the name of religion divide mankind into sects and separate man from man, community from community, nation from nation. All the prophets of the world desire the unification of mankind. All those who are burdened with tradition-worship seek a thousand ways to preserve their compartmental aloofness. . . . Conventional religion is a curse to mankind.[125]

At stake for Dhalla in his promotion of Reformist Zoroastrianism was more than a new spirituality and social consciousness. For him, theological reform was necessary in order to generate individualism and, through individualism, secularism, democracy, and the end of particularism. Not surprisingly, Dhalla argued that modernity was a stage on the road of human evolution, not the monopoly of the West; modernity is universal. "Western culture of the twentieth century does not mean the culture of any one of the four directions of the world nor of only one of the continents of the earth, but it is a world-culture belonging to the new age—the newest, the latest, all-embracing, universal and fully experimented."[126]

The question of religious universalism, like the question of ritual, was one that sharply divided Reformists and Orthodox. As we saw above, Dhalla overtly accused the Orthodox of religious particularism, which he viewed as resting on false consciousness of God's intent. Sanjana's position was characteristically Orthodox in his insistence that any departure from Zoroastrian tradition was tantamount to "racial suicide." He prioritized community cohesion, not individual enlightenment, and viewed Reformists' advocacy of theism and deism as divisive and, ultimately, fatal. Sanjana's insistence on the Zoroastrian origins of modernity differs radically from Dhalla's view that the ultimate stage in the evolution of mankind will be religious commonality, a commonality that implicitly spells the triumph of interiorized individual piety and with it the defeat of ritual as a primitive manifestation of historical difference. This explains Dhalla's passionate claim that "conventional religion is a curse to mankind."

Reformists also differed strongly from the Orthodox over the issue of conversion. This distinction was a function of Reformist emphasis on Zoroastrianism as a universally valid, modern religion, rather than ethnically, historically, or tradition bound. At issue was the basis of Zoroastrian identity—was it faith, historically contingent tradition, or a sectarian identity rooted in ethnicity? The various conversion cases of the early twentieth century pitted Reformists and Orthodox against each other in what were ultimately irreconcilable claims surrounding the identity of the Parsi community.[127] Conversion cases revolved around the competition between religious and ethnohistorical bases of Parsi identity. Who was a Parsi? Was conversion to Zoroastrianism even permissible? There were three possible resolutions to these questions. First, ethnohistorical factors determined Parsi identity. "Parsiness" was based on having been born into a certain community that defined itself in ethnohistorical *and* religious terms. In other words, the terms *Parsi* and *Zoroastrian* were synonymous. Ethnicity and religion could not viably be distinguished one from the other. This position lent itself to claims of Zoroastrianism as both a race and a religion. Iranian Zoroastrians, in addition to Indian Zoroastrians, were therefore included in the definition of *Parsi*. This resolution was promoted by the Orthodox, who, like Sanjana, believed strongly in the preeminence of community cohesion and identified Parsis as a sectarian group that could not be dissected into "religious" and "ethnic" components. They were the children of ancient Iran. They were the inheritors and preservers of a historical legacy, racial purity, and religious "truth" that could not be assumed by "foreigners" through conviction alone.

The second possibility was to distinguish between "Parsi" as an ethnohistorical identity and "Zoroastrianism" as a faith. In this case, one could convert to Zoroastrianism, but one could not become a Parsi, except through birth to Parsi parents. In the infamous watershed Parsi Panchayat Case of 1906–8, Justice Davar argued that since the community had not accepted conversions in recorded memory, this rejection should serve as legal precedent, even though the court acknowledged that theologically, Zoroastrianism did accept, if not encourage, conversion. Ultimately, this second solution prevailed in the Parsi Panchayat Case of 1906–8 that distinguished the *right to convert* to Zoroastrianism (as a faith) from the *right to belong* to the Parsi (ethnic) community. The second judge in the 1906–8 case, Judge Beaman, concurred with Davar's position, arguing that in the Indian context, the Parsis functioned as a caste and thus were in effect closed to conversion. The judges did not deny the right of non-Parsis to convert to Zoroastrianism, but did deny these newfound Zoroastrians the right to consider themselves members of the Parsi community, which effectively excluded them from enjoying any rights pertaining to such membership. The inverse, of course, could also exist, namely, one could conceivably be born a Parsi (and thus be ethnically Parsi), yet convert *away from* Zoroastrianism (as a faith). This alternative was not much discussed in the case, since at issue was the right of converts to be considered Parsis and thus to partake of Parsi rights to community resources. Nonetheless, you will remember that this position was taken by Dhanjibhai Nauroji, the Zoroastrian boy who converted to Christianity as a result of the influence of Rev. John Wilson, discussed in chapter 2.

The third possibility was to assert the primacy of faith as a determinant of Zoroastrian-Parsi identity. This position privileged faith over any ethnohistorical community identity. In so doing, it insisted on the recognition of faith as a matter of conscious individual choice, rather than an identity into which one was born. In keeping with Reformist views of the historical context of tradition, this position effectively relegated community identity to the sentimental attachment to tradition. To quote Dhalla once again, "Tradition is not religion."[128] In this reading, the ethnohistorical community of the Parsis was characterized by the *unconscious* practice of *sectarian identity,* in contradistinction to Zoroastrians who were composed of individuals with a *consciously* upheld commitment to Zoroastrian *faith.* Advocates of this position believed that one must *consciously choose* to be Zoroastrian, whether of Parsi parentage or not. Converts should be accorded all rights and privileges of the Parsi community. Reformists, who rallied behind this position, naturally insisted that individual faith, not community identity, be paramount in determining rights to access religious sites. They also firmly believed that any claims to an ethnohistorical identity imperiled the nature of faith as consciously chosen and upheld, pitting the unconscious performer of sectarian difference against the conscious spirituality inherent in

Zoroastrianism. This stance paralleled the distinction between ritual observance and the internalization of piety, between external adherence and spirituality as the ultimate intent of God.

Whereas studies of the several conversion controversies in the early twentieth century have understandably centered on legal rights and conflicting notions of community identity, I would like to underscore the connections between contestations over identity and changing conceptions of religion in this period. Reformist Zoroastrianism recast religion as a matter of conscious, individual choice—a function of spiritual connection to God that expressed itself as social ethics. Religion was no longer a particularism that privileged identity in a community, no longer a claim to a historical lineage and ethnic distinction. Reformists redefined religion as the consciousness of the Divine, manifest in the internalization of piety. They therefore insisted on the *right* to convert as tantamount to the right to religious enlightenment. They also endorsed conscious individual commitment to Zoroastrian teachings implicit in the act of conversion that they found sorely lacking in the community.

The Parsi Rediscovery of Ancient Iran

> Centuries of contact with a weak and idle race have not exercised any perceptible influence upon the habits of industry for which the ancestors of the Parsees were remarkable.
>
> —DOSABHOY FRAMJEe, *Parsees: Their History,*
> *Manners, Customs, and Religion* (1858)

In the middle of the nineteenth century, Parsi reform-minded philanthropists took the first steps toward reestablishing ties with their coreligionists in Iran.[1] What began as an effort to improve Iranian Zoroastrians' living conditions quickly mushroomed into a full-blown operation to reorganize and reform the Iranian Zoroastrian community, as well as to revise their legal status vis-à-vis the Islamic state. Parsis arrived in Iran with the funds, international political connections, and organizational capacity to implement these changes. In their efforts to revitalize their Iranian brethren, Parsi reformers and philanthropists radically changed the Iranian Zoroastrian community, leaving behind the footprint of their own, Reformist, context. They initiated community organization and religious reform along Indian Parsi lines, although these were refracted through the different conditions and experiences in Iran. Iran also played a central part in the Parsi imagination. Parsi histories that emerged in the nineteenth century begin with the "myth" of ancient Iranian grandeur, followed by the story of Parsi exile from the fatherland. These new histories, written in the context of religious reform, illustrate profound connections between religion, race, and civilization as they revolve around the myth of exile and return.

Renewal of Contact Between Iran and India

The nature of the contact between the Iranian and Indian Zoroastrian communities changed during the course of the eighteenth century. Deteriorating conditions in Iran led to increased Zoroastrian migration from Iran at the end of the century. These same conditions altered the relationship of the Parsi community to their fellow religionists. Ever since Parsi emigration to India, the Iranian Zoroastrian community, the "original" Zoroastrians, had been imbued with a certain religious authority. Over the centuries, emissaries had been sent to Iran in order to clarify religious questions or to seek authority or knowledge of texts.

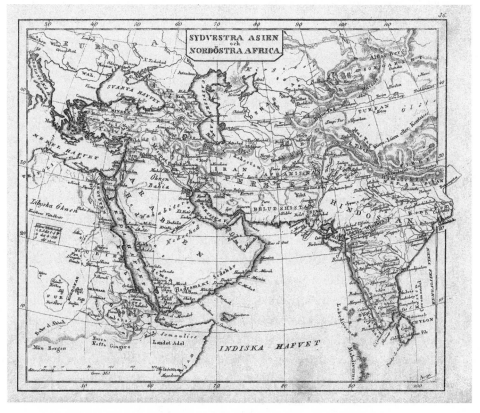

14. Swedish map of Iran and India, Fullständig Schol-Atlas, Stockholm, 1867.

In 1722 an Iranian *dastur* arrived in India from Kerman with the response to a religious question from the Parsis—a *rivayat*. Dastur Jamasp Hakim Vilayati, a scholar of both Pahlavi and Avestan languages, enjoyed such authority among the Parsis that he was asked to resolve a dispute concerning *dakhmeh* ritual. He brought a previously unknown religious text to the Parsis, the Nirangestan, and remained in India for a year to train high priests.[2] During his residence in India, Dastur Vilayati discovered that there was a one-month discrepancy between the Parsi and Iranian Zoroastrian religious calendars. Owing to the enormous importance of the calendar for calculating appropriate ritual observances, this finding ushered in an intense controversy in the community, dividing those individuals who would adhere to the existing Parsi practice (the Shahenshahis) from those Parsis who believed that the Iranian Zoroastrians were more likely to have maintained correct practice over the centuries (the Qadimis). Those in the Iranian camp, in addition to those priests trained by Dastur Vilayati, tended to be poorer artisans and lesser-known merchants. The Parsi *dasturs* held sway among those groups that were more closely tied in with their own authority and prestige, such as the larger merchant families in Surat.

The Qadimis wrote to Iran asking for further confirmation, but received no response. Nearly a generation later, in 1768, the nephew of Dastur Darab (one of Velayati's Parsi students and high priest of the Qadimis) was commissioned by the Qadimis to travel to Iran to pursue the issue. Dastur Mulla Kaus spent the next twelve years in Iran with his son, Mulla Feroze, studying astronomy and astrology with Zoroastrians in Yazd and Kerman. While in Yazd he consulted with a general assembly of Zoroastrians at the fire temple. The last of the *rivayats* was compiled from the seventy-eight questions he put to this assembly.[3] Still seeking more information on the calendar issue, Mulla Kaus traveled to Isfahan, where he spent three years with Muslim scholars studying Arabic and Persian, as well as astrology, philosophy, logic, grammar, Islamic theology, and medicine.[4] After successfully making an astrological prediction for the Iranian shah, Karim Khan Zand, he served at his court in Shiraz for several years, then spent three years in Baghdad before returning to India. His son, later called Mulla Feroze, was educated as a Zoroastrian priest in Yazd by the leading *dastur*. Upon leaving Iran, Mulla Feroze was an expert in Pahlavi, Avestan, Persian, Turkish, and Arabic (although he reportedly had forgotten his native Gujarati), as well as a trained Zoroastrian priest. Back in India, Mulla Kaus briefly served as high priest of the

Qadimis before retiring and relinquishing his position to his son. Mulla Feroze became a renowned scholar and had accumulated a library of more than eight hundred manuscripts by the time of his death in 1830.

The mission of Mulla Kaus and his son to Iran in 1768–80 is indicative of the relationship between the Parsis and the Iranians at the time. It was still the Iranian Zoroastrians who served as the repository of authority, knowledge, and texts for Parsis. Certainly, the divide between the Qadimis and Shahenshahis indicates that Iranian authority was not absolute and that the Parsi priests held sway in large segments of the Parsi population. Nonetheless, in an attempt to acquire more information, or authority, it was to Iran that the community turned. Mulla Kaus's experience in Iran indicates a high level of learning and scholarship in the Iranian community. It is significant, however, that he turns elsewhere—to Islamic scholars—for additional scientific study. The fact that he spent years studying with ulama and served at the court of the shah suggests a level of tolerance toward Zoroastrians that would not always exist by the end of the century.

The mission to Iran served as a turning point, although it was not understood as such at the time. The Iranian community that received Mulla Kaus and Mulla Feroze declined significantly, becoming almost unrecognizable in an account by a European observer some seventy years later. The report in question was a letter addressed to John Wilson by Danish Zoroastrian scholar Professor Westergaard that appeared in the *Oriental Christian Spectator* in May 1848. His description of the Zoroastrian communities of Yazd and Kerman differed radically from those depictions that had become familiar to the Parsi community from the Mulla Kaus mission. According to Westergaard, there were only one thousand Zoroastrian households in Yazd, and they lived in conditions "below the lowest Hindus." His account of their religious knowledge was even more alarming: "Of their religion they know nothing whatever; in the temple they light the fire only for a few hours during the beginning of the night. They consider smoking as improper for the Dastur only; and the Dastur himself offered me a kullan [a water pipe] in his own house."[5]

Westergaard maintained that many religious texts had been lost and that the few texts that the community preserved were poorly understood by the priests he met in Yazd. The Zoroastrians of Kerman fared even worse and were gradually converting to Islam. Scottish missionary John Wilson, the editor of the *Oriental*

Christian Spectator, appended a note to the article, asking why "the opulent Parsis of Bombay don't send a mission of inquiry to their brethren in Yazd and Kirman."[6] This article caused an enormous uproar in both the Qadimi and the Shahenshahi Parsi communities. The Qadimis in particular were threatened, since they had staked their position on the calendar dispute on the basis of Iranian authority. If, the Shahenshahis challenged, the Iranian Zoroastrians were in such a poor state of religious knowledge and practice, how could they possibly serve as authorities on ritual matters?

Westergaard's account of the dismal state of the Iranian Zoroastrian community was also alarming owing to the deeper religious danger it portended. The Iranians, whether their opinion was accepted in all matters of ritual or not, had always been a source of religious knowledge and texts. They had also represented the "original" community, admired as much for their endurance throughout the centuries of Islamic rule as they were as repositories of Zoroastrian religious teaching. The loss of this "original" community of Zoroastrians would be devastating, and Westergaard's suggestion that they were being lost, not only to ignorance, but to Islam, caused much consternation. For the Parsis, the age of Iranian authority was over, to be replaced only in part by a turn to European scholarship. The publication of this article, the increasing flow of Zoroastrian refugees from Iran during this same period, and the Parsis' own growing economic prominence in Bombay sparked a renewed interest in Iran. This time, however, Parsi interest stemmed from a concern to protect and assist the Zoroastrian communities there rather than to seek knowledge.

In 1853 Parsi merchants established a group dedicated to improving the conditions of Zoroastrians in Iran. This organization, the Society for the Amelioration of Conditions in Iran (SACI), set as its goal the lifting of Islamic legal restrictions on Zoroastrians (as non-Muslims) and the associated non-Muslim tax, the *jazieh.* There had already been a fund established some twenty years previously in order to provide financial assistance to Iranian refugees.[7] The society, however, was the first organized means for changing legal and living conditions for Zoroastrians in Iran. It is not certain whether Parsis were contacted by their coreligionists in Iran for help with the *jazieh* tax or whether they initiated assistance unrequested.[8] The first society representative to Iran was Maneckji Limji Hataria (1813–1890). Hataria, a Bombay Zoroastrian who worked for the British on commercial issues, enjoyed British citizenship and had been searching for an opportunity to visit Iran—the historic homeland of the Zoroastrians. In 1854 Hataria journeyed to Iran and settled in Tehran to begin lobbying for the repeal of the *jazieh* tax. He remained in Iran until his death in 1890, only once journeying back to Bombay between 1863 and 1865.[9]

The Infamous *Jazieh* Tax

Of all the restrictions imposed upon the Zoroastrians in Iran, the *jazieh* tax was considered the most onerous. This hardship was in part owing to the fact that the community itself had shrunk significantly over the course of the troubled eighteenth century while the total amount owed the government remained calibrated according to earlier population figures. It was also because the local governors permitted the tax to be arbitrarily increased, some sources claiming that the amount due was doubled or even tripled during Naser al-Din Shah's reign (1848–96).[10] According to statistics compiled by Hataria, the Zoroastrian population of Yazd at the time of his arrival was approximately 6,596 persons, of which only 200 could fully pay the tax and as many as 320 people had difficulty paying any portion of it.[11] Hataria took over the payment of the full amount with funds provided by the SACI. Parsis would continue to foot the bill for the *jazieh* for twenty-eight years until the tax was finally abolished in 1882.

Hataria was ultimately successful in convincing the shah to repeal the *jazieh* tax, in large part owing to his political acumen and ability to enlist foreign diplomats as erstwhile allies. British officials were encouraged, both by Hataria and by Parsis in India, to lobby the shah on behalf of Zoroastrians in Iran. British foreign consul Ronald Thompson, Major Rawlinson, ambassador to Iran E. B. Eastwick, as well as British members of Parliament all urged the shah and members of his court to abolish the tax. The Comte Arthur De Gobineau, a longtime French resident and scholar in Iran, also took sides with Hataria and the Zoroastrians in this matter. Hataria also sought to establish good relations with Iranian political and religious elites in order to further his goals. He was on intimate terms of friendship with a number of ulama, with whom he dialogued on theological matters. Hataria's own correspondence is replete with references to the *jazieh* as inconsistent with an Islamic sense of justice. He also pointed to the fact that the Armenians in Tabriz, with the aid of the Russians, had been freed of their own *jazieh* tax burden some years previously. Hataria wrote frequently to British representatives in Iran with stories of kidnapping and forced conversion of Zoroastrian girls that were brought to his attention by Zoroastrians in Yazd and Kerman.[12]

In 1882 Naser al-Din Shah abolished the *jazieh* tax by royal writ. Hataria hosted a garden party at the home of Haji Zaher al-Dowlah[13] in Tehran to celebrate. Foreign ambassadors, Parsis, Iranian royalty, and Armenian merchants were all present at the festivities, which included both Persian and "English variegated sweets." The shah's son and commander in chief of the Persian forces, Na'eb al-Sultan Amir Kabir, sent his own band of musicians to entertain the guests. A translation of the shah's *farman* appeared in the *Bombay Gazette* on November 16, 1882. It read, in part: "The Zoroastrians residing at Yezd and Kerman, who are the descendants of the ancient population and nobles of Persia . . . by the issue of this Royal Firman we order and command that the same taxes, assessments, revenues, and all other Government imposts, trading dues, &c., which are taken from our Mohomedan subjects residing in the towns and villages of Yezd and Kerman shall be taken in like manner from the Zoroastrians who also reside there; and nothing more nor less. . . . [T]he exaction of the sum of eight hundred and forty-five Tomans (Ts. 845), which was annually levied under another name from the said community will be abolished."[14] Hataria did not neglect to thank his British allies and gallantly credited them with his success. Petit, chair of the *jazieh* committee of SACI, also wrote letters of appreciation to the British officials, warmly thanking them for their assistance: "I feel sure that had it not been for the British influence at the Court of Teheran such a happy result could not have been so successfully accomplished."[15]

Despite the effusion of delight with the shah's formal rescindance of the tax, discrimination against Zoroastrians continued. The *jazieh* even continued to be collected by local officials in Yazd for some time.[16] Over the course of the nineteenth century, as the court increased the degree of governmental centralization, the question of the Zoroastrians, and religious minorities more broadly, was inseparable from the ongoing contest between royal authority and local autonomy. The ulama in particular resisted royal attempts to infringe on the Islamic-based legal system—part of the perpetual contest between royal and ulama prerogatives in the legal domain. Religious minorities were the site of these battles over authority, and their harassment and persecution need to be viewed in this light. Even as late as 1898, Naser al-Din Shah's son and successor,

Mozzafar al-Din Shah, issued a *farman* again, insisting that the Zoroastrians not be subject to shari'a-based indignities.[17]

The shahs' willingness to support the reduction of shari'a-based restrictions on religious minorities was also owing to Zoroastrian international political capital and their growing commercial wealth—both a function of closer ties with the Parsis in India. This combination of the extension of central authority, international political pressure, and commercial incentives made it more likely for the shah to find it in his interest to protect religious minorities against local oppressors. This equation would continue throughout the nineteenth century and well into the twentieth century in Iran.

The Establishment of the Anjoman

Following his success regarding the *jazieh,* Hataria concerned himself with organizing the Zoroastrian community. He traveled to Yazd and Kerman and established governing groups modeled after the Parsi Panchayat in the Zoroastrian communities of Yazd and Kerman as well as Tehran. These groups, or *anjomans* as they would be termed in Persian, functioned both to intermediate between Zoroastrians and the wider society and polity as well as to regulate internal community affairs.

In 1884 the Yazd Anjoman was constituted with wealthy merchants, the head *mobed,* a schoolteacher, and the head villager (the *kalantar*) as members.[18] A similar *anjoman* was founded in Kerman shortly thereafter. Both of these organizations were charged with consolidating the community and providing charitable assistance to Zoroastrians. In a written dialogue between Hataria and members of the *anjoman* in Yazd, Hataria's concern for the organization, accountability, and functions of the *anjoman* is clear. He urged members to be financially accountable and to ascertain the community's financial needs. He advised the *anjoman* to take appropriate measures to provide a monthly food allowance and clothes to the needy, to decide on the priests' salary, and to determine the costs of building a new fire temple and elementary schools.[19] The Kerman Anjoman established a dowry fund for poor girls, opened an orphanage, rebuilt a decaying fire temple, and founded a girls' school and a community space to celebrate religious ceremonies.[20]

Education and Religious Reform

In keeping with Parsi convictions concerning the importance of European-style education for both boys and girls, Hataria initiated the establishment of such schools in Iran. Traditional Zoroastrian schooling provided basic literacy. Children were taught some religious prayers by rote only. In addition to providing basic literacy and some knowledge of the Avesta and religious obligations, these new schools also taught sciences, mathematics, and home economics for the girls.

To encourage further learning, Hataria brought twelve local students from Kerman and twenty from Yazd to Tehran. These students and their successors were recruited to continue their studies in Bombay, although they did so with very mixed success.[21] By 1900 more than fourteen such "new" European-style schools were established for Zoroastrians in Iran.[22] The funds for the majority of these schools were provided by individual Parsi benefactors, in addition to SACI funds.[23]

Hataria was keenly interested in reforming Iranian Zoroastrian religion. He observed that Iranian practices were not identical with the ones followed in India and attributed this discrepancy to the dearth of religious texts and the generally poor state of religious knowledge and leadership in Iran. He thus used Parsi practices as the yardstick and attempted to bring Iranian practices into accord. In this regard, he aligned himself with Parsi Reformist ideas of "true" religion. Hataria conceived of reform as a process of purification whereby superstitions and non-Zoroastrian (read: Islamic) practices would be purged and forgotten practices reinstated. In his own account *Travels to Iran: A Parsi Mission to Iran* (1865), Hataria outlined his views on the importance of religious and social reforms.

The source of the problem, according to Hataria, was the lack of religious knowledge among the laity and the priests alike: "The problem of availability of mobeds in Iran is very acute. Those who are there are not very enlightened and they are not even well versed with some of our rites and customs. There is a great need to improve the conditions of the mobeds there: to educate them properly so that they may be better able to serve the community. . . . [A]s the mobeds remained uneducated, they could not guide the *behdins* [Zoroastrian believers] on the right lines in religious matters. They often believed in superstitious elements and introduced superstition into the religion. Thus the real tenets of our good religion were set aside and false beliefs crept in."[24]

Hataria clearly believed in the reinstatement of "lost" practices and the purification of Zoroastrianism from historical accretions of Islamic or Arab origin. For that reason, he sought to revive a number of practices that contributed to community solidarity that had been abandoned: the keeping of the Bahram fire, the coming-of-age ceremony of the investiture of a shirt and a rope-cord belt (*sadre pushi*), the viewing of a corpse by a dog (*sag did*), proper rituals associated with burial, and the reading, rather than only reciting, of the Avesta.[25] He wrote that historic and religious "languages like Avesta, Pahlavi and Persian need to be revived." Like the Parsi Reformists in India, Hataria argued for change as a "return" and emphasized Zoroastrianism as a monotheistic and fundamentally moral religion.

There were also non-Zoroastrian practices that Hataria urged the community to stop. Such practices included drinking wine in the daytime, dancing and playing music at someone's death, performing Muslim marriage customs, polygamy, religiously sacrificing animals, eating cow and camel meat, and wearing Muslim clothes.[26] In his writings and in his actions, Hataria demonstrated his desire that Iranian Zoroastrians continue to follow basic Zoroastrian rituals, customs, and traditions like their Parsi brethren. This concern should not be seen as an Orthodox emphasis on ritual, but rather the promotion of basic practices in order to preserve the Zoroastrian religion as well as community cohesion and identity.

Professor Jackson, traveling to Iran in the early twentieth century, witnessed many changes in Zoroastrian practices that he attributed to the Reformist Parsi influence. Jackson noted that overall, Zoroastrian practices and customs in Iran tended to be simpler than the ones of the Parsis, if they were even practiced at all. For example, he noted that "there is practically no religious ritual performed in Persia."[27] Two ceremonies considered essential to Parsis, the coming-of-age investiture of Zoroastrian garments (*sadre pushi*) and the *Barashnum* purifications, were largely ignored in Iran. Describing the *sadre pushi*, Jackson wrote that there was no real formality—children just put on the garments when they could recite parts of the Avesta properly—and that in Yazd it was uncommon for Zoroastrians to wear the prescribed garments. In both cases, he believed that the Parsis, whom he repeatedly termed more "advanced" than their Iranian counterparts, were strongly encouraging both these practices in Iran.[28] Jackson also noted that animal sacrifice among Iranian Zoroastrians was gradually being abandoned because the Reformist Parsis from Bombay insisted that it was un-Zoroastrian and adopted from Islam. The practice of polygamy was also attributed by Parsis to Islam and as a result was also discouraged. Jackson even speculated that some of the very "monotheistic" views of Zoroastrianism were owing to the influence of the Bombay Parsis.[29] Certainly, Reformist Parsis were having an impact on Iranian religious practices and beliefs in their attempt to bring Iranian practices into line with their own.

Hataria's Mission

Parsi philanthropic contact had an enormous impact on the Iranian Zoroastrian community. The influx of funding and political expertise led directly to the improvement of Zoroastrian legal status, financial resources, as well as community organization and educational and religious facilities. The growing political authority of the *anjomans* to intermediate on behalf of the entire Zoroastrian community with the larger polity constitutes a watershed in Zoroastrians' ability to advance their interests. Growing commercial contacts with the Parsis also meant that the Iranian Zoroastrians developed financial resources of their own. These two trends, community organization and the growth of commerce, would quickly lead to the flourishing of the Zoroastrians and their entrance into the political and social elite of the capital in the twentieth century. The wider political climate of secularization and the assertion of central authority, however, were just as critical for providing acceptance for the improvement of the Zoroastrians' legal and thus financial and political standing.

A comparison of the Iranian Zoroastrian experience of reform with the experience of their Parsi coreligionists at this early stage suggests three areas of similarity and difference. First, in both the Indian and the Iranian cases, the growth of the merchant class and the associated primacy of lay as opposed to priestly authority are clear. This trend was less pronounced in the Iranian case, however, since the merchant class and political organization of the *anjomans* were still in their infancy. At the turn of the century, Jackson observed that authority in the Zoroastrian community was neatly divided between lay and religious, with the *anjoman* dominated by merchants. He met with the eighteen members of the *anjoman* as well as the leading priest during his visit to Yazd. He described the *anjoman* as "the synod of leading men in the Gabar [Zoroastrian] community."[30] He also explained that the priests' religious authority was "tempered" by the fact that they enjoyed no coercive power. Their rulings on religious matters could be and were ignored.[31] This disregard is in clear distinction to the *anjoman,* which enjoyed political, social, as well as financial resources at its disposal.

Second, the threat to the Zoroastrian priests that Hataria's reforms (whether organizational, educational, or religious) spelled is clear from the nature of opposition he encountered. Although never discussed explicitly, opposition to Hataria is alluded to in his own work *A Parsi Mission to Iran.* He described "mobeds of the old school" refusing to use a new *dakhmeh* that the Bombay Parsis had financed, on the grounds that "the new one was constructed in modern style and thus was not in keeping with our religion." More specifically, the problem appeared to concern the materials used in construction. The opposing *mobeds* argued that "stone walls are modern, adopted from western countries, and thus they are unfit for a *dokhma.*" Hataria dismissed his opponents as ignorant, insisting that "this wrong belief is due to want of education." Nonetheless, these *mobeds* obviously had their own traditionalist constituency among the local Zoroastrians since Hataria recorded that "there was a row and controversy between the supporters of the old *dakhmeh* and the upholders of the new one." Reading between the lines of Hataria's account, it is apparent that the opposition he encountered was substantial. Although his political influence, social standing, and financial resources enabled him to effect many changes within the community, it was not an easy matter to convince all Zoroastrians that the Parsis' practices were authoritative. Resistance to change, although probably related to the shifting status of the priests, was articulated as resistance to religious innovation—always a potent charge.

It must also be underlined that the Iranians and the Parsis experienced very different impetus and sources for reform. The Parsis found their society impacted by British imperialism and the associated influence of British cultural norms, education, and social and political agendas. The Zoroastrian religious tradition was deliberately and expertly challenged by European scholarly and missionary beliefs. In reaction, therefore, the Parsis were driven not only to reexamine their tradition, but to do so largely on their opponents' terms. The Iranians experienced religious reform in a very different manner. On the one hand, religious reform was *imported* rather than *generated* in a domestic context. Iranian conditions did not spur reform, whether religious, political, or educational. To the extent that they, too, were influenced by the Parsi reform agenda, they were also impacted by European religious concerns, but one layer removed.

On the other hand, the Parsis were not the outsiders in Iran that the British were in India. Although not Iranian born, and certainly originating from a different religious and political context, the Parsis were *coreligionists* and by *origin* Iranian. They not only believed in their common history, but were accepted as such by the Iranian Zoroastrians. Whereas the Indian context generated the rise of the merchants, the Parsis promoted the rise of the merchants in Iran. And whereas Parsis generated the nature and scope of their own religious response to European attacks, the Iranians were handed these terms already formed and authoritative. As Zoroastrians, the Parsis arrived in Iran with an authority and a legitimacy that no other group possessed. This point should not minimize, however, the extent to which Iranian reforms (religious or otherwise) stood on their own. Over time, as the Iranian Zoroastrian community developed politically, socially, and financially, they would begin to assert independence from the Parsis. They also made their own choices in reexamining their religious traditions— choices that often, but not always, resembled the ones first arrived at in India.

The Rediscovery of Ancient Iran

The project of Parsi reform rested on the premise of historicism—on the idea that the pure kernel of Zoroastrianism had over the course of history become encrusted with foreign accretions, and that reform therefore consisted of the archaeological cleansing of historical detritus to recover the original, essential truth of Zoroaster's message. Accordingly, Parsi Reformists and religious studies scholars were invested in the rediscovery of true Zoroastrianism. This aim was necessarily a project of historicizing Zoroastrian practice, even as the project itself denied its own historical context. This recovery effort involved the exploration of the Zoroastrian past, both as a religion (what were the essential beliefs) and as a community (how had the religion been practiced over time). It is no coincidence, therefore, that Parsi Reformists in the mid-nineteenth century began to write new histories of the community in search of this pure, essential past. Of course, this recovery of the *Zoroastrian* past was also one of rediscovering the ancient *Iranian* past. Ancient Iran, already the ancestral homeland of the Parsis, was imagined as an idealized ahistoricized past, one in which the essential truths of Zoroaster's message manifested themselves in civilizational superiority. Parsis emphasized their own connection to this past by means of the trope of exile—an exile that defined the Parsis by race and religion as authentically Iranian.

Two of the earliest Parsi reformist histories written in the mid-nineteenth century were Dosabhoy Framjee's *Parsees: Their History, Manners, Customs, and Religion* (1858) and Maneckji Hataria's *A Parsee Mission to Iran* (1865). Framjee's account is perhaps the first history of the Zoroastrians written in the nineteenth-century context of religious reform by a leading Reformist. It was widely read and frequently alluded to in subsequent histories, and it clearly illustrates the emerging confluence of race, religion, and civilization that would become hallmarks of later Zoroastrian histories. Framjee wrote his history expressly in order to introduce Zoroastrians to the British. He therefore dwelled on those elements of Zoroastrian-ness that he believed were most important to emphasize to a British audience. Framjee's emphasis on ancient Iranian history as embodying the essence of Zoroastrian religion and civilizational character thus must be read in the context of his deliberate alignment of Parsis with the British, in religion, civilization, and, ultimately, "progress." Hataria's account of his travels also contains much commentary on a "mythologized" ancient Iran, in order to locate idealized religious and civilizational characteristics in that period and to explicitly connect Parsis to an Iranian homeland.

From the outset, Framjee outlined the profound connection between race, religion, civilization, and progress: "Parsis are a distinct race, and that neither in their religion nor in their habits of life, do they assimilate with either the Mahomedans or the Hindoos. . . . Western civilization has had great influence on their characters. . . . [I]t must be evident that the Parsees form a striking exception to the other [Oriental] races."[32] In this remarkable passage, Framjee posited that religion was inseparable from race. Religion distinguishes Zoroastrians from other "races" and is the cause of their predisposition toward "Western civilization" (read: progress). Framjee was clearly of the conviction, whether consciously or unconsciously, that certain forms of religious belief and practice were generative of internal dispositions and sensibilities; in other words, "true" religion produces progressive "habits of life," values, and belief systems as it molds individual characters. Framjee eagerly claimed essential "racio-religious" difference from both Hindus and Muslims in an attempt to align Parsis with the British. Remember too that Framjee was writing this history in the context of religious reforms that were rationalized as purifying Zoroastrianism from Hindu (and, in the Iranian context, Muslim) elements that had been unwittingly assimilated over time.

Chapter 1 of Framjee's history, titled "Historical Sketch," is composed of five sections that undergird his conception of Parsi history. Although Framjee does not subtitle the sections, they are clearly distinguishable as: "Iran Before the Conquest," "Conquest," "Iran After the Conquest," "Exodus," and "Parsees in India." Iran before the conquest is described in superlatives. The vast Persian empire was one "whose grandeur, magnificence, and glory were unequaled by any nation of ancient times; whose kings were at once the most powerful of monarchs, and the wisest and most beneficent of rulers."[33] This empire was then destroyed by "Mahomedan" conquerors. The conquerors exhibited qualities necessitated by their religious beliefs: "Toleration in religion is unknown to the haughty, uncivilized barbarian believers of the Koran. Bigotry is the highest virtue demanded of the Mahomedan, and one which secures for him favour in the eyes of his prophet and his God."[34] In Framjee's understanding, faith determines values, and prophets pass on essential characteristics of religious belief, in the case of Islam: bigotry, intolerance, and brutality. This belief is borne out by Framjee's assertion that owing to subsequent persecution and hardship, the majority of Zoroastrians converted to Islam and consequently "lost their good characters."[35] It is also worth noting in this regard that Framjee identified the conquerors as Muslims, not Arabs. Religion generates civilization, not vice versa, and as such is the dominant signifier of difference.

Framjee's explanation of Zoroastrian exodus from Iran to India occupies a central and lengthy place in the chapter. It clearly draws much of its narrative from the *Qisseh-ye Sanjan,* the Zoroastrian history of migration from Iran composed in 1599. In Framjee's day, the *Qisseh* was regarded as authoritative, although many scholars since have cast aspersions on its accuracy.[36] According to Framjee, despite hardship and persecution, some Zoroastrians remained true to their faith and, in order to safeguard it, "sought asylum in the country of the Hindoos."[37] It was thus a matter of the preservation of the faith that led the Parsis to India: "Rather than abandon the faith they had inherited from their fathers, they had voluntarily made themselves exiles for ever [*sic*] from the land that gave them birth, and were now at the mercy of strangers for a home."[38] India is described as a prayed-for "deliverance."[39] Framjee differs, in emphasis, from the *Qisseh.* The passage in the *Qisseh* concerning the decision to depart Iran reads:

A wise *dastur* there was in that domain,
> a master in the science of the stars.

He looked in his old tables of the heavens,
> And said, At last our life is finished here.

It is correct for us to leave this land.
> We must now make an exit from this realm,

Or else we shall all fall into a trap.
> To reason were in vain, a foolish thing.

So it is better we set off for Hend,
> And that we leave behind the wicked devils.

Let everyone escape henceforth to Hend,
> to save our lives and for Religion's sake.[40]

The *Qisseh* privileges avoidance of persecution as the primary impetus for Zoroastrian departure from Iran; Framjee emphasizes *preservation of true religion* as the rationale. The story thus subtly changes from one of flight to one of exodus, one of self-preservation to one of guardianship of religious purity.

Following the traditional narrative established by the *Qisseh-ye Sanjan*, Framjee recounted the negotiation between the newly arrived Zoroastrians and the prince of Sanjan who ultimately decided to allow the Zoroastrians to reside in India. Framjee faithfully provided the legendary sixteen articles of Zoroastrian faith that are recorded in the *Qisseh* and have been understood by the Zoroastrian community as accurate representations of their beliefs upon arrival in India. However, Framjee proffered a radical reinterpretation of these articles of faith. He argued that they must be read in the context of the desperate attempt by the Zoroastrians to remain safely in India. He suggested that the Zoroastrians were prepared to dissimulate their own beliefs in order to satisfy Hindu sensibilities: "They concealed from the Prince all that would have appeared extraordinary or offensive to him and his subjects, and supplied, in place thereof, ceremonies which had an origin exclusively Hindoo."[41] Framjee's gloss here allows him to problematize the description of Zoroastrianism contained in the *Qisseh* and to insist that, in line with Reformist convictions, Zoroastrianism was monotheistic and decidedly less ritualistic than described. Considering the reform effort under way to rid Zoroastrianism of "Hindu superstitions," it is not surprising that Framjee explains any commonalities with Hindu practices as of much later provenance and insists that at the time of arrival in India, Zoroastrianism was "correctly" practiced. It also allows Framjee to explain the Parsi adoption of Hindu language, dress, and marriage ceremonies as pragmatic concessions in return for safety, rather than essential to Zoroastrian belief. Now, under the British policy of religious tolerance, the Parsis can finally afford to jettison "foreign" practices. The last part of chapter 1 describes the Parsis as having lived peacefully and loyally in India. Since the arrival of the British in India, however, Framjee narrates that the Parsis have become an exceptionally industrious, prosperous, and successful minority.

The remainder of Framjee's *History* concerns the Indian period and stresses Parsi achievements and shared sensibilities with the British, which has been discussed in earlier chapters. It is worth noting that in chapter 2, "The Parsees in Persia," Framjee takes the opportunity to stress the racio-religious difference between Zoroastrians and Muslims, implicitly aligning the former with the British:

> The physical and moral condition of the Parsees in Persia have remained unchanged since the time when they called the country their own. Centuries of oppression have not been able to destroy the *strong, muscular and hardy* appearance of the Zoroastrian. He is greatly superior in strength to the modern *effeminate and luxurious* Persian; and is ever willing to work could he find employment. Centuries of contact with a *weak and idle race* have not exercised any perceptible influence upon the *habits of industry* for which the ancestors of the Parsees were remarkable. *The Zoroastrian is taught by his religion to earn his bread by the sweat of his brow, whereas the Molsem [sic] is taught to believe, that he will be the favoured of God by becoming a fakir and living on alms.* It is a fact creditable to the *blood* which flows in Zoroastrian veins, that the *race* has not degenerated by contact with those by whom fate has surrounded them. The same may be said of their moral conduct.[42]

What is most notable here, and is a constant theme in Framjee's *History*, is the assertion of difference between the Zoroastrians and other "Oriental" races. In the preceding passage, Framjee constructs a dichotomy between the strong, muscular Zoroastrian and the effeminate Muslim; between industry and sloth; between work as God's intent and predestinarianism; and between morality and immorality. In this distinction he is profoundly influenced by British Protestant sensibilities in his efforts to claim that Zoroastrianism, reformed and rationalized, is similarly progressive and conducive of enlightened "sensibilities and dispositions."

Hataria's *Parsi Mission to Iran* is a record of his travel to Iran, not a Zoroastrian history per se, and thus cannot be compared exactly in form or in content to Framjee's history of the Zoroastrians. Nonetheless, Hataria evidences a similar connection between religion, race, and civilization to Framjee's *History*. Through his focus on ancient Iranian history as a uniquely Zoroastrian heritage, Hataria, like Framjee, presents a transcendental Zoroastrian identity—one that is fastened to a time and place (ancient Iran) and thus transcends exodus, separation, and subsequent history. Iranian and Indian Zoroastrians, as a racio-religious group and bound together through shared history, are indelibly connected to Iran, and to each other. Hataria, not surprisingly, spends a good deal more time discussing ancient Iran than does Framjee. Whereas Framjee accords ancient Iranian "grandeur" and greatness, Hataria mythologizes it. As noted by Michael Stausberg, Hataria's description of ancient Iran as a "garden of paradise" and the "sign of heaven" portrays Iran as a "mythic" country.[43] I would argue that this "myth" of ancient Iran allows Hataria to construct ancient Iran ahistorically, as more civilized, more scientifically advanced than the present. Whereas Framjee writes that ancient Iran "was unequalled by any nation of *ancient times*," ancient Iran in Hataria's rendering is more civilized than the *present*: "The ancient Iranians were far superior and civilized than the people of today. . . . Modern science of today is filled with awe at their equipment and their constructions. . . . [T]he ancient Iranians were far advanced in all ways of life."[44] Hataria's version of ancient Iran thus functions as more than a past example of greatness; it is a yardstick against which to measure the shortcomings of the present and a template upon which to model the future. Note too that past greatness is measured according to contemporary criteria of "civilization and progress," that is, science, hygiene, brotherhood, morality, piety, and political domination. Hataria thus denounces a positivist rendering of human history, instead positing a model of rediscovery of the past as a way forward to the future. The connection between the past and the future defines the interim period—precisely the period of Islamic rule—as an anomaly, an intermission, a gap that can be bridged through the reappropriation of ancient Iranian civilization. Not surprisingly, Hataria was in dialogue with Iranian intellectuals interested in ancient Iran, such as Prince Jalal al-Din Mirza and Mirza Fath Ali Akhundzadeh. Bayat, Marashi, and Stausberg have noted correspondence between them and have suggested that Hataria may have played a seminal role in sparking an interest in the "modern" possibilities of ancient Iran among Iranian protonationalists.[45]

Hataria follows closely Framjee's emphasis on the causal connection between religion and civilization, noting that prosperity derived from "the inhabitants observ[ing] the rules of piety and purity of body, mind and soul."[46] Hataria also follows Framjee in emphasizing the violence of the Arabs, contrasting them with "peace-loving" Iranians. In Hataria's account, the violence is also connected to tyranny and corrupt administration. Although Hataria does not explicitly condemn Islam as the cause of Arab barbarism, he implies it when he notes that Zoroastrians, for lack of *proper religious education,* also became aggressive. Arabs, and implicitly Muslims, are faulted for lack of education, lack of culture, and, consequently, lack of civilization. Nonetheless, Hataria hesitates to condemn Islam outright. Instead, he writes that it was Arab hordes and "other barbaric

15. Roman Emperor Valerian at the feet of Shah Shapur, Nakhsh-e Rostam, wood-engraved print from Elisee Reclus, *The Universal Geography, the Earth and Its Inhabitants,* edited by E. G. Ravenstein (London: Virtue & Co, ca. 1885).

tribes" (like the Mongols) who destroyed Iran.[47] Elsewhere, he concedes that persecution of Zoroastrians in Iran was not condoned in Islam: "Many a time, the Muslim officers who wield power in Iran went off track of Islamic rules as taught to them by their Prophet Mohammed."[48] Given the level of visceral accounts of the barbarism of the conquest and subsequent Islamic rule, this statement reads as a tactical pussyfooting around a condemnation of Islam for the sake of political exigency or, at the very least, a profound ambivalence where Islam is concerned.

Hataria and Framjee also concur on the story of exile and separation. On the one hand, Zoroastrian exile to India was one of loss, of separation from the Iranian fatherland. On the other hand, it is a triumphal story of the preservation of religion, of race, and of civilization. It is a victory of survival despite the conquest, one that both ensures a permanent link to the homeland and offers the possibility of full redemption through a return to Iran or, conversely, a return of ancient Iranian splendor. Hataria's *Mission* is in many ways cast as a return and the beginnings of the rediscovery and reclamation of the ancient past. Hataria's collection of ancient coins and artifacts and his careful notation of ancient Zoroastrian sites complement his own role as regenerator and renovator of the Zoroastrian community in Iran. In his *Mission,* Hataria hopes that this collection, forty years in the making, will be preserved "in a fitting place and augment[ed] by the research work of other scholars so that the collection may be a permanent and everlasting treasure"—a treasure and testimony to ancient Iranian civilization.[49]

Writing on twentieth-century Parsi history, Patel and Luhrmann have both noted that the Parsi identification with Iran makes them an exilic community, which profoundly shapes their relationship to India—as a minority caught between British affiliation and Indian independence, between India as home and India as exile.[50] But what I want to emphasize here is that the beginning of this consciousness of a shared historical past that took on these new connotations emerged out of the religious reform movement that subjected tradition and history to new scrutiny—and in so doing reconstructed both.

Such early histories made important and lasting connections between religion and "civilization and progress" and generated a deep intimacy between ideas of race and nation that remained characteristic of Parsi conceptions of self in the twentieth century. Perhaps the individual that illustrates these tendencies most forcefully was Dinshah Jeejeebhoy Irani (1881–1938). In a life that spanned the Parsi reform movement, Irani worked with both the Rahnuma Mazdayasnan

Saba and the Gatha societies and was a trustee for important fire temples. He also founded the Iranian Zoroastrian Anjoman (1918) and the Iran League (1922), where he served as lifelong president and vice president, respectively.[51] Irani was thus profoundly engaged, both intellectually and socially, with Reformist circles in India and deeply committed to preserving and furthering Parsi connections to Iran. In 1932, as the leader of a Parsi delegation, he was invited by Reza Shah to Iran and awarded the honorary *Neshan-e Elmi* educational distinction.[52] Irani exemplified the Parsi community's passionate interest in ancient Iran and in revivifying ancient greatness through religious piety and devotion. In a telling letter to his son, Irani made explicit the enduring connections between ancient Iranian civilization and his Reformist vision of Zoroastrianism: "I have taught you the passages from the Gathas. . . . Daily I have been trying to infuse in you an undying love for our religion, and for our ancient fatherland—Iran. . . . I wish to see you grow up, a true scion of the ancient Iranian race . . . devoted to Truth, perfectly righteous, manly and noble . . . serving with your life and soul the cause of your ancient land, the cause of your great religion, and serving humanity. . . . [Y]ou will realize the great Truth that our existence here is to make ourselves Super-men, nay God-like, with the development of the Divine Attributes which are His, but which it is our birth-right to attain to and possess."[53] In this passionate testament to his son, Irani clearly believes that ancient Iran, Zoroastrianism, and race are firmly and unassailably bound together. Although this passage certifies Irani as influenced by Reformist visions of spiritualized, rational religion, his emphasis on Zoroastrians as a race with both historical and religious parentage brings him much further in line with the Orthodox position on the indivisibility of religion, history, and race than it does with Dhalla and other Reformists who emphasize faith over any ethnohistorical or racial components of identity.

7

Iranian Nationalism
and the Zoroastrian Past

There are not wanting those who credit the Shah with entertaining thoughts
... of the restoration of the ancient Zoroastrian worship.
                —US State Department, letter by RIVES CHILDES,
                          April 26, 1935

Twentieth-century Iran witnessed the fruition and intensification of nineteenth-century reform efforts. Islamic law was largely, although not entirely, secularized, providing greater legal equality and the end of sartorial and other socioeconomic restrictions on religious minorities. Iranian nationalism was adopted as the ideology of state in order to promote concepts of the modern citizen and popular sovereignty. Iranian nationalism, owing to its identification with the pre-Islamic (and thus Zoroastrian) past, also created a special relationship between the state and the Zoroastrian community. Modernity was mapped onto a reimagined past, and the Zoroastrians held special status as the "authentic" Iranians unsullied by intervening years of decline, conversion, and distance from cultural origins.

The Turn of the Century

State efforts at increasing centralization and secularization continued over the course of the nineteenth and twentieth centuries. Iranian political stability and European imperialism brought with them renewed European interest in Iran. This new context had a very real impact on the Iranian Zoroastrian community. The "Great Game" between Russia and Britain, and European aggressive political and economic policies more generally, lent Iran increasing international importance. More and more Europeans, primarily belonging to the diplomatic and commercial communities, took up residence in Tehran. The Parsis, too, had representatives in Tehran who cultivated European diplomats and harnessed their support in attempts to secure improved legal rights for Iranian Zoroastrians.

Renewed contact by the Parsis with their coreligionists in Iran spurred Iranian Zoroastrian entrance into trade and commerce, a niche formerly prohibited them. Parsi funding and support, combined with an easier trade route to Bombay, led to the predominance of Zoroastrian mercantile activities with India.[1] This preference continued throughout the Reza Shah period, even as Zoroastrians gradually expanded into the domestic market.

Increased centralization also implied increased secularization of the legal sphere. Although no formal, systematic changes occurred in the Islamic shari'a or the existing court system before Reza Shah became king, religious minorities (including the Zoroastrians) were eased of some of their restrictions, at least in theory. Minorities in Tehran could count on the Qajar shahs' protection, whereas those in the provinces still suffered under the authority of local governors and populations who sometimes refused to comply with royal orders. Reza Shah accomplished a much tighter degree of centralization, but the divide between conditions in the capital and in the provinces continued to be relevant for minorities throughout his reign.

The increasing centrality of Tehran, as the seat of both domestic authority and international connections, grew over the course of Reza Shah's reign. Despite Reza Shah's attempts to control and integrate the country as a whole, the capital remained the center of modernizing, Westernizing policies and benefited unequally from economic development and the expansion of the bureaucratic and professional middle class. Zoroastrians were attracted to the capital for a variety of reasons. Individual entrepreneurs arrived in the capital at the turn of the century primarily for commercial reasons and were quickly followed by a stream of others drawn by the economic incentives that the new Zoroastrian merchants held out.

Before the Constitutional Revolution, the Zoroastrians lived predominantly in the southern towns of Yazd and Kerman and their environs.[2] There were 50 Zoroastrian merchants living in Tehran by 1850, and Zoroastrian villagers used to travel to the capital in groups of 200 or so to seek summer work in the gardens north of the city.[3] The first Parsi representative to Iran, Maneckji Limji Hataria, encouraged Zoroastrian merchants to move to Tehran, where he assured them they would receive more government protection and be the objects of less prejudice.[4] With the lifting of bans on trade, Zoroastrians did come to Tehran, and by 1880 the number of Zoroastrian merchants in the capital had tripled to 150. The number doubled again in only a decade. By 1892 the Parsi Society for the Amelioration of Conditions in Iran estimated the number at 295.[5] Although in the span of fifty years the Zoroastrian population of Tehran increased more than five times, they remained a small minority in the capital, which enjoyed a total population of approximately 200,000 at the turn of the century.[6] By 1912 the number of Zoroastrians in the capital had mushroomed to 500.[7] Statistics for 1927 and 1937 are 800 and 1,500, respectively.[8]

Europeans, following a much-worn path of supporting minority groups, helped the Zoroastrians, both politically and financially. A Russian bank gave loans to small Zoroastrian businesses and helped the first of the recent Zoroastrian immigrants to launch their banking operations.[9] Minorities filled new niches, and the Zoroastrians concentrated on banking and trade with India. Zoroastrians, because of their minority status and their connection with Parsis and Europeans, were also more open to foreigners and foreign institutions than the majority Muslim society. For example, a Zoroastrian girl attended a European mission school in Tehran as early as 1878, whereas the first Muslim girl did not attend until nearly twenty years later, in 1896.[10]

The expansion of commercial and banking activities, coupled with sponsorship by the Parsis, led to the rise of large merchants among the Zoroastrians and the gradual emergence of a Zoroastrian community in Tehran.[11] By the turn of the century, there were as many as six large and an equal number of small Zoroastrian businesses in the capital.[12] The largest of them was the merchant house of Arbob Jamshid Jamshidian. Originally from Kerman, Jamshidian received help from Iranian government officials and Russia in establishing his business. He engaged in trade involving Russia, India, and nine provincial centers in Iran and enjoyed the privilege of selling cloth to the shah's household. Jamshidian preferred to employ fellow Zoroastrians and recruited them in the southern towns of Yazd and Kerman, encouraging them to immigrate to Tehran. By 1905 he employed more than one hundred Zoroastrian workers in Tehran alone.[13]

Jamshidian cultivated the notion of social responsibility for his workers and participation in the Iranian community at large. In so doing he established an informal community centered on his merchant house. He provided housing, financial loans, medical services, and a weekly dinner to his employees. On the Zoroastrian holiday of the New Year (*Nowruz*), he gave presents to each Zoroastrian family.[14] He purchased land north of Tehran that he irrigated and employed Zoroastrians in farming.[15] He also contributed generously to philanthropic ventures for the benefit of the entire Zoroastrian community: In 1907 he built a public hall for the celebration of Zoroastrian religious holidays and helped fund the building of the Zoroastrian temple—the *Adorian*. He brought Mobed Mehreban from Yazd and provided a vehicle to transport the dead to the *dakhmeh*. A *dadgah* fire was maintained in his home until the completion of the Zoroastrian temple in 1908.[16] He also built a public bath and in 1908 built Jamshid-e Jam—the first formal Zoroastrian schoolhouse in Tehran.

Jamshidian's sense of community contributed greatly to the sense of loyalty and communal identity of the Zoroastrians in Tehran. It should also be noted that Tehran, as a new residence of Zoroastrians, did not have established community networks or authorities, either political or religious. This fact enabled Jamshidian and other Zoroastrian merchants to exercise authority in the community, without threatening, or being threatened by, existing political elites or a Zoroastrian priesthood. The fact that Zoroastrian immigrants to the capital were merchants or employed by merchants also facilitated the breakdown of previous determinants of social status. Family background and status were superseded (although not replaced) by generations of self-made wealthy merchants who came to wield considerable authority both within the community and vis-à-vis the Iranian state.

Jamshidian, as the unofficial mediator between the growing Zoroastrian community and the larger Iranian society, was also careful to cultivate good relations with fellow Muslim merchants, the court, and important officials. He had public water fountains established throughout Iran on major trade routes, gave generously to Islamic religious institutions, and offered gifts and dinners to eminent Muslims. He enjoyed a national reputation for both honesty and generosity and became the first Zoroastrian representative in the first Iranian Parliament in 1905 following the Constitutional Revolution.[17] According to Napier Malcolm,

"Arbab Jamshid . . . is probably more able to influence the Persian Government in favour of his countrymen than are the Indian Parsis from Bombay."[18]

The Constitutional Revolution

A number of the most important Zoroastrian merchants in Tehran actively participated in the Constitutional Revolution. At first glance, the Zoroastrian reliance on and indebtedness to the central state in the form of the shah would seem to mitigate against any revolutionary predilections. The Zoroastrians certainly looked to the shah to protect their recent gains, both economic and legal, as well as to enforce them in the provinces. The Zoroastrians as a religious minority benefited from royal protection vis-à-vis the population at large and as such were not naturally inclined to majority rule, without assurances of protection.

An appreciation of the shah's role in maintaining their welfare, however, did not ultimately outweigh the merchants' affinities with the revolution's goals. The Zoroastrian merchants were seduced by the revolution's promises on a variety of grounds. First, they were encouraged by the pro-British Parsis to side with the revolution.[19] Both Arbob Jamshid and Arbob Shah Jahan contributed money to buying guns from India for the revolutionaries.[20] Zoroastrian merchants also had shared interests with many Muslim merchants and revolutionary sympathizers who looked forward to the limitation of the shah's arbitrary rule and the imposition of a more rationalized commercial and political environment. The promise of representation and a constitution also may have suggested a limitation of the power of the ulama, not just of the shah, that would certainly have been welcomed by Zoroastrians. As a token of respect, and perhaps to assuage ulama fears of minority rights, Arbob Jamshid gave a substantial gift to Sayed Abdollah Behbehani, a prominent ayatollah and proponent of the revolution.[21]

Zoroastrians were also encouraged by the rhetoric of the more radical elements among the revolutionaries. A growing nationalism, articulated by Kermani, Akhundzadeh, and others, suggested an enhanced role for the Zoroastrians in a new state. The promotion of a revived pre-Islamic Persian identity and the identification of Islam as a source of backwardness were implicitly, if not explicitly, welcomed by Zoroastrians as alternatives to the Islamic emphasis on political legitimacy, law, and social identity. Akhundzadeh, who called for the purification of Persian from Arabic words and the national celebration of the Zoroastrian holiday of *Nowruz,* also praised the Zoroastrians as the repositories of Iran's glorious past and promised them full social and political equality.[22] This newly constructed nationalism with its emphasis on the pre-Islamic (Zoroastrian) past as the essential building block for progress and civilization gave the Zoroastrians not simply a newfound tolerance in an Islamic state, but a more honored place in a new society.

The constitution, as it was eventually formulated, was radical in that it ensured equality of treatment for all Persians, including religious minorities. At the same time, the Islamic foundation of the state and primacy of Muslims were firmly reinforced. The ulama were accorded new rights of oversight in the constitution, allowing them virtual veto power over any legislation. This fundamental contradiction—between a secular notion of equal rights regardless of religion and the reaffirmation of ulama authority in ascertaining compliance of all legislation with the shari'a—manifested the divides among constitutionalists, as well as the uncontained power of the ulama.

Particularly in comparison with Ottoman legal rulings of 1836, 1856, and 1876, the Iranian Constitution lacks any genuine commitment to a secular state. For example, Article 8 apparently establishes equality under law: "The people of the Persian Empire are to enjoy equal rights before the Law." However, Islam remained the official religion, and all law became firmly subject to religious law, *as interpreted by the ulama.* The legal, now *constitutional,* primacy of Islam and Islamic law are provided for in Articles 1 and 2 of the Supplemental Fundamental Laws of October 7, 1907. Article 1 reads: "The official religion of Persia is Islam, according to the orthodox Ja'fari doctrine of the Ithna 'Ashariyya, which faith the Shah of Persia must profess and promote." Article 2 establishes a five-person committee of ulama (the Ecclesiastical Committee) to ensure that all laws promulgated are in accordance with their interpretation of Islamic law:

> At no time must any legal enactment of the Sacred National Consultative Assembly, established by the favour and assistance of His Holiness the Imam of the Age (may God hasten his glad Advent!), the favour of His Majesty the Shahinshah of Islam (may God immortalize his reign!), the care of the proofs of Islam (may God multiply the like of them!) and the whole people of the Persian nation, be at variance with the sacred principles of Islam or the laws established

by His Holiness the Best of Mankind [the Prophet Muhammad]. . . . It is for the learned doctors of theology . . . to determine whether such laws as may be proposed are or are not conformable to the principles of Islam. . . . [T]he decision of this Ecclesiastical Committee shall be followed and obeyed.[23]

Despite the inherent theoretical contradictions in the constitution, the Zoroastrians initially benefited. Minorities were guaranteed protection of life and property and were each able to elect one member to parliament. Arbob Jamshid was selected, and Zoroastrians were included in the celebrations.[24]

During the counterrevolution, Zoroastrians and other minorities became a target of violence, since they represented the challenge to the Islamic state that minority rights entailed.[25] Many powerful ulama opposed minorities being accorded equal rights in an Islamic state. Although the constitution was eventually restored, it remained largely ignored throughout the Pahlavi period. Nonetheless, many of the rights accorded minorities for the first time in the constitution were reinstated later by Reza Shah as part of his attempts at secularization.

Zoroastrian participation in the Constitutional Revolution—often at great danger and expense—indicates how strong their interest in economic rationality and the limitation of arbitrary government was. The revival of ancient Iran as a basis for a modern identity and the impetus for a secular legal system were strongly advocated by nationalists. These two issues—pre-Islamic Iran and secular law—threatened the prerogatives of the ulama and challenged the preeminence of an Islamic conception of state. The constitution itself did not usher in a secular legal system, and in fact it may be argued that the ulama actually increased their authority through the ratification of their veto power over all legislation deemed in conflict with shari'a law. Many progressive ulama, however, did support the constitution in the name of an end to arbitrary government.

The constitution exacerbated the uneasy relationship of the ulama to the central government. On the one hand, the reigning shahs had long identified with an Islamic state and sought legitimacy on those grounds, whether boasting of their own religious credentials in the form of lineage (the Safavids, for example) or as the guardians of an Islamic state in accordance with Islamic law (as did the Qajars). In return, the ulama enjoyed an unchallenged monopoly on interpretation of religious tradition, scriptures, and law. The Qajars, presiding over a much weaker and less centralized government than their Safavid predecessors, lost some authority at the expense of a stronger ulama. They nonetheless were accorded Islamic legitimacy. The attempt at secularization altered this relationship and fundamentally pitted the ulama against the constitution.

Rulers in Islamic states have always enjoyed some amount of leeway (depending on their ability to take it) in the matter of legislation. The constitution, however, while not challenging the ulama's virtual powers, challenged their theoretical monopoly on legislation. Simply put, the constitution enshrined *both* the ulama's legislative veto power *and* the right of Iranian subjects through the medium of elected parliamentary representatives to legislate. The inherent and irreconcilable tension written into the constitution, thus, was between God's sole right to legislate (as interpreted by the ulama) versus society's right to do so. This dichotomy led to serious opposition to constitutionalism, as most famously articulated by Ayatollah Nuri.[26] Though challenged by other ulama, Nuri's position continued to dominate the majority of ulama opinion and contributed to their suspicion of "republican" and "democratic" government as antithetical to an "Islamic" state that ultimately facilitated Reza Shah's assumption of the throne, rather than the establishment of a republic.[27]

The Establishment of the Zoroastrian Anjoman

The Zoroastrian Anjoman of Tehran was formally reestablished in 1905 by a group of Zoroastrian merchants consciously drawing on the promise of the revolution. Although first formed in 1898, the Anjoman remained informal and without effective leadership. Kay Khosroji Khan Saheb, the Parsi delegate to Iran, and Kay Khosrow Shahrokh, an employee of Arbob Jamshid Jamshidian, together with fourteen other Zoroastrian merchants, met in the Zoroastrian section of the bazaar and pledged to form a society.[28] In the inaugural statement, the revolution is drawn on as inspiration: "Since the success of every people depends on cooperation, the Anjoman should be founded. Especially in the Zoroastrian religion, the Anjoman has seen stress as well as discussion and cooperation. . . . Now that the government and Parliament have developed a constitutional system, we should give every effort to develop our anjoman along formal lines."[29] This group of merchants proceeded to manage elections for the first formal *anjoman*, which comprised fourteen "outstanding members" of the community elected by the male Zoroastrian population for a term of two years. The next elections for the *anjoman* in 1908 resulted in the election of eleven merchants, one teacher, one builder, and one employee of the national telegraph company. Unlike the *anjoman* in Yazd, a *mobed* was not automatically included in the membership.[30]

The Tehran Anjoman functioned much as the provincial *anjomans* and Parsi *panchayats* did, serving to manage community properties and activities as well as operating as a mediator both within the Zoroastrian community and vis-à-vis the Iranian state and society.[31] The *anjoman* was the ruling body of the Zoroastrian community and oversaw Zoroastrian legal matters (divorce, marriage, internal financial disputes, and so on). The *anjoman* had a strong mandate to help the community (even providing social welfare to needy Zoroastrians) as well as to manage the public image of the community with the larger Iranian state and society.[32] The profession of elected members indicates the continued importance of merchant leadership and the power they wielded in their community.

Just as the *anjoman* managed Zoroastrian community affairs, the Zoroastrian representative to the Majles (parliament) represented the community's interests directly to the Iranian state. Deepening fissures within the community—between "modernists" and "conservatives"—exploded over the 1915 election of the representative to the Majles. Former representative Arbob Jamshid Jamshidian had resigned after his bankruptcy and was replaced temporarily by Kay Khosrow Shahrokh. Shahrokh subsequently ran for election against Mister Khodabakh. These two contenders represented the divisions within the Zoroastrian community in this period.

Shahrokh, originally from Kerman, had been educated at the American mission school in Tehran, as well as in Parsi schools in Bombay. Upon his return from India, he worked as a teacher in the newly founded Zoroastrian schools in his hometown for many years, eventually becoming principal of the schools. His education, both in Protestant and in Reformist Parsi schools, familiarized him with Parsi reform ideas concerning religion and the importance of education in creating "modern" citizens. He believed in equal access to education and improved rights for women and was deeply committed to a Zoroastrianism reformed of outdated customs. Upon moving to Tehran, he worked for Arbob Jamshidian.

Khodabakh, Shahrokh's principal challenger, originated from Yazd. He, like Shahrokh, had been educated in Bombay and similarly returned to Iran conversant in Reformist Parsi ideas. He, however, maintained a more conservative view of religion, insisting on the importance of a strict adherence to Zoroastrian

نمای آدریان تهران
از راست بچپ: مهربان شاهپور ـ بهمن کیخسرو ـ مهربان مهر ـ افلاتونشاهرخ ـ شهریاربهرام ـ کیخسرو شاهرخ ـ اسفندیار افسرکشمیری
ـ ؟ ـ خدارحم آبادیان ـ شهریارخدامراد فرارونی ـ خدا رحم اسفندیار ـ ؟ ـ

16. Adorian in Tehran, Iran, with prominent Zoroastrians seated in front (*right to left*): Mehraban Shahpour, Bahman Kay Khosrow, Mehraban Mehr, Aflatoun Shahrokh, Shahriyar Bahram, Kay Khosrow Shahrokh, Esfandiyar Afsar Kashmiri, unidentified, Khodarahm Abadiyan, Shahriyar Khodamorad Fararouny, Khodarahm Esfandiyar, and unidentified. From the back cover of Mahnameh-ye Zartoshtian, *Nowruz*, 2536 shahanshahi.

religious law. His relatively conservative religious views labeled him as a conservative, yet his progressive social views alienated the old elites and religious leaders in Yazd. The fissures in Zoroastrian society—between Tehran and the provinces, between Yazd and Kerman, and over such politically charged issues as social and religious reform—were deeply felt in the early twentieth century and manifest in this election.

Shahrokh won by default, since Khodabakh was murdered shortly before the 1915 elections.[33] Shahrokh was continually reelected as the Zoroastrian representative in parliament throughout the Reza Shah period, ultimately serving until his death in 1940. His national prestige, proximity to the court, and continued service to the Zoroastrian community were renowned. His repeated reelection also indicated the solidarity of the Zoroastrian community which characterized the community in the pre-1941 period.

The Late Qajar and First Pahlavi Period

The period 1870–1941 witnessed formerly unimaginable changes in the Zoroastrian community and concomitantly the community's relationship to the Iranian state. The modernization programs initiated under Naser al-Din Shah, although often suffering from royal ambivalence, inaugurated a period of change in government institutions. More important even than actual accomplishments, the late Naseri period was a watershed in terms of intellectuals' conceptions of the modern state, secularism, constitutionalism, and the relationship of state and society.[34]

The gradual extension of state protection for religious minorities, developing notions of citizenship, and a newfound emphasis on the potential of pre-Islamic Iran to serve as a bedrock for the construction of a modern state combined to fundamentally alter the status of Zoroastrians in Iran. State actions and nationalists' focus on the pre-Islamic period accompanied the Zoroastrian community's own burgeoning educational, institutional, and religious reforms. Within one generation the Zoroastrian community went from living in rural isolation in the villages surrounding Yazd and Kerman to becoming a prosperous, respected, and increasingly powerful minority in the capital.

The Zoroastrian community in the period 1870–1941 was defined by three interrelated developments. First, this era saw the emergence of the Zoroastrian *anjomans* and the gradual domination of the Tehran Anjoman under relatively cohesive and continuous leadership. A founder of the Tehran Anjoman after the Constitutional Revolution, Kay Khosrow Shahrokh solidified the *anjoman*'s authority in the community under his continued leadership, which he preserved throughout his lifetime. Although subsequently challenged by the growth and variety of new Zoroastrian community organizations in the 1950s and 1960s, the first half of the twentieth century was a period of consolidated authority and leadership.

Second, the community was dominated by the merchant laity. This fact held true both for *anjoman* leadership as well as for national representation. Kay Khosrow Shahrokh exemplified this control by serving not only as the head of the

Tehran Anjoman but also as the Zoroastrian representative to the Majles from 1907 until his death in 1940. His leadership also extended beyond politics into the realm of religion. When Maneckji Limji Hataria first began work among the Zoroastrians in the early nineteenth century, he decried the priesthood as uneducated, illiterate, and lacking political authority in the community. Despite increased contact and funding between the Iranian and Parsi Zoroastrians, and an attempt to both reform religious education and improve the livelihood of the priests in Iran, the results remained modest. Certainly, the Zoroastrian community in twentieth-century Iran boasted of learned priests who had been educated in India and were abreast of contemporary religious studies and fluent in Zoroastrian religious texts and traditions. Nonetheless, the priests remained few in number and were never in a position to challenge the authority and leadership of the wealthy Zoroastrian merchants. This situation was true both in India and more especially in the much smaller community in Iran. As noted by Hinnells in the context of migration to Bombay, Iranian Zoroastrian migration to Tehran resulted in a similar situation of merchant authority in the absence of established priestly institutions.

Laity leadership meant that *anjoman* leaders such as Shahrokh wielded enormous influence over not only the institutional and political life of the community but its religious life as well. Lay leaders engaged in religious commentary based on their own reading of religious texts. Authority of the religious establishment thus was challenged not only by lay community leadership, but also by the newly claimed authority of this lay leadership to comment decisively on religious matters. Shahrokh in particular, like his intellectual forebearers in India, was a religious reformer and actively sought to modify the conception and practice of Zoroastrianism. As discussed in the next chapter, although most famous for his political leadership, he was also a religious modernizer and endeavored to define modern Zoroastrianism in Iran.

Third, this period witnessed the gradual emancipation of Iranian Zoroastrians from Parsi control. Although there remained powerful ties that bound these two communities together, an improved economic situation combined with consolidated leadership of the Iranian Zoroastrians under Kay Khosrow Shahrokh allowed them to take independent positions regarding religious and community priorities. Such independence signified both the weakening of Parsi economic leverage and control and also the Iranian community's intellectual and political maturity.

Authoritarian Modernization

Reza Shah's modernization program changed the nature of the relationship between state and society.[35] The promotion of centralism and secularism accorded religious minorities more rights than they had previously enjoyed in the Qajar period. Reza Shah's advocacy of modernization as Westernization and his reliance on Iranian nationalism to buttress his policies profoundly altered the state's identity and the conception of its citizens. All religious minorities benefited from the Pahlavi de-emphasis of Islam as the principal pillar of law, state identity, and legitimacy. The Zoroastrian community in particular was profoundly associated with, and affected by, this modernization program.

Reza Shah's program is rightly termed *authoritarian modernization*. It was "authoritarian" in the sense that it was imposed by the state onto society. It was not generated by popular will, but imposed by the political power of the state and, ultimately, Reza Shah. This state of affairs also meant that the program did not develop organically. It was thus in many respects artificial and perceived as such by a population not always prepared for it and, concomitantly, not always receptive to it. "Modernization" implied the deliberate and antagonistic rejection of "traditional." The very term *modern* exists only insofar as it is able to sustain itself with the creation of an opposite: *tradition*. The claim to modernization rested on the creation of this, largely artificial, dichotomy and on its substantiation through active definition and concomitant rejection of the "traditional." In other words, both of these categories were constructed through definition and survived through mutual opposition.

"Authoritarian modernization" was composed of the separate, although interdependent, elements of modernization, centralization, secularism, and Iranian nationalism. Modernization was characterized by state centralization with the consciously utilitarian use of Western institutions as models. Unlike earlier generations, intellectuals and politicians in the post–World War I period largely understood modernization as entailing Westernization. Ideas of modernization were markedly less syncretic and deliberately selective than they had been in the prewar period.[36]

Modernization involved the adoption of some degree of Western political and cultural forms, including clothing; ideas concerning companionate marriage, family structure, and women's public participation; and Western-style education. Reza Shah, like his role model, Ataturk, was concerned with appearing Western and thus "civilized." The identification of "modern" with "Western" meant that "indigenous" and "traditional" were defined as "backward." The creation of these antagonisms had long-term pernicious effects. One of the outcomes was to force all discussions concerning modernity into an "either-or" situation of choosing sides between "modern" (as Western) or "traditional." This division resulted in a growing schism over the cultural content of Iranian modernity such that Westernization was posited as inauthentic, as opposed to Islam, which was claimed to be "authentic." The forcing of categories created an antagonism that reified the respective positions on culture and the nature of Iranian modernity. This discord meant that the language of opposition was articulated as a contest over "authenticity" and "cultural traditions," even when the basis of the opposition primarily concerned political prerogatives.

Centralization was arguably the central pillar of Reza Shah's program. Centralization was simply the age-old competition between center and edge, shah and alternative authorities: local governors, border areas, tribes, and the ulama. Reza Shah substantially increased his authority through the development of modern communications, infrastructure, and a modern military. He increased his control of the country and population through a policy of the forcible settlement of tribes. The power of the ulama was curtailed by the secularization of the educational and legal systems, formerly their preserve.

Secularization in the Reza Shah period was a means to further the goal of centralization and the expansion of state power vis-à-vis alternative authorities, not as an end in and of itself. Secularization was incomplete and did not entail full equality of law or the elimination of Islamic-based laws, nor did it include the rejection of Islam as a state religion. Rather, Reza Shah intruded into and captured a much larger amount of control in the areas of education and law than the Iranian state had ever been able to previously. The adoption of a national, compulsory educational system was envisioned as providing three specific benefits; first, to educate bureaucrats that could staff a growing state administration; second, to foster a sense of national identity and solidarity; and third, to promote loyalty toward Reza Shah and the Iranian state.

Reza Shah's modernization program was deliberately designed to further his own power. It was not intended to engage with the process of developing and nurturing democratic, representative, and participatory institutions. Unlike

Ataturk, Reza Shah made no real attempts to develop citizens or the institutional, cultural, and political structures that could sustain them. It is often pointed out that Reza Shah was dissuaded from establishing a republic by some ulama anxious to avoid a system that they believed threatened Islam. Whatever the secrets were that passed between Reza Shah and his ulama interlocutors, Reza Shah's crowing as the first Pahlavi monarch certainly was indicative of his fundamental relationship to modernity and citizenship.

Modernization remained superficial, artificial, and deeply lopsided. Changes largely resulted in Reza Shah's own economic and political aggrandizement. Modernization remained primarily an urban phenomenon and in many ways contributed to the development of cultural schisms in the population between those individuals who allied themselves with modernity as Westernization and those who rejected the program as alien and inauthentic. Reza Shah was initially given a mandate by the political elite to provide law, order, and national security in an attempt to prevent Iran's political dissolution and colonization by European powers. Reza Shah relied principally on a vastly expanded military and on a limited stratum of officials with a personal investment in his reign. Over time, he alienated large segments of the population, including the political elites.

State promotion of modernization, centralization, and secularization involved the propagation of Iranian nationalism as a legitimizing ideology. Ideas of Iranian nationalism had been developed over a long period of time, beginning in the nineteenth century, by a number of secular intellectuals such as Akhundzadeh and Taqizadeh. Reza Shah appropriated some of the principal ideas developed by these intellectuals and others in order to legitimize and promote his political program of authoritarian modernization.

In the particular context of the post–World War I Middle East, nationalism was understood as the sine qua non of powerful, "modern" states. Nationalism had proved its potency by its firm establishment in Europe and subsequent European colonialism and in its role in the dissolution of the Ottoman Empire into a multitude of nation-states. Turkey, the only other country in the Middle East that was not colonized, also believed strongly in the imperative of developing nationalism as prerequisite for a modern and independent state. Iranian nationalism included a spectrum of ideas concerning Iranian identity, not limited to those tenets chosen by Reza Shah for adoption and official promotion.

In its broad brushstrokes, Iranian nationalism involved the premise that pre-Islamic Iranian greatness was inherently compatible with goals of modernization. It facilitated secularism by positing an alternative authentic identity for Iran, focusing on its historical past.[37] Iranian-ness was thus imagined as primordial and transcending any one time period. Iran could therefore be unshackled from Islamic institutions. Doing so allowed the state to promulgate secularization while sidestepping charges of being inauthentic. Some proponents of nationalism went so far as to blame current weakness on the ulama and Islamic institutions, if not on Islam as an alien, Arab imposition. Iranian nationalism also legitimized change as "return" to original greatness, rather than the adoption of new or foreign institutions. It claimed modernity as attainable through the glorification of the pre-Islamic past.

Iranian Nationalism and Zoroastrian Identity

Reza Shah's program of authoritarian modernization profoundly impacted Iranian religious minorities, none more so than the Zoroastrians. Religious minorities had typically benefited from state protection against local authorities and religious leaders. A strongly centralized state, therefore, increased their ability to claim their rights and seek redress against injustices. These rights were fundamentally improved with the secularization of the legal system and the restriction of shari'a-based legal codes. The reduction of prejudicial laws and sartorial and other restrictions enabled religious minorities to engage in activities formerly denied them. They were allowed freedom of dress and movement, as well as participation in the national economy, military, politics, society, and culture. The deep support of minorities for the Pahlavi monarchs was a function of their recognition that their fortunes were in many ways tied to state protection.

A Parsi traveler to Tehran in 1932 had the following enthusiastic, and anticlerical, remarks to make on Reza Shah's centralization and secularization program:

> When Reza Shah ascended the throne, the country was groaning under the tyranny of the Mullahs and the brigands. The brigands have been completely routed; nay, as if by a talisman, the highwayman of yesterday is turned into the yeoman of today. As for the Mullahs, they were once the true rulers of Iran, being able to support or smash any government and to stifle any measure

of reform likely to undermine their hold on the ignorant and superstitious masses. Those days are gone. Under the new rules a Mullah's turban is no longer regarded as the sole proof of one's qualifications to be a priest. He has to prove his knowledge and innate worth. This in itself has thinned the ranks of those inveterate enemies of progress. The few that remain have been relegated to their legitimate position in the state. . . . [U]nder the present constitution all the subjects are equal before the law.[38]

Reza Shah's government attempted to restrain what it termed "superstitious" religious practices. An American diplomat in Iran reported in 1931 that "particular emphasis was laid on the enlightened efforts of the central government and police authorities to rid [the celebration of Ashura] of the more barbarous and fanatical practices with which it has been traditionally observed."[39] In fact, self-styled "modern" Iranians abandoned many religious practices in this period. The same diplomat remarked on the association of religion with cultural backwardness and the resulting chasm between the "modern" and "traditional" segments of the population: "Among modern, European-educated Persians the observance of these many religious holidays is looked upon as but one more example of their undesired heritage from a mulla ridden past. 'We got rid of seven of them a year ago,' one official of the Persian Foreign Office said as he firmly helped himself to a supper of sliced ham, 'and the sooner we do away with most of the others, the better it will be for everyone.' This point of view is not new, but I find it interesting as indicative of the now full grown assurance which is felt in Persian official circles that the Shah's policy of modernization can be imposed on his still primitive people."[40]

The period 1928–40 witnessed increasing measures to wrest control of the legal sphere from the ulama. The state successfully monopolized the court system and completed the rationalization and homogenization of the legal code. It was the state, not the ulama, that now staffed the courts and determined legal rulings.[41] However, despite the adoption of some Western legal codes, law in Iran was not fully secularized. Personal status law remained shari'a based. Religious minorities were asked to codify their own religious law codes for implementation in state courts. Personal status was defined to include "matters pertaining to the family, marriage, divorce, wills, inheritance, relationships, guardianships."[42] Religious identity continued to determine the Personal Status Code to whom each person was accountable and meant that the content of personal status laws continued to be religious rather than secular.[43]

Islam remained the religion of state, and despite very real improvements, disabilities for non-Muslims continued. There were restrictions on the level of participation of non-Muslims in government positions. For example, Article 58 of the Supplemental Fundamental Laws of October 7, 1907, stated, "No one can attain the rank of Minister unless he be a Musulman by religion, a Persian by birth, and a Persian subject." Islam was not eliminated as the religion of state, and the teaching of legal superiority of Muslims over non-Muslims in schools was obligatory.[44]

Modernization, secularism, and centralization impacted all non-Muslim minorities similarly. Jews, Christians, and Zoroastrians enjoyed significant improvements in their rights and liberties vis-à-vis the state, law, and society. The association of modernization with Westernization and the concomitant de-emphasis of the Islamic component of Iranian identity allowed more room for minorities to participate in the nation and to be identified as Iranian rather than "foreign." The adoption of Iranian nationalism as the state ideology, however, involved the Zoroastrian community in unique ways that affected their own identity as well as their relationship to the state.[45]

Iranian nationalism linked modernity and national greatness with the pre-Islamic past. This imagined past had three essential attributes: it was modern, it was retrievable, and it was accessible. It was modern in the sense of embodying, if not originating, modern ideas or at least premised as compatible with modern ideas and institutions. It was retrievable in the sense that it could be "resuscitated" and brought back to be grafted onto the present. And it was accessible in the sense that it was imagined as being the legacy of all Iranians—in other words, that all Iranians, regardless of ethnicity or religious identity, were equally its inheritors. This past thus was imagined as embodying the essence of modern Iranian national identity.

There were many complications with this construction of the past. First, modernity (as social progress, gender equality, science, monotheism, and so on) had to be projected ahistorically on the past, thus distorting it. Second, its retrieval depended on the selective claiming of elements from the past. This selection was carried out by the promotion of selective literature, by the emphasis on Persian language as the national language, and by identifying "true" markers of this reconstructed past in the form of historic sites. It was in this context, for example, that Ferdowsi's tomb was "discovered" and a new monument constructed and dedicated to him by the shah on behalf of the nation.[46]

The question of accessibility was the thorniest of the three issues. The premise that all Iranians shared equally, as inheritors, in the ancient past was a difficult one to maintain. It depended on the construction of the past as primarily historic as well as religiously and ethnically neutral. Which of course it was not. This reclaimed and reconstructed past was in fact ethnically Persian and religiously Zoroastrian.

The appropriation of the ancient past for the purposes of creating modern national identity manifested itself in the adoption of Zoroastrian religious symbols and celebrations as *national, nonreligious* symbols and celebrations. Reza Shah sought Kay Khosrow Shahrokh's advice in choosing Zoroastrian names for the calendar months, adopted the Zoroastrian *Fravahar* symbol on government buildings (including the national bank and the Ministry of Justice), and encouraged the use of old Zoroastrian names.[47] The promotion of the Persian-Zoroastrian past was taken to such lengths that the American chargé d'affaires in Tehran anticipated the official adoption of Zoroastrianism in Iran: "There are not wanting those who credit the Shah with entertaining thoughts, in the movement which he has initiated of rehabilitating the past of Iran, of the restoration of the ancient Zoroastrian worship, which was the earliest religion of the country, as the religion of modern Iran.... [I]t would seem by no means impossible that the Shah might well come to give something more than passing consideration to the restoration of the ancient Aryan Worship as a culminating measure of his State policy."[48] Although this official clearly misread the shah's intentions, he accurately reflected the deep connections between Zoroastrians and Iranian modernization.

Tensions over the nature of the past were deeply intertwined with questions concerning the nature of Zoroastrian identity in the present. On the one hand, Zoroastrians were viewed as the repositories of this ancient, now "national," heritage, and thus as the most "authentically Iranian" of all Iran's peoples. Such authenticity was sometimes associated with racial purity, which distinguished Zoroastrians from "Arabs" (as well as, incidentally, the majority of the Iranian population.) This correlation was a complete shift from Islamic notions of difference and identity in which religious identity was paramount. Zoroastrians were

17. "Ruines de Persepolis (Perse)," lithograph. First appeared in Ernest Breton, *Monuments de tous les peuples, décrits et dessinés d'après les documents les plus modernes* (Brussels: Librarie Historique-Artistique, 1843).

identified with this idealized past and as such enjoyed an enormous increase in respect. One member of a Parsi delegation noted with some surprise the changed attitude of Iranians toward Iranian Zoroastrians: "The angle of vision towards the great Iranian Prophet and his followers was entirely changed. Shocking epithets and derision of his name gave place to most respectful and eloquent tributes, and the present generation of his followers began to be considered as brothers and sisters who had suffered untold wrongs which neither they nor their forbears ever deserved."[49]

Yet on the other hand, this past, although claimed by all Iranians as their rightful heritage, was really a Zoroastrian past. Moreover, the past was the subject of intensive selectivity and ahistorical reconstruction. The claim that this past was religiously and ethnically neutral created some ambivalence about the identity of the Zoroastrian community: Was it primarily an ethnic group, the historical heir of the pre-Islamic past? Or was it defined by religious belief? These questions revolved around the contest between particularism and universalism, between sectarian and national identity.

The tensions over identity and the ancient past also involved the Zoroastrian community's relationship to state and society. Zoroastrian religion, as articulated by Kay Khosrow Shahrokh, emphasized the commonality of all religions. This stress enabled the promotion of national identity for all Iranians, since it de-emphasized sectarianism and particularism and instead emphasized equality of citizenship. This prioritization was countered by the retention of Islam as a religion of state and religious-based identity in the legal and political spheres. These tensions would remain, unresolved, throughout the Pahlavi period.

Kay Khosrow Shahrokh

Rational Religion and Citizenship in Iran

Which religion should I choose when there are so many true religions about?
—KAY KHOSROW SHAHROKH (1874–1940)

Kay Khosrow Shahrokh in many ways defined his time, both as the product of new influences and as the agent of change himself. In addition to serving as the head of the Zoroastrian *anjoman* in Tehran and as Zoroastrian representative to the Majles for thirteen sessions, he was deeply engaged in religious issues. He saw himself as a religious reformer. He authored two treatises on Zoroastrianism that were used ubiquitously in Zoroastrian schools. Significantly, they were also read by a wider segment of the Iranian population as the first real introduction to Zoroastrianism by a well-known and respected national figure. Shahrokh believed strongly in the need for Zoroastrian religious reform and religion's profound relationship to citizenship, nationalism, and Zoroastrian identity. He believed that rational religion was generative of modern citizens since it served as an ethical prompt to social responsibility and participation necessary for citizenship. Rational religion also de-emphasized ritual as the public performance of sectarian difference and instead emphasized religious universalism and equality between citizens in the public sphere. His articulation of modern Zoroastrianism became the reigning orthodoxy for the rest of the century.

Shahrokh the Reformer

By the time of Shahrokh's birth in Kerman in 1874, the Society for the Amelioration of Conditions in Iran under the leadership of Hataria had already begun work on community organization, the establishment of new schools, and the upgrading of the *dakhmeh*. Shahrokh early on experienced the results of increased contact and direct involvement of the Parsi reformers in philanthropic projects under way in Kerman. For family reasons, Shahrokh moved to Tehran at age sixteen and remained there for four years. During this time he attended the American Protestant missionary school, where he learned English, became familiar with the New Testament, and sought answers to questions of religious truth and identity.[1] His interest in religion that was shaped by the dual influences of Parsi reform projects in Kerman and American Protestantism in Tehran was only heightened by a subsequent year spent in Bombay, where he attended the famous Jamsetjee Jeejeebhoy Parsi school.[2] These three contexts of religious inquiry and reform were formative for his own religious journey and his understanding of "modern" religion's new relationship to state and society.

The Parsi society SACI in Bombay appointed Shahrokh as principal and teacher at a new Parsi-funded school back in Kerman and paid for his return journey there. Shahrokh remained in this position for the next eleven years, and was active in furthering new educational initiatives. He established new schools for boys and girls, served as secretary of the Kerman Anjoman and fought against shari'a-based discrimination. As recounted later in his memoirs, Shahrokh persisted in riding a horse to Governor Prince Farmanfarma's residence to teach him English, despite the very real personal danger he incurred by transgressing this traditional shari'a-based Muslim prerogative.[3] In fact, it was not until 1923, some forty-two years later, that Reza Shah issued a decree permitting Zoroastrians to ride horses.[4]

Shahrokh encountered similar Muslim prejudice and Zoroastrian fears when he insisted on defying traditional dress codes for Zoroastrians. Ever since his return from Bombay, he had refused to abide by minority sartorial restrictions. Shortly after his arrival in Kerman, he introduced school uniforms at the Amelioration boys' school, in addition to a school anthem. Shahrokh deftly forestalled Muslim opposition to the sartorial codes by inviting Muslim dignitaries to the school, including Governor Farmanfarma, where they were duly impressed with the students.[5] Although never stated explicitly, the officials' favorable opinion of the students was consistent with the new, modern schools' literacy rates, organization, and student discipline that compared favorably to *maktab* (traditional) education.[6] Zoroastrian fears of retribution were not assuaged by this favorable response by the governor, however. The Zoroastrian Yazd Anjoman tried to convince Shahrokh that such a sartorial travesty would indubitably lead to reprisals against the Zoroastrian community. Shahrokh refused to back down, however, and subsequently urged Zoroastrians to defy dress codes as well—something that they were reluctant to do.[7]

These instances of defiance attest to Shahrokh's personal courage. But they are also indicative of larger forces afoot. Shahrokh had by this time experienced life in Tehran, where religious minorities were less constricted by shari'a-based disadvantages and where the court stood as an enforcer (and thus typically protector) of minority rights. He had also lived in Bombay, where the legal system was not Islamic and where British rule enforced religious tolerance. Shahrokh had thus grown accustomed to living without sartorial restrictions or legal discrimination against minorities. More important, he recognized that the modernization measures championed by the court in Tehran were in fact part of a larger contest between royal and ulama authority. He also clearly saw that in this contest, religious minorities had everything to gain from the triumph of

18. National Bank, Tehran, Iran, built ca. 1935, architect H. Heinric. Photo taken by Talinn Grigor, 2007.

the central government. The larger social and political reforms meant the whittling away of Muslim shari'a-based prerogatives and the advocacy of equal legal rights. Although obviously written with the benefit of hindsight, Shahrokh's memoirs emphasize that the issue of minority rights was a function of the contested boundaries of central authority and that minorities understood this fact and frequently appealed to the shah or the local governor to inveigh against local religious prejudices.[8] Shahrokh remained a staunch advocate of minority legal rights. As the Zoroastrian representative in the Majles from 1909 to 1940, he continually championed the principle of legal equality. In one speech to the Majles, Shahrokh defended the rights, and responsibility, of non-Muslims to serve in the armed forces. As reported by the American Legation, Shahrokh stressed "the feeling of all Persians for their fatherland, regardless of their religion."[9]

Religious Reform and Modernization

Shahrokh's interest in religion went beyond championing minority legal rights against Islamic restrictions and local prejudices. In his memoirs he describes himself as a religious seeker and admits to having nearly converted to Christianity.[10] His four years at the American Protestant School in Tehran had such an enormous impact on him that even after his year among Reformist Parsis in Bombay he continued to attend Christian mass in Kerman.[11] He exhibited "a strong Christian belief" at that time and debated about which religion to "choose." Recalling his dilemma, Shahrokh wrote that ultimately he "chose" Zoroastrianism partly as a result of his own identity. In a curious story, Shahrokh recounted a chance meeting with a Muslim clergyman who introduced himself after one of these Sunday masses. This Sheikh Yahya chided Shahrokh for his lack of knowledge of Zoroastrianism, offering to teach him its doctrines and urged him to follow his own, Zoroastrian, religion.[12] Even after this conversation, Shahrokh records his continued religious confusion: "I thought about his words for several days: which religion should I choose when there are so many true religions about?"[13] This frank admission of religious indecision reveals not only Shahrokh's honesty, but also his fundamental understanding of the nature of religious belief and identity. In his memoirs, Shahrokh testifies to an almost deist conception of religion, one based firmly on the centrality of ethics and morality: "When one studies and understands the principles of all religions, one finds that there are no differences.

The only difference is that each shows a different path to the same destination, but God and moral principles are the same in all."[14]

Shahrokh accumulated the tools of religious inquiry, including English and Arabic, and took seriously his quest for understanding religion in a comparative framework. In addition to his study of Christianity, he read the Quran and claimed to have learned the entire Avesta by heart.[15] His time in Bombay and his important government positions in Tehran that sometimes required travel abroad put him in intimate contact with leading currents of religious thought. In addition to familiarity with Christianity, he was conversant with Zoroastrian religious debates in India, as well as with the larger field of religious studies in the West.

Shahrokh distinguished himself as a religious reformer. He not only achieved changes in religious practices, but reconceived of and promulgated Zoroastrianism in Iran. Although often consistent with the Parsi reform movement in India, Shahrokh was an independent thinker and willing to disagree. Not infrequently, he ran into religious opposition, whether from the ulama, more traditional Zoroastrians, or Parsis. One issue in particular brought him into conflict with fellow Zoroastrians and set him apart as a reformer: the use of *dakhmehs*.

The *Dakhmeh* Debate

The *dahkmeh* used by Zoroastrians in the early twentieth century in Tehran was of recent provenance. Considering that there had not been a sizable Zoroastrian population in the city until the twentieth century, it is not surprising that there was no *dakhmeh* in use until 1893 when the third Parsi representative of the Amelioration Society, Kay Khosrow Khan Saheb, had an ancient *dakhmeh* rebuilt.[16] What is surprising is that within a generation, it was completely abandoned. The story of Kay Khosrow Shahrokh deciding in 1935 to establish a Zoroastrian cemetery outside the city and receiving royal approbation and assistance in doing so is well known and often recounted as testimony to the friendly relations between Reza Shah and the Zoroastrian community.[17] What are less well known are the motivations surrounding this radical departure from traditional Zoroastrian practice.

Shahrokh might be accused of exaggeration in asserting that he had "since a young age . . . been against the practice of exposure of the dead in the dakhma [*sic*]."[18] However, his motivations ring true. He provides three reasons for the abandonment of the *dakhmeh*. First, its use was unhygienic. Second, it was actually a misunderstanding of Zoroaster's preaching. Third, the growth of Tehran had brought the city's environs close to the *dakhmeh*, with the disagreeable consequence that corpses suffered desecration at the hands of Muslim hooligans.[19] This combination of pragmatic, "scientific," and religious rationales characterizes Shahrokh as a religious Reformist.

In terms of the actual motivation of the Tehran Zoroastrian community, the desecration of Zoroastrian corpses and rumors that they were being used in medical autopsies were doubtless of primary importance.[20] Shahrokh's initiative was embraced by the Tehran Anjoman, and the Zoroastrian community quickly raised sufficient funds to buy land for the cemetery and to build appropriate buildings there.[21] More significant as a window onto Zoroastrian reformism, however, are Shahrokh's claims of scientific proof and insight into "pure" or "true" Zoroastrianism. In his rationale, Shahrokh asserts that cemeteries were more "hygienic." Medical science was frequently cited in the early twentieth century as authoritative and was not surprisingly claimed by his opponents as well. These claims, of course, say much less about hygiene itself than they do about the authority attributed to scientific "proof."

The bulk of his argument, however, rested on his claim to religious "truth" through a historicization of Zoroastrianism. In an argument typical of Parsi Reformists and contemporary religious studies scholarship alike, Shahrokh asserted that Zoroaster himself never advocated the use of *dakhmehs*. Calling forth Western linguistics and the scholarly consensus that the message of Zoroaster had been corrupted after his death, Shahrokh argued that the use of *dakhmehs* was not in fact authentic Zoroastrian doctrine, but rather a later aberration. Other reform-minded Zoroastrians agreed. According to Farhang Mehr, their arguments paralleled Shahrokh's, deconstructing Zoroastrian tradition. "Pointing to the tombs of Persian kings, they tried to justify the change by arguing that since a form of entombment of the dead was practiced by Zoroastrians in ancient times, using cemeteries would not go against tradition."[22]

In addition to Shahrokh's obvious fluency in religious studies' conceptions of Zoroastrian history, what is important to note here is his presumption that Zoroaster's *intentions* could be ascertained by recourse to *logic*. Religious reformers' frequent recourse to a religion's "true essence" or intent (whether textual or prophetic) in fact rested on their own claims to be able to *ascertain this essence or intent* through rational thought. Rationalism was always claimed as incontrovertible and always concurred with reformers' own views of the "truth" or "essence" of the religion. Claims to science and empiricism were related to the rational retrieval of meaning—of traditions, of texts.

Orthodox Parsis were deeply troubled by Shahrokh's abandonment of the *dakhmeh* in Tehran and his encouragement of the Kerman and Yazd communities to follow suit, so much so that they commissioned an essay that insisted on the value of the *dakhmeh*. This tract, "Dokhma: A Scientific Method of Disposal of the Dead among Zoroastrians," was sponsored and published by the Iran League, an organization that encouraged ties between Parsis and their coreligionists in the homeland of Iran.[23] In the introduction, the secretary of the Iran League, Kaikhosrow A. Fitter, pleaded in the name of "ancient and hallowed custom" for the Iranian Zoroastrians to rethink their decision. He even went so far as to threaten a "complete alienation" between the Parsis and the Iranian Zoroastrians if they did not. The introduction states that the purpose of the tract was to "bring

19. Police headquarters, Tehran, Iran, ca. 1934. Photo taken by Talinn Grigor, 2003.

forward the most convincing proofs, both from their [Zoroastrian] sacred books, and from the opinions of some of the most enlightened Westerners in favour of the sanctified and old custom of 'Khurshid Nigirishne' [use of the *dakhmeh*]."[24]

The tract itself is a compellation of opinions and quotations from leading Parsis, Western travelers, scholars, and medical doctors attesting to the advantages of the *dakhmeh*. The majority of testimonials attest to the superiority of the *dakhmeh* on the basis of "scientific proof" and "hygiene": for example, "Burial Dangerous to the Living—an eminent writer on Hygiene, Dr. E. A. Parkes, could not but comment upon the system of burial as the most insanitary [*sic*]: 'it is a matter of notoriety that the vicinity of graveyards is unhealthy.'"[25] Dr. Rudolf Pock of the Austrian Plague Commission is quoted: "I find that the Parsi system of the disposal of the dead bodies is the best from a hygienic point."[26] *Scientific American* is also quoted as warning against graveyards where "disease producing organisms" have been found alive and "as active as ever" even "after the lapse of several hundred years."[27] No less of an authority than Lord Randolph Churchill himself is marshaled to the cause: "Funeral obsequies, conducted in accordance with the teachings and precepts of *Zoroaster* . . . are entirely agreeable to the principles of a *pure religion* . . . and powerfully supported by physiological science and experience."[28]

More interesting than the claims of science, however, are the arguments based on text and tradition. The introduction asserts several telling dichotomies: "We deeply regret the replacing of religious commandments by 'local' considerations; 'ancient customs' by new fashions; 'religion' by intellectual views; 'scientific hygiene' by considerations of worldly views."[29] Implicitly, therefore, "Dokhma" claims the authority of tradition, true religion, and (of course) science. Not surprisingly, all the textual support for the use of *dakhmehs* was culled from the Vendidad, a section of the Avesta considered of much later provenance than Zoroaster's time and thus largely rejected as a source of authority by Reformists.

The meaning of the charge of Shahrokh's "replacing of religious commandments by 'local' considerations" is clarified by the parallel assertion that Iranian Zoroastrians were "adopting the Semitic method of burial." Both of these claims, like Shahrokh's own, rely on the historicization of Zoroastrian tradition. Although they disagree in their conclusions, such claims of change over time within Zoroastrianism lay open room for interpretation concerning "true" and "authentic"—and thus "pure"—Zoroastrianism. Reformists and more orthodox

Zoroastrians naturally differed on the weight they assigned to tradition, with Reformists arguing for the purification-recovery of the "essence" of Zoroastrianism from local accretions, misinterpretation, and divergence. The Orthodox authors of "Dokhma" claim to be protecting tradition from just such a divergence. Despite the vehemence of "Dokhma" and calls for Zoroastrian unity in the maintenance of "customs and traditions," no abiding schism between the Parsis and Iranian Zoroastrians resulted from the *dakhmeh* dispute. In Tehran, in recognition of Zoroastrian injunctions against pollution, graves were "lined with rocks and plastered with cement to prevent direct contact with the earth." Reformist Zoroastrians in Yazd and Kerman built similar cemeteries, although the *dakhmehs* remained in use there until the 1970s.[30]

Although the *dakhmeh* dispute provided some insight into Shahrokh's ideas of Zoroastrian tradition, it is his two works on Zoroastrianism that reveal his notions of the nature and function of modern, rational religion and his profound reconceptualization of Zoroastrianism.

Conceptualizing Modern Religion

A'ineh-ye A'in-e Mazdasna (The Mirror of the Religion of Mazda) was published first in 1907 and again in 1921.[31] This text was styled as a catechism for the explicit purpose instructing Zoroastrian children in their religion. The second edition included a glossary of Zoroastrian terms in order to facilitate its reading by non-Zoroastrians. The second work, *Forough-e Mazdasna* (The Light of Mazdaism) was published in 1924 and was widely used in Zoroastrian schools. Shahrokh credited these books with helping improve Muslim attitudes toward Zoroastrianism.[32]

Shahrokh's conception of modern religion shared the basic premises of Parsi reformers in India as well as Western scholarly assumptions of the time. Shahrokh, like the Parsis, was profoundly influenced by Western scholarly notions of evolutionism, context, and the historical development of human consciousness of religion over time. His writings evidence a fluency in religious studies ideas of the time, as well as the new consensus concerning Zoroastrian religious history. Shahrokh conceived of "modern" Zoroastrianism as defined by the following four characteristics: monotheism, the individual's spiritual relationship with God, the de-emphasis on ritual, and the corresponding re-emphasis on ethical behavior in society. This conception of rational religion and the interiorization of piety were intimately tied to Shahrokh's understanding of the role of the citizen in the modern state.

By the twentieth century when Shahrokh composed his two works, the superiority of monotheism was so far unchallenged as to be taken as a given. Moreover, Zoroastrianism had been claimed as monotheistic by generations of Western scholars and insisted upon as well by Parsi reformers and scholars. Despite the recent scholarly consensus, Shahrokh was still at pains to insist on it. He brought up the issue of monotheism no fewer than fifteen times in *Forough-e Mazdisna,* citing Haug and other Western scholars as evidence.[33] This emphasis is indicative of the resiliency of Muslim prejudice against Zoroastrianism as a dualistic and thus "untrue" religion. As dualistic, Zoroastrianism could not be accepted as a revealed religion in the Abrahamic tradition, making Zoroastrians thus ineligible for *dhimmi* status. The claims that Zoroastrianism was a dualistic religion were thus at least partly rooted in anti-Zoroastrian polemic as well as the justification for ongoing shari'a-based discrimination.[34]

There was also a more fundamental, theological reason for Shahrokh's insistence on monotheism: God's relationship to believers. This relationship was described as a spiritual one, based on the individual's consciousness of God. This spiritual relationship was repeatedly emphasized as a primary characteristic of Zoroastrianism and was consistent with scholarly convictions. Protestant scholarship had successfully claimed rational religion and its promotion of moral individual actors as the most evolved and thereby the most progressive of all religions. Shahrokh spent no time on the characteristics of God (apart from the notion of sole creator) or on specific practices or beliefs enjoined on believers. In emphasizing spirituality, he implied that God is the fountainhead of man's morality and ethical behavior—the reason for ethical action in this world. The relationship hinged on man's recognition (and the spiritual understanding that gives rise to this recognition) that God enjoins man to ethical behavior.

Ritual as a means of affecting the Divine is completely absent in Shahrokh's explanation of the beliefs and practices of Zoroastrianism. Rituals as a means of "performance" of religious "duties" as understood in orthodox Zoroastrian ethics are also absent. Instead, Shahrokh describes "prayer" as a prompt—a continued mindfulness of God's desire to have man behave ethically in this world. Prayer is also enjoined in order to ask for God's forgiveness for failings and to request God's guidance in becoming a more moral person—deeply Protestant ideas of the nature and purpose of prayer. The only instance of a specifically Zoroastrian practice is when Shahrokh encourages the wearing of the *sadre* and *kushti.* Their use serves two purposes: first, as prompts to be mindful of God when praying and, second, as symbolic markers of Zoroastrian identity. Shahrokh specifically urges Zoroastrians to be proud to wear them, particularly in remembrance of the difficulties that Zoroastrians faced as minorities in an Islamic state. They are not accorded any "truth" or functional value in and of themselves, but only in their larger utility toward individual consciousness of God and community identity maintenance.

Shahrokh, like Parsi reformers, emphasized the internalization of ethics in the consciousness of God and in a commitment to ethical behavior. He essentialized Zoroastrianism by extrapolating its "intent," "purpose," and "function." What becomes important is the social function of religion. The purpose of religious education, as envisioned by Shahrokh, is to train ethical individuals, not to teach Zoroastrians how to perform required religious rituals. This view is a radical departure from more Orthodox emphases on Zoroastrian particularism and "truth." Yet the explicit interiorization of modern religion does not imply a diminution of its importance. Privatization in this regard also meant religion's conscious incorporation into *all aspects of lived experience.* God's moral agency thus becomes the totality of man's actions, rather than being "performed" in only ceremonial and thus limited times.

Related to the essentialization (or the extraction of religious intent, purpose, and function) in rationalized, modern Zoroastrianism is Shahrokh's emphasis on universalism. He understood the term in two ways. On the one hand, he posited a universal essence to all religions. Not only is Zoroastrianism described as consistent with and similar to Christianity and Islam, but it is *essentially* the same. All religions, thus, are essentialized down to the same core: morality. Particularism and the truth-value of religions are relegated to the "historic" or traditional and useful only in maintaining community identity. On the other hand, Shahrokh did claim a special universality, and thus modernity, for Zoroastrianism as the origin of monotheism and as the origin of modern ideas and conceptions concerning religion. He touted Zoroastrianism as an ideal religion for today's modern world that was universally applicable to all. This stance had important implications for his understanding of citizenship and Zoroastrian identity.

Shahrokh's deist conception of religious universalism presupposes religious equality. The interiorization of piety and the ethical foundations of individual responsibility found in his two works create the parameters of citizenship and social progress. In his view, rational religion actually promotes citizenship since it equalizes all individuals and makes social participation and responsibility equally incumbent. Although he does not specifically address the question of citizenship, his catechism is similar to J. J. Modi's in that it posits a clear causal connection between the interiorization of piety and the development of modern citizens. The privatization of piety entailed the de-emphasis of the performance of religious difference as sectarianism, instead enabling religious equality and common participation in public as citizens.

Conclusion

Religion and the Creation of Pious Citizens

Over the course of the period 1830–1940 Zoroastrian reformers in India and Iran arrived at a remarkable consensus concerning the form and function of enlightened (that is, rational) religion. What had begun as an act of self-defense against Protestant missionaries and their claims to ownership of "true" religion developed into a comprehensive theological reform movement. Armed with both the destructive and the creative capacities of historicism, reformers reevaluated their own religious Tradition. They molded Zoroastrian belief and practice according to contemporary ideas of rational religion and its potential to create pious citizens. Reformers radically reconceived of the nature of religion as a human phenomenon that altered Zoroastrianism's relationship to its own tradition as well as to other religious traditions. They fundamentally reshaped the way that individual Zoroastrians understood their history and their religious customs and practices. Self-styled Orthodox Zoroastrians, while disagreeing with their Reformist brethren on a number of central issues, were themselves also profoundly affected by new ideas of historicism and evolutionism. Quite simply, Zoroastrianism as understood and practiced in 1940 was qualitatively different from its understanding and practice in 1830.

Rational religion was recovered and resuscitated from the ancient "core" of Zoroastrianism through the twin processes of historicization and essentialization. Its principal characteristics included monotheism, a stress on the individual's spiritual relationship to God, and a denunciation of formalism and ritual. Ethics, formerly understood and the practice of prescribed rituals that aided God and God's supernatural minions in the ultimate battle between good and evil, was recast as ethical behavior in this world. The rationalization of ritual involved discerning God's intent, which was cast as moral responsibility. In other words, individual moral responsibility toward oneself, toward others, and toward society was cast as divinely ordained.

The central feature of rational religion, and its chief attraction, was its causal relationship to social change. Rational religion was believed to be generative of "progress" and "civilization." In other words, certain beliefs concerning the nature of an individual's relationship to God, and the resulting modes of practice, were believed to create different sorts of individuals and consequently different kinds of societies. Society and, by extension, states were believed to be stronger and more powerful through the agency of particular forms of religious belief and practice. Reformers were convinced that there could be no social change without religious change.[1] The individual was thus the motor for social change. As such, religion had a formative role in shaping the character of individuals who would then be active in society. Rational religion emphasized that God's intention for mankind was to behave ethically in society. Reformers thus presumed to be able to discern God's intentions and to identify the "essence" or "true" core of their religious traditions and texts. They held that ethical behavior did not entail participation in and allegiance to a particular religious community, nor yet was it embodied in correct performance of ritual. Rather, reformers repeatedly insisted that God's intent was for individuals to behave ethically *in society*. The generation of the modern state thus depended ultimately on the creation of pious citizens. It was the deliberate, conscious assumption of ethical responsibility of the individual in society that was so fundamental to reformed religion. Ritual and performance were believed to lack, or even obscure, individual moral consciousness and to circumscribe ethics to limited performances and ritual duties. The truly pious, according to the new understanding of religion, imbued all their worldly actions with a conscious responsibility toward God and moral behavior.

This focus on the individual character also explains the emphasis on the family and the role of women as mothers and thus targets of social reform. Women's role in the religious and moral education of children as future citizens is a common theme in Reformist literature. Karkaria vehemently pursued this idea when he asserted that "a State is based on the family, and before trying to reform the former, attempts must be made to improve the latter."[2] The social condition of women in particular was a cause of much concern. Karkaria explained that "a people with their homes debased, their women ignorant and superstitious, a people trammeled with all the old-world prejudices and subject to the most cruelly one-sided customs and usages, can never hope to enjoy or exercise high political privileges. All endeavours in this direction, without fulfilling the *preliminary conditions of moral and social reform,* must end in disappointment if not in disaster."[3] Moral reform—in other words, the introduction of rationalized, interiorized piety—was a sine qua non for substantive social and political change.

Even the more self-consciously Orthodox priest Dastur Sanjana, in the conclusion to his article "The Position of Zoroastrian Women in Remote Antiquity," made a similar causal connection between the moral education of women and national "progress." He wrote, "'Let France have good mothers and she will have good sons,' was a happy remark of the Emperor Napoleon. The literary attainments of the mother, her fitness to perform her household duties, *her example of a moral and religious life,* are more beneficial to posterity, *to the future progress of a nation,* than the impressions produced by the father. Moral and religious instruction ought, therefore to form the chief element in the education of women of every country; for without religion there is no moral obligation, and *without the sense of a moral obligation, no sympathy or unity with the family, the race, or community.*"[4] Rational religion, believed to be more consciously moral than performance-oriented religions, was therefore the key to progress, of the individual and, through the individual, the nation.

The premise of rational religion was that it created modern citizens and was thus generative of modern society and modern states. In reformers' ideas of the citizen, certain features were prominent: They understood citizens to enjoy equality in society and in relationship to the state. Citizens primarily identified as members of a nation, rather than as members of specific religious or ethnic communities. They also imagined citizens as being both *participatory in* society as well as *responsible toward* society. Collectively, citizens embodied the state in the sense of identity, solidarity, and nationalism, and in that the state's legitimacy derived from the citizens—they are the raison d'être of the state. Rational religion was believed to promote the formation of citizens by consciously weakening sectarianism through an emphasis on the similarity or even universality of religions. Sectarian identity and loyalty were superseded by identity with the state and solidarity with fellow citizens. Rational religion downplayed religious community, instead promoting national community, commonality among citizens, and equal participation. In Iran the development of modern citizens along these lines was retarded by the lack of fully secular law, equal political participation, and nonreligious state legitimacy.[5] Iran remained Islamic; law continued to be determined according to religious community and enforced according to religious laws. The continued emphasis on religious community as a source of fundamental difference in citizenship in Iran prevented equality of citizenship, and thus equality of participation and identification with state and society.

A new relationship developed between the private and the public spheres, religion, and the nation. Rational religion discouraged the public demonstration of religious community, or sectarian identity, through religious performance. Such performance emphasized individuals' primary identity as a member of a religious community. Similarly, it reinforced the notion of the religious community as the object of responsibility and solidarity. Rational religion altered these relationships. Community membership gave way to national membership; sectarian identity gave way to national identity. In this manner, religion became a matter of *private observance,* rather then *public performance.* There are several reasons for this shift in emphasis. First, the public emerged as the site of citizens' demonstration of equality, national (shared) identity, and solidarity. Second, religion as practiced in the private sphere centered on the individual's *relationship with God,* rather than the individual's *participation in a sectarian community.* Religion as identity was subsumed under national identity. National identity, not sectarian identity, was performed and thereby demonstrated in public.

The project of religious reform created new public spaces that went hand in hand with the emergence of citizens. The theological priority given to individual consciousness of God meant that individuals were entitled to discern God's intent through interpretation of sacred texts. The individual's hermeneutical authority effectively ended the religious establishment's monopoly on interpretation and on the construction of truth. It also eroded clerical institutional and social authority, as new secular and public spaces of religious debate emerged. Debates surrounding religious texts, morality, education, and civics arose largely outside of governmental or clerical control. These areas were secular spaces in the sense that they were not exclusive to one religious affiliation or associated with a religion of state. However, these new public spaces were occupied by the self-consciously pious. Secular did not entail the absence of religion, merely the privatization of particularism. The new journals, educational and religious scholarly societies, as well as philanthropic organizations asserted the value of civic participation that facilitated the development of citizens and ideals of civic duty. Civic duty was founded on the premise of individualized piety and the notion of secular public space. The new citizens that emerged from these spaces were a product of civic virtues of social responsibility and participation in generating "civilization and progress." They were also a product of individualism, hard work, merit, and the emphasis on character development that were so much a function of rationalized religion.

The emphasis on the nation, with concomitant performances of national solidarity, commonality, and identity, was also reinforced in Iran by attempts to nationalize (and thus homogenize) clothing and language. Persian was consequently adopted as the national language. Clothing, like religion, ceased to symbolize difference and instead became a matter of "private" choice. A telling example of this change is a remark by Reza Shah's prime minister Teymourtache to the German minister in 1939. Commenting on the multiple purposes of the "law on uniform dress," he explained, "We want to drive the clergy out into the open, eliminate those who have been masquerading as clergy, and otherwise *foster national unity* by eliminating a variety of special clothing which heretofore has served to identify an individual as being a resident of Tabriz, or Meshed, et cetera, rather than a Persian. . . . [O]nce our point is definitely won, full liberty will be accorded the individual in the matter of choosing his own dress, *provided his choice falls on something modern*."[6] He was not the first to voice this sentiment. Nationalists like Hosein Kazemzadeh and Mahmud Afshar had long sought to erase difference through clothing change and the establishment of Persian as a national language. They understood these factors to be paramount in the creation of national identity and solidarity. In an article in the journal *Iranshahr* the author lamented the obstacles in the way of national solidarity: "The problem of communalism is so serious that whenever an Iranian traveling abroad is asked his nationality, he will give his locality—not the proud name of his country. *We must eliminate local sects, local dialects, local clothes, local customs, and local sentiments.*"[7]

The implications of the privatization of religion were manifold. One result was that religious difference, or, put differently, identification with a religious community, was understood as a matter of allegiance to a particular *historical* tradition. Since all religions were premised as containing the same essence, the same moral message, difference therefore was circumstantial, rather than a matter of "truth" value. This situation created unresolved tensions, as it pitted religious commonality against religious particularism. Kay Khosrow Shahrokh poignantly illustrated this point when he explained that his decision to choose Zoroastrianism "from so many true religions" was owing to the circumstance of his being born Zoroastrian.[8] The notion of religious commonality posed real challenges, particularly for minority religious communities like the Zoroastrians, since it weakened their sense of community solidarity and made it difficult to insist on intramarriage. Zoroastrian loss of members to intermarriage became a real cause of concern for the Zoroastrian community in Iran in the 1960s and 1970s.[9]

Most important, the privatization of religion should not be understood as the marginalization, or lessening, of the role of religion. At first glance, the removal of religious performance from the public sphere and the primacy of national over religious sectarian identity *seem* to imply a lessening of the role of religion. Certainly, they suggest the privileging of the public sphere and the notion that religion is reduced in the process of privatization. This interpretation is misleading. I would argue instead that the de-emphasis of religious difference and identity was intended to weaken sectarianism and religious particularism. However, rational religion presumed to influence *all behavior* in private and public through the individual's conscious assumption of ethical responsibility. Rather than diminishing the role of religion, rational religion claimed to inform all spheres of life. In fact, one of the roles of rational religion was to eliminate the specific relegation (and thus in a sense *limitation*) of the "religious" to the performance of rituals. Rational religion sought to imbue all individual actions with a constant mindfulness of God. In so doing, it appropriated *both the public and the private spheres*. Religion then was redefined to mean not sectarian identity, but individualized piety.

ششم فروردین ، خورداد فروردین ماه ، زادروز

اشو زرتشت سپنتمان

را به همه بهدینان جهان شادباش میگوئیم

20. Zoroaster, from inside front cover of Mahnameh-ye Zartoshtian, *Nowruz* 1354 Khorshidi.

The Language of Debate

By reshaping their own religious tradition along rational lines, Zoroastrians were not seeking to abandon it under the guise of reform. Rather, they were genuinely convinced that their own tradition had the capacity to assume these new forms. Reform was understood not as the Protestantization of religion, but rather as a corresponding "reformation." The claim to "true" religion was thus not only a tactical effort to legitimize change as return to origin or "indigenous" essence, but an expression of the idea of the *form* of rational religion as universal. There was, naturally, no shortage of reformers who attributed change to the agency of the West and who believed that Westernization was the key to modernity and social change. To take one example, Karkaria, in his biography of noted social reformer B. M. Malabari, explained the effects of the British on India: "Even greater than the triumph of material progress is that is that of mental and moral advance. England has had the rare satisfaction of awakening the torpid Hindu intellect from the sleep into which it had been thrown by the fierce foreign rule of the Mahomedans. . . . [I]n its far-reaching importance this new period of the *Eclaircissement* in modern India may be compared to the awakening of the European mind from the inactivity of the Middle Ages at the time of the Renaissance."[10] Upon closer examination, however, it is apparent that Karkaria simultaneously claims that India has the ability to assume a new form and that this form exists in its indigenous essence. Although he attributes agency to the British, it is India itself that consequently *undergoes* an Enlightenment. This attribution significantly tempers the presumption that modernization involves Westernization. Agency and impetus are clearly distinguished from capacity. In this reading, modernity, by way of "modern" rational religion, was universally accessible through the adoption of certain forms of religious belief and expression. Modernity was not imitative, or culturally Western, and could be achieved by means of rationalizing Zoroastrianism or, in the broader case of India, rationalizing Hinduism.

Religious Rationalization: Beyond Zoroastrianism

Religious reform, and the subsequent construction of rational religion, is particularly apparent in the Indian and Iranian Zoroastrian communities. There are several reasons for its special visibility. First, no other religious community engaged in such an intense conversation with missionaries and European scholars as did the Zoroastrian community. The resulting dialogues are unique as sources and indicative of the profound impact of Protestant religious assumptions concerning modern, evolved, or "true" religion on the Zoroastrians. Second, Zoroastrianism as practiced in the 1800s, both in Iran and in India, placed particular emphasis on ritual and performance. It was thus singled out for attack by scholars and missionaries and as a result subject to radical revision by reformers seeking to reshape it according to the characteristics of "true" or evolved, modern, rational religion. Third, the Zoroastrian community played a unique role in both India and Iran vis-à-vis the state. In Iran, the Zoroastrian connection to Iranian nationalism and the ancient past was exceptional. Nationalism's claims to modernity and the state's privileging of the Zoroastrians further encouraged religious change and the eager promotion of the state's modernization program by the Zoroastrians. In the case of India, the British discovered in the Zoroastrians a community of intermediaries. This special relationship encouraged Zoroastrian attempts to distinguish themselves from Hindus and Muslims as having greater cultural and religious affinities with the British. As Hinnells perceptively points out, the British-Zoroastrian affinity ran both ways.[11] The Zoroastrians became the most Anglicized of Indian communities and served as intermediaries for British rule. Yet at the same time, it was the British who greeted the Zoroastrians with feelings of affinity. Religion was at the center of perceptions of commonality. The British considered Zoroastrianism closer to their own monotheism than Hindu religion, and even went so far as to articulate racial similarity. Captain Hamilton, writing in 1716, was impressed with their racial purity: "They never marry into foreign Families, which makes them retain their native fair Complexion, little inferior to us *Europeans*."[12]

The Parsis and the British colluded in constructing mutual similarity, Parsi exceptionalism, and difference from the Hindu majority. George Viscount Valencia, writing in 1804, asserted that the Parsis "form an important barrier against the more powerful castes of India."[13] Parsi reformers also testify to this reciprocal relationship. Karkaria asserted that "the Parsis have thus been the most prominent community among the natives: it is scarcely possible to conceive of the public life in Western India without them. They have, therefore, attracted the attention of Europeans to an extent commensurate with their abilities and importance. Christian missionaries have sought them specially . . . with the hope of influencing the other Indian communities through the Parsis."[14]

Karkaria continued his observations of the effects of the special Parsi-British relationship. He noted that as a result of their mutual attraction, the Parsis became known as the most Westernized of all the Indian communities, even assuming different physical characteristics: "In physical matters, too, Parsis are rapidly evolving robuster qualities of body, which will in the long run make them the equals of many Western nations, and on which Western supremacy rests. In social matters they easily take the lead of their Hindu countrymen, as they are singularly free from those narrow views of caste which hamper the latter."[15] The Zoroastrians, for their part, eagerly embraced religious (and to some extent racial) similarity with the Christian British as a claim to being more civilized, deliberately differentiating themselves from the pagan Hindu population. The connection between religious commonality and civilization propelled the Zoroastrian reform movement and encouraged religious change.

Yet Zoroastrians were not the only community to take up the gauntlet of religious reform. Ideas of rational, or modern, religion were pervasive in this period and fundamentally influenced many religious reform movements. In India the Hindu Brahmo Samaj, Prarthana Samaj, Arya Samaj, and Paramahansa Mandali movements shared very similar characteristics to the Zoroastrian reform movement. They all emphasized monotheism, religious universalism or theism, and individual morality and likewise rejected religious performance as a way of affecting the divine.[16] Religious reform movements in this period typically claimed to be recovering "true" original religion from sacred texts and rejecting tradition as historical detritus. Reformers argued that modern or "true" religion was in fact implicit in their own traditions, although unfortunately it had become obscured over time. As the Brahmo Samaj representative explained before members of the World's Parliament of Religions of 1893, "Our society is a new society; our religion is a new religion; but it comes from far, far antiquity."[17] Reform was, therefore, a recovery of the essential, rather than the adoption of the new, foreign, or inauthentic. In line with a recovery of ancient "essence," these movements also focused on rediscovering ancient history. Religious reform aimed at rationalization was typically concerned to establish cultural and religious origins for modernity, insisting on an essential capacity for civilization and progress, rather than seeking to legitimize change as the adoption of foreign or Western forms.

Another commonality across religious reform movements in India was the belief that religious change was a necessary prerequisite for substantive social change.

To take but one example of the most prominent Hindu reform movement, the Brahmo Samaj, its founder, Ram Mohan Roy (1774–1833), was particularly drawn to Unitarian Christianity. Writing to a friend in 1817 he admitted that he "had found the doctrines of Christ more conducive to moral principles, and more adapted for the use of rational beings, than any other which have come to my knowledge."[18] A year after founding the British Indian Unitarian Association in 1827, Roy changed his tactics. Rather than encouraging conversion to Christianity he believed it crucial for reasons of authenticity and cultural resonance to provide a Vedic foundation for religious reform and accordingly established the Brahmo Samaj in 1828.[19] Roy radically reconstructed Hindu practices in order to emphasize consciousness of God, spirituality, social responsibility, and religious universalism. He aimed "to lead the Hindus back to the Vedanta," yet this claim to be restoring religion allowed him to reshape it into what he termed "Hindu Theism."[20] As declared by a representative of the society, "Our monotheism . . . stands upon all Scriptures. . . . [T]here was in our hearts the God of infinite reality, the source of inspiration of all the books, of the Bible, of the Koran, of the Zend-Avesta, who drew our attention to his excellencies as revealed in the record of holy experience everywhere."[21] In a radical divergence from contemporary Hindu practice, Roy completely rejected the worship of idols as part of religious practice. Prayer meetings were designed to encourage civic and social responsibility by way of individual consciousness of God and internalized piety. It was decreed that "no sermon, preaching, discourse, prayer or hymn be delivered . . . but such as have a tendency to the promotion of the contemplation of the Author and Preserver of the Universe, to the promotion of charity, morality, piety, benevolence, virtue and the strengthening of the bonds of union between men of all religious persuasions and creeds."[22]

In the Middle East, Islamic Modernists shared many of these central ideas of rational or "modern" religion. I am in complete agreement that reformers' insistence that Islam was not essentially inimical to modernity served important tactical uses. I would even agree that in the case of some reformers, tactical uses were paramount.[23] However, Islamic Modernism entailed more than a superficial whitewashing of "backward" practices and superstitions. Its more serious advocates understood religious reform as an intellectual project of shaping new subjectivities and of safeguarding religious relevance in the modern period. Islamic Modernism involved substantive theological revision based on the new consensus surrounding the nature and function of religion and its foundational place in creating a modern society.

For example, in an essay titled "And Seek Their Counsel in the Matter" (1869),[24] Ottoman reformer Namık Kemal argues that Islam, contrary to contemporary practice, calls for popular sovereignty, consultative government, and the protection of individual freedom. According to Kemal, "Regardless of time, place, and circumstance, state authority should be realized in the way which will least limit the freedom of the individual."[25] Kemal's objective is the well-being of the nation and the Islamic *ummah* (community of believers). Kemal's argument rests on a reinterpretation of key Quranic verses and presumes that the Quran is reconcilable with "natural law." Kemal's very first sentence reads, "Being created free by God, man is naturally obliged to benefit from this divine gift."[26] I take seriously his project of defending modern political institutions as not only reconcilable with but essential to Islam. In important ways, Kemal's reinterpretation of the Quran implied substantive differences with "traditional" exegetical theory.

The dominant discourse of the rejection of "superstition" and the denunciation of the ulama as upholding religious beliefs and practices inimical to rationalism, science, and hygiene should be understood in this context. Religious reform was based on the conviction that religious truth must necessarily be compatible with scientific truth and that Islam must be the basis of morality, civilization, and progress, regardless of social, political, or cultural context. Like Zoroastrian and Hindu reformers, Islamic Modernists too historicized tradition and sought a timeless religious "essence" in the Quran. They insisted that God's intent was retrievable from the Quran and sought to identify enduring truths and distinguish them from contextual interpretations that had become canonized. In short, Islamic Modernists attempted to liberate God's intent from history. Tradition was seen as inhibiting rational and critical thought and consequently the ability to discern God's intent. For example, Qasim Amin, in his famous reform treatise *The Liberation of Women* (1899), connected sociopolitical backwardness to the absence of critical inquiry that resulted from the myth of tradition. Amin denounced tradition as masquerading as "true" religion and thus inhibiting progress: "What present-day Muslims ... call Islam is in reality a conglomeration of many ideas, customs and traditions that have no relationship to the *genuine, true, and pure religion.* . . . Thus it is the medley of beliefs, traditions, and morals that people call religion and consider to be Islam that is in fact the obstacle to progress."[27] Amin carefully distinguished between religion *as practiced* and *true* religion. Muslim and Zoroastrian reformers, typified by Amin, advocated the abandonment of tradition (and thus "traditional" interpretations) in favor of a return to the original text—in the case of Islam the Quran, in the case of Zoroastrianism the Avesta.

The realignment of religion with science, though not a principal concern of Zoroastrian Reformists, was a central objective for Islamic Modernists. They attempted to realign religion with science, both in terms of new theorems and, more important, in terms of empirical method. "Science," in the view of reformers like Qasim Amin and Jamal al-Din al-Afghani, was *the* source of Western strength. Al-Afghani explained European colonialism as a consequence of science: "In reality this usurpation, aggression, and conquest has not come from the French or the English. Rather it is science that everywhere manifests its greatness and power."[28] He specifically blamed the Islamic religious establishment for its failure to recognize the universality of science and thus its compatibility with Islam. "Our ulama these days have divided science into two parts. One they call Muslim science, and one European science. . . . They have not understood that science is that noble thing that has no connection with any nation. . . . [T]hose who forbid science and knowledge in the belief that they are safeguarding the Islamic religion are really the enemies of that religion. The Islamic religion is the closest of religions to science and knowledge, and there is no incompatibility between science and knowledge and the foundations of the Islamic faith."[29]

Anticlericalism contributed to the profound loss not only of the religious establishment's religious authority, but of their social authority as well. Not surprisingly, the Muslim and Zoroastrian religious establishments were blamed for social and political backwardness and were accused of hindering the critical thinking and freedom of thought essential to constructing a modern society and state. Reform, so closely related to the reevaluation of tradition, could not have been imagined without this new awareness of historicism. Anticlericalism was also intimately connected to institutional secularization. Political reform in the Middle East entailed centralization and the secularization of law and education. Reformers sought to wrest control of education and law from the Muslim religious establishment and place them firmly under the aegis of the central state.

Their desire to rationalize and control law, and to nationalize and universalize education, formed the rationale behind secularization. Until this time, law and education had been monopolized by the ulama. Law was primarily Islamic law, and education was religious knowledge derived from Quranic interpretation— both of which were defined and interpreted by the ulama. The secularization of these two "religious" institutions entailed the usurpation of religion by the state and consequently required a reconsideration of religious traditions as law and education were reformulated and repromulgated.[30]

Centering Religion in the Construction of Modernity

The project of rationalizing religion is a missing link in the history of modernization movements in the Middle East and India in the nineteenth and early twentieth centuries. We cannot understand the modernization project without the very central and *causally generative* role that "modern" religion was believed to play in constructing citizens and promoting national identity and secularism. Religion was central to modernity in the Middle East and India, not peripheral. Yet scholarship on the emergence of the modern state and citizen in the Middle East does not include religion as an integral component of modernity. There is no recognition of the role that reformed rationalized religion was intended to play in the construction of citizens and modern society. This dearth is less true for India; indeed, I concur with the pioneering work of religious studies scholar Peter Van der Veer on Britain and India, who insists that religious change was fundamental to the creation of modernities.[31] Religious reform needs to be accorded centrality as *generative in and of itself of modernity.* Nor has there been any recognition of religious reform as a *shared phenomenon* across religions in Middle Eastern scholarship. Religious modernism is seen as Islamic, rather than a more universal response to larger questions of constructing modernity in the Middle East and India. But why has religion been seen primarily as tactical or at least peripheral to modernization in the Middle East? Why is Islamic Modernism seen as a project of *reconciling* religion with new values and institutions, rather than as a theological reform movement that was believed to be *causally generative* of these institutions and values?

I would suggest that there are several overlapping reasons that have contributed to the undervaluation of the role of religion in shaping modern citizens, national identity, and secular states. The first goes back to the thorny problem of origins and authenticity, as they played themselves out in competing definitions of civilization and progress. Modernization and reform were indissolubly connected to the competition over the cultural origins of modernity—as contested both *between* West and the Middle East as well as *within* each of these societies. This struggle led to the bifurcation of notions of modern-traditional, which were in turn enhanced by projections of morality onto this equation. This confluence had the regrettable consequence of reinforcing certain binaries, such as the one that accuses Westernization and modernization of being inauthentic and immoral as opposed to Islam, which is posited as ultimately moral and authentic. The lifeblood of this dichotomy arose not simply from Orientalism but also from its refraction and appropriation into debates between different factions in the Middle East. For example, in Iran opponents of reform themselves employed Orientalist categorization to delegitimize reformers as Westernizers and thus as imitative and inauthentic.[32] This dichotomy enjoyed a momentum of its own, one that had important implications for the process of scripting modernity in the Middle East. Most important, it contributed to the difficulty that religious reformers had in legitimizing new forms of religious practice as authentic and moral, as opposed to imitative and foreign or immoral. In the same vein, it also led to the positioning of modernity as somehow demanding an absence of religion, a rejection of faith as implicitly antimodern and reactionary.

A second contributing reason was that for many of the political sponsors of modernization, whether shahs, prime ministers, or parliamentarians, the process was one of combating the ulama. They pitted themselves against the ulama—institutionally, socially, culturally, and intellectually. Centralization of state power and secularization cut deeply into ulama prerogatives, modes of authority, and their monopoly of the creation of religious truth. From the vantage point of political modernizers, the ulama stood in the way of equality of law, representative government, secular education, and the development of a participatory public with a strong sense of national identity. The newly emerging class of journalists and secular literati competed with the ulama for social authority and leadership. They saw the ulama as stalwart defenders of religious particularism and a barrier to the development of a national consciousness. They also blamed the ulama for "superstition" and the preservation of tradition that stood in the way of legal equality for minorities, women's rights, scientific innovation, and public health.

Anticlericalism thus segued into profound religious antipathy. Those individuals who advocated modernization identified their opponents as the religious establishment and religious beliefs and practices more generally. They were profoundly anticlerical, but also took the position that worship too was reactionary. Modernizers thus frequently saw themselves as secular defenders of a modernity predicated on the rejection of religion. This view accounts for the assumption that piety must necessarily be antimodern in form and content. It also explains why the history of modernization and the associated construction of modernities in the Middle East are based on the assumption that religion was at best peripheral to this process. How could secularism and the privatization of religion be consistent with the formation of pious citizens? And how could the rise of individualism, legal equality, and the rejection of religious particularism have theological premises? This book argues that this was precisely the case and insists that to write religion out of the construction of modernities distorts our understanding of the religious foundations of modernity. We must appreciate religious reform movements as profoundly participatory in the construction of modernity and acknowledge the theological basis for many "modern" ideas of state and society.

We must also recognize the ways in which religious reformers escaped the bounds of the modern-versus-traditional, authentic-versus-inauthentic, moral-versus-immoral equation. They were creative and sophisticated, constructing new possibilities for a modern-authentic-moral religion. Religious reform also transcended the confines of universalism as understood and propagated by many of their Christian interlocutors. Universalism, for the Protestant missionaries active in India and the majority of Western religious scholars in the early twentieth century, was a Christian preserve. In other words, despite the recognition of religion as a universal human phenomenon, and religious difference as a function of historical context, the claim that Christianity was the most evolved and progressive religion and would ultimately serve as the universal religion of mankind lurked behind much of the missionary and scholarly presumptions concerning "true" and rational religion. Zoroastrians were never seduced by the claims of Christianity. Zoroastrian reformers created alternative possibilities for rational religion as a latent potential embedded in Zoroastrian scripture, a potential released through theological reform. Yet there is more to this rejection of Christian universalism than the assertion that rational religion was implicit in Zoroastrianism. As Uday Mehta has theorized, Western claims to superiority had a philosophical basis in ideas of universalism. Western forms of knowledge, political institutions, and of course religion were understood as definitions, as templates for others to adopt. This stance left no room for the possibility of alternatives and categorized other societies and cultural forms as necessarily "provisional."[33] The reforms that generated rational, or modernist, religion (whether Zoroastrian, Hindu, or Muslim) did more than construct an "indigenous solution" to modern religion; in their insistence on "alternatives," they went beyond a facile understanding of the modern and engaged in a sophisticated discourse surrounding modernity that has yet to be fully mined.

Religious rationalism and the fundamental theological shift that this movement spawned also offer insight into a current story. I do not believe that we can understand contemporary piety movements that have drawn such recent attention without taking into account what they are responding to and reacting against.[34] These piety movements are reacting *not* to religion as it was practiced prior to the religious reform movements, but rather to *exactly these notions of rational religion* that led in many instances to the almost complete abandonment of practice, as ethics became an individual matter of spirituality—and an abstract, universal one at that. Contemporary piety movements have seized hold of rational religion's emphasis on interiorized consciousness and piety, even as they reject the notion of ritual as irrelevant. They thus are the product of rational religion, even as they reject some of its implications.

Notes

Bibliography

Index

Notes

Introduction: Modernity, Religion, and the Production of Knowledge

1. Uday Singh Mehta, *Liberalism and Empire: A Study in Nineteenth-Century British Liberal Thought*.

2. On the difference in locations of the sacred between Calvinists and Catholics and their associated sensibilities, see Natalie Zemon Davis, "The Sacred and the Body Social in Sixteenth-Century Lyon."

3. I am in dialogue here with Mohamad Tavakoli-Targhi on the question of what constitutes modernity and the modern period in Iran. I agree with him that "modernity may be envisaged as an ethos rather than a well-demarcated historical period," and specifically posit the recognition of historicism as the watershed between traditional and modern. See Tavakoli-Targhi, *Refashioning Iran: Orientalism, Occidentalism, and Historiography*, 9.

4. On the reexamination of religious and gender traditions in early-twentieth-century Iranian women's journals, see Monica M. Ringer, "Rethinking Religion: Progress and Morality in the Early Twentieth-Century Iranian Women's Press."

5. In my previous book, I explored at some length the demise of the ulama's intellectual monopoly on authoritative interpretation of sacred texts as a result of educational reform. I had not considered, however, the theological premise behind the authority of individual interpretation. See Monica M. Ringer, *Education, Religion, and the Discourse of Cultural Change in Qajar Iran*.

6. The idea of modernity as a product of the formation of new individual characters is omnipresent in the twentieth-century women's press. See Ringer, "Rethinking Religion."

7. Benedict Anderson, *Imagined Communities: Reflections on the Origins and Spread of Nationalism*.

8. Pamela Voekel, *Alone Before God: The Religious Origins of Modernity in Mexico*, 7.

9. Mehta, *Liberalism and Empire*. See esp. 191–92, 200–201.

10. S. Bhattacharya, "Paradigms Lost: Notes on Social History of India."

11. Tavakoli-Targhi, *Refashioning Iran*; Ali Behdad, *Belated Travelers: Orientalism in the Age of Colonial Dissolution*; Peter Van der Veer, *Imperial Encounters: Religion and Modernity in India*; and Peter Van der Veer, ed., *Conversion to Modernities: The Globalization of Christianity*. For a general discussion of Orientalism and its theorists, see Alexander Lyon Macfie, ed., *Orientalism: A Reader*.

12. Mohamad Tavakoli-Targhi, "Women of the West Imagined: Persian Occidentalism, Euro-Eroticism, and Modernity."

13. Van der Veer, *Imperial Encounters* and *Conversion to Modernities*.

14. In the context of educational reform debates in nineteenth-century Iran as they involved the determination of prerequisites for modernity, see Ringer, *Education, Religion, and the Discourse of Cultural Reform*.

15. On the Western construction of modern time and consequent claim to be chronologically ahead of the non-West, see Tavakoli-Targhi, *Refashioning Iran*.

16. Pierre Bourdieu, "Cultural Reproduction and Social Reproduction" and "The Genesis of the Concepts of Habitus and Field."

17. Edward Said, *Orientalism*.

18. Van der Veer, *Imperial Encounters*, 4–5.

19. James Mill, *History of British India* (1817), cited in ibid., 5. James Mill was the father of John Stuart Mill. Both father and son served in India in the East India Company.

20. Voekel, *Alone Before God*, 10.

21. Paul Kléber Monod, *The Power of Kings: Monarchy and Religion in Europe, 1589–1715*, 7, 4.

22. The dates of King Gushtasp's legendary reign remain unclear. Sources for the life of Zoroaster describe legendary kings that scholars have attempted to associate with historical figures, not always successfully. The Persian epic *Shahnameh* by Abolqasem Ferdowsi composed in the tenth century was considered a historical source for Zoroastrian history, even in the twentieth century, as evidenced by Kay Khosrow Shahrokh's use of it in compiling his own synopsis of the history of Zoroastrian kings.

23. The principal sections of the Avesta are the Yasna, Visprat, Videvdat, and Yasht. The five Gathas form a part of the Yasna.

24. See, for example, Martin Haug, *Essays on the Sacred Language, Writings, and Religion of the Parsis;* James Hope Moulton, *The Treasure of the Magi: A Study of Modern Zoroastrianism;* and Mary Boyce, *Zoroastrians: Their Religious Beliefs and Practices*.

25. John Wilson, *The Parsi Religion*.

26. Susan Stiles Maneck, *The Death of Ahriman: Culture, Identity, and Theological Change among the Parsis of India*.

27. Prior to the Islamic period, Zoroastrian literature did not focus much attention on Zoroaster and did not regard him as a teacher or prophet. By the thirteenth century, the idea of Zoroaster as the bringer of divine revelation in the form of a text, the Avesta, became firmly cemented. See William R. Darrow, "The Zoroaster Legend: Its Historical and Religious Significance," esp. 175–76.

28. D'Herbelot, on p. 931 of his *Bibliotheca Orientalis* published in 1697, attested, "The ancient Persians have it that Zoroaster was more ancient than Moses, and there are Magi who even maintain that he is none other than Abraham and often call him Ibrahim Zardusht," as cited in J. Duchesne-Guillemin, *The Western Response to Zoroaster*, 9.

29. On Jews in Iran, see Daniel Tsadik, *Between Foreigners and Shi'is: Nineteenth-Century Iran and Its Jewish Minority*.

30. Napier Malcolm, *Five Years in a Persian Town*, 53.

31. N. K. Firby, *European Travellers and Their Perceptions of Zoroastrians in the 17th and 18th Centuries*, 25.

32. Ibid., 26.

33. Ibid., 42.

34. Ibid., 62.

35. Ibid., 50.

36. Ibid., 72.

37. Ibid., 74.

38. Ibid., 77.

39. Ibid., 79.

40. Ibid., 80–81. Sir John Malcolm reported that the Zoroastrians joined the Afghan invaders in the hopes that they would be remembered for their service, but as a consequence, Nader Shah and Aqa Mohammad Qajar engaged bloody reprisals on the community. For this and alternate Zoroastrian traditions concerning the events, see Dosabhoy Framjee, *Parsees: Their History, Manners, Customs, and Religion*, 32–36.

41. Malcolm, *Five Years*, 41.

42. Mary Boyce, *A Persian Stronghold of Zoroastrianism*, 11.

43. There is a wide discrepancy in the population data for this period. For example, James Bassett, traveling in the same period, gives a total number of between four and five thousand. Bassett, *Persia, the Land of the Imams: A Narrative of Travel and Residence, 1871–1885*, 313. Joseph Knanishu records as many as fifteen thousand. Knanishu, *About Persia and Its People*, 220–21. Parsi representative Maneckji Limji Hataria provides a figure of between seven and eight thousand in *Travels to Iran: A Parsi Mission to Iran (1865)*, which is confirmed by C. J. Wills and Thomas Edward Gordon, who both note eight thousand Zoroastrians in Iran. Wills, *Persia as It Is: Being Sketches of Modern Persian Life and Character*, 229; Gordon, *Persia Revisited (1895)*, 1:194. A. V. W. Jackson, traveling in the early twentieth century, cites statistics compiled by Parsi representative Ardeshir Reporter of eight thousand Zoroastrians in Yazd out of a total Yazd population (including villages) of sixty thousand and only eleven thousand Zoroastrians in all of Iran. Jackson, *Persia, Past and Present: A Book of Travel and Research*. Napier Malcolm's belief that the population of Yazd consisted of thirty to forty thousand people and the surrounding villages constituting fifty to sixty thousand is in line with Reporter's data. His estimates of the Zoroastrian population are larger, citing fourteen hundred Zoroastrian "houses" in Yazd in 1905, which would bring the number up considerably. Malcolm, *Five Years*, 44. In midcentury there were some fifty Zoroastrian merchants in Tehran; this figure rose rapidly to nearly three hundred by 1892, according to the Parsi Amelioration Society figures cited in Janet Kestenberg Amighi, *The Zoroastrians of Iran: Conversion, Assimilation, or Persistence*, 147. These figures accord with the rise in population over the course of the nineteenth century.

44. Boyce, *Persian Stronghold*, 3–4.

45. See Amighi, *Zoroastrians of Iran*, 111; and Hataria, *Parsi Mission to Iran*.

46. Amighi, *Zoroastrians of Iran*, 86–87, quoting M. M. Murzban, *The Parsis of India, Being an Enlarged and Copiously Annotated, Up to Date English Edition of Mlle. Delphine Menant's "Les Parsis."*

47. Zoroastrians were not allowed to trade until 1860. Malcolm, *Five Years*, 45–49.

48. Maneckji Hataria stated in *Parsi Mission to Iran* that Zoroastrian religious clothing of the *sudreh* and *kusti* was also prohibited.

49. E. G. Browne, *A Year Amongst the Persians: Impressions as to the Life, Character, and Thought of the People of Persia Received During Twelve Months' Residence in That Country in the Year 1887–1888*, 2:370.

50. Ibid., 381.

51. Bassett, for instance, records that minorities were persecuted as a result of the opening of Christian missions. Bassett, *Land of the Imams*, 335. Most observers, however, note a general increase in tolerance of minorities, although a clear differentiation between the shah's capital and the provinces. See, for example, Wills, *Persia as It Is*, 229; Gordon, *Persia Revisited (1895)*, 80–81; and Malcolm, *Five Years*, 51.

52. See Michael Fischer, "Zoroastrian Iran: Between Myth and Praxis," 431; and Malcolm, *Five Years*, 49.

53. George N. Curzon, *Persia and the Persian Question*, vol. 2, pt. 2, 241–42. See also Ella Constance Sykes, *Persia and Its People*, 122.

54. Malcolm, *Five Years*, 50.

55. Browne and Eastwick both relate stories of forced conversion, as does Maneckji Hataria. See Browne, *Year Amongst the Persians*, 2:447–48; Edward Backhouse Eastwick, *Journal of a Diplomate's Three Years' Residence in Persia*, 1:230; and Hataria, *Parsi Mission to Iran*.

56. Browne, *Year Amongst the Persians*, pt. 2, 370–71.

57. Ibid.

58. In one such instance, Zoroastrians in Yazd appealed to Amir Kabir concerning a robbery, and he ordered the governor to have the lost property restored. Amighi, *Zoroastrians of Iran*, 90, citing R. Shahmardan, *Parasteshgah-e Zartoshtian*. Malcolm reports a series of similar incidents, which continued throughout the century, indicating the persistence of local and central contests of authority. Malcolm, *Five Years*, 47–55.

59. Curzon, *Persian Question*, pt. 2, 241.

60. Malcolm, *Five Years*, 54.

61. Ibid., 50.

62. Pars, or "Fars" as it is pronounced in post-Islamic Persian, is a province in Iran. It was the origin of the Greek appellation of "Persia" to Iran and the reason that Europeans continued to call the country "Persia" until Reza Shah officially changed the name to "Iran."

63. The *Qisseh-ye Sanjan* of 1599 was written by Behman Kaikobad Sanjana. It has convincingly been called "thoroughly fictitious" by M. S. Irani in "The Story of Sanjan: The History of Parsi Migration to India, a Critical Study." The *Qisseh-ye Zartushtian-e Hendustan* was written between 1765 and 1805 by Shapurji Maneckji Sanjana of Navsari. There is still much scholarly controversy surrounding the date and reason for the arrival of these Iranian Zoroastrians to India. For a

discussion of the various theories and a translation of the text, see Alan Williams, *The Zoroastrian Myth of Migration from Iran and Settlement in the Indian Diaspora: Text, Translation, and Analysis of the 16th Century "Qesse-ye Sanjan," "The Story of Sanjan."* See also Jesse S. Palsetia, *The Parsis of India: Preservation of Identity in Bombay City,* 3; and G. K. Nariman, "Was It Religious Persecution Which Compelled the Parsis to Migrate from Persia into India?" For a typical Zoroastrian account of the migration that relies on the *Qisseh-ye Sanjan,* see Framjee, *Parsees,* 7.

64. See Andre Wink, *Al-Hind: The Making of the Indo-Islamic World;* and Maneck's concurrence in *Death of Ahriman,* 15–25.

65. Over time, Gujarati split into two dialects, the one used by the Hindus and the one used by the Parsis. In the nineteenth century, the Hindus increasingly incorporated older Sanskritic terms, while the Parsis added English and Persian to their dialect of Gujarati, making them mutually almost unintelligible. Missionaries in India translated the Bible into *both* Gujarati dialects. See Rustomji Pestonji Karkaria, *India: Forty Years of Progress and Reform, Being a Sketch of the Life and Times of Behramji M. Malabari,* 55–57.

66. H. Yule, ed. and trans., *The Wonders of the East by Friar Jordanus,* 1:21, cited in Maneck, *Death of Ahriman,* 33.

67. Akbar also introduced a new calendar with Zoroastrian names for the months and days. For a comprehensive discussion of Iranian and Indian Zoroastrian influence on Akbar, see Jivanji Jamshedji Modi, "The Parsees at the Court of Akbar and Dastur Meherji Rana" and "Notes on Anquetil DuPerron on King Akbar and Dastur Meherji Rana." See also Sven S. Hartman, *Parsism: The Religion of Zoroaster,* 12–13.

68. An account of the life of this Parsi priest—Meherji Rana—was written by his descendant Dastur Erachji Sohrabji Meherji Rana, librarian at the Mulla Feroze Madressa, in 1881, titled *Mahyar Name.*

69. Maneck, *Death of Ahriman,* 39.

70. A list of the twenty-six major *rivayats* and the name of the Parsi letter carrier to Iran are found in Shahpurshah Hormasji Hodivala, *Studies in Parsi History,* 343–44. For the last *rivayat,* see Mario Vitalone, *The Persian "Revayat" "Ithoter": Zoroastrian Rituals in the Eighteenth Century.*

71. Maneck, *Death of Ahriman,* 36–37. See also Palsetia, *Parsis of India,* 23–24.

72. The sacred fire was relocated in 1492. Palsetia, *Parsis of India,* 23.

73. Maneck, *Death of Ahriman,* 38–39.

74. Ibid., 41. For the history of this and other subsequent *panchayats,* see J. G. Drummund, *Panchayats in India.*

75. Maneck, *Death of Ahriman,* 86, 92.

76. There are a number of theories as to why the Parsis ended up being the principal brokers between Indian and European trade companies. Scholars point to such reasons as the absence of caste-related inhibition to interaction with foreigners, their commercial niche, and the fact that as a minority it would be in their interest to cultivate outside connections as some of the most convincing explanations. On these theories, see ibid., 86–88; and Eckehard Kulke, *The Parsees in India: A Minority as Agent of Social Change.*

77. This estimate was by Dutch sea captain J. S. Stavorinus and published in his travel account, *Voyages to the East Indies,* 2:494, as cited in Maneck, *Death of Ahriman,* 91.

78. The British moved their headquarters to Bombay in 1687. According to the 1780 census of Bombay taken by the Bombay Grain Committee, Parsis made up 3,087 of the total population of 33,444. See Palsetia, *Parsis of India,* 51.

79. Maneck, *Death of Ahriman,* 162, citing a certain British Lieutenant Moore.

80. Ibid.

81. The Parsis were not alone. Religious reform movements with similar characteristics arose among other religious communities as well. See J. N. Farquhar, *Modern Religious Movements in India;* and Kenneth W. Jones, *Socio-religious Reform Movements in British India,* 138–50. See also Christine Dobbin, *Urban Leadership in Western India: Politics and Communities in Bombay City, 1840–1885;* and Manilal C. Parekh, *The Brahma Samaj: A Short History.*

1. Bombay and Murmurs of Reform: Religion as "Civilization" and "Progress"

1. As pointed out by Dobbin, Bombay had always been an important port on the western littoral of India. However, trade had been interrupted by domestic turmoil and was gradually revived in the eighteenth century under British influence. Dobbin, *Urban Leadership in Western India,* 1.

2. John R. Hinnells, "Parsis and the British," 5.

3. Great Britain attempted to acquire Bombay from the Portuguese as early as 1626, but it was not until the marriage of British Charles II and Portuguese Catherine of Braganza in 1662 that Britain received Bombay as part of Catherine's dowry. Bombay was subsequently transferred to the British East India Company in 1668.

4. According to Hinnells, sea piracy and ongoing influence of the Portuguese on the mainland hindered immigration to Bombay until the 1730s. Ibid., 8.

5. This insight is from ibid.

6. M. D. David, *History of Bombay, 1661–1708* (Bombay, 1973), as cited in ibid., 6–7.

7. Dobbin, *Urban Leadership,* 1.

8. "[A person] unobservant of that decency which enlightened people shew [sic] to the religious ceremonies of the Natives of India, had lately entered one of the repositories for their dead . . . [and consequently, in order to dissuade anyone else from doing this], whoever shall obtrude themselves on the temples, Tombs or Government, will be suspended from the Honourable Company's service." Signed by William Page, Secretary, February 29, 1792, as cited in Hinnells, "Parsis and the British," 6.

9. Ibid., 16.

10. *A Narrative of the Operations of Captain Little's Detachment,* 379–83, as cited in ibid., 11–12.

11. Their popularity with the British was also owing to the fact that the Parsis were very careful not to compete directly with British commercial interests. Since the East India Company dominated European trade with India, Parsi firms concentrated on trade eastward, particularly the opium trade with China. When they did engage in British commercial enterprises, it was typically

as suppliers, middlemen, and landlords. See Hinnells, "Parsis and British," 9. By 1805 Parsis owned more firms (eighteen) in the city than did any other community, including Hindus (fifteen) and Europeans (nine). See ibid., 13–14.

12. "Minute on Indian Education" (1835), quoted in *Speeches by Lord Macaulay*, edited by G. M. Young (Oxford, 1935), 359, as cited in Kulke, *Parsees in India*, 82.

13. Framjee, *Parsees*, 151–52. By the mid-nineteenth century, the number of Parsis in India was approximately 111,000. This number is high in comparison with other accounts that estimate the Parsi population of 1833 at 20,184 out of a total population of 234,032. See George Smith, *The Life of John Wilson*, 49, quoting an official census.

14. Maneck, *Death of Ahriman*, 163. On legal changes in the Parsi community, see Palsetia, *Parsis of India*, 197–276.

15. These five initial members were Banaji Limji, the three sons of Ruseam Manock, and Jamsetjee Jeejeebhoy Modi. See Maneck, *Death of Ahriman*, 163. Kulke, *Parsees in India*, 61, gives the date for the establishment of the Panchayat as 1728. According to Palsetia, the first *panchayat* was established by the Parsis of Navsari in 1642, and the first official Parsi *panchayat* of Bombay was established sometime between 1725 and 1733. Palsetia, *Parsis of India*, 26, 69.

16. For the history of the Bombay Panchayat, see Kulke, *Parsees in India*, 62–63; and Palsetia, *Parsis of India*, 63–90.

17. The British officially recognized the Panchayat of Bombay as the internal government of the Parsis in Bombay in 1787. See Palsetia, *Parsis of India*, 26.

18. Kulke, *Parsees in India*, 63, quoted from *Parsee Prakash*, 1:56.

19. For a complete list of punishment options, see Kulke, *Parsees in India*, 63.

20. The Report of the British Commission is reproduced in Sohrab Davar, *The History of the Parsi Punchayet of Bombay*, 9–13. For other explanations of the report, see Maneck, *Death of Ahriman*, 165–67; and Palsetia, *Parsis of India*, 70–73.

21. Report of the British Commission cited in Maneck, *Death of Ahriman*, 165–67.

22. Kulke, *Parsees in India*, 65.

23. On the 1796 Panchayat ruling, see Maneck, *Death of Ahriman*, 167.

24. Ibid., 168.

25. Letter from an unnamed British official to the Commissioners for the Affairs of India, April 30, 1832, in Davar, *History of the Parsi Punchayet*, 60–61.

26. Maneck, *Death of Ahriman*, 172.

27. Ibid., 175.

28. The Parsi Benevolent Institution established by Sir Jamsetjee Jeejeebhoy in 1849 merged with the Panchayat in 1851.

29. Kulke, *Parsees in India*, 61.

30. *Indian Spectator*, December 30, 1894, quoted in ibid., 77.

31. Some scholars have suggested that Parsis had less caste requirements that prevented them from mixing with non-Parsis than Hindus or Muslims. Typically, this explanation is given for Parsi exceptionalism and openness to European practices. There is evidence, however, that rather than

not having barriers to socializing with Europeans, these barriers were, with encouragement and incentives, crossed by the Parsis. This fact leads me to privilege the theory that Parsi attitudes and sensibilities *changed* and to seek to account for it.

32. The society became the Public Board of Education in 1840. See Smith, *Life of John Wilson*, 32–33, for the history of this society.

33. Bombay Education Society Reports, 1:4, cited in Maneck, *Death of Ahriman*, 183–84.

34. Smith, *Life of John Wilson*, 143–44.

35. Lynn Zastoupil, "India, J. S. Mill, and 'Western' Culture," 115–16.

36. Maneck, *Death of Ahriman*, 184.

37. Framjee gives the date of establishment of the institution as 1855 in *Parsees*, 194. Palsetia suggests a date of 1849 in *Parsis of India*, 122.

38. Maneck, *Death of Ahriman*, 185.

39. Palsetia, *Parsis of India*, 131.

40. See D. C. Jessawalla, *The Story of My Life*, esp. 103–4.

41. The Anglicists included James Mill, author of the multivolume *The History of British India*. His even more renowned son, J. S. Mill, while initially agreeing with his father, gradually moved into the Orientalist camp after his father's death. J. S. Mill served in the India Office of the East India Company from 1823 to 1858. On the Mills and their educational policies, see Martin I. Moir, Douglas M. Peers, and Lynn Zastoupil, eds., *J. S. Mill's Encounter with India*.

42. James Mill, an Anglicist, argued against the "evils of aristocratic and priestly influence in Europe and India." See Zastoupil, "India, J. S. Mill, and 'Western' Culture," 112.

43. Penelope Carson, "Golden Casket or Pebbles and Trash? J. S. Mill and the Anglicist/Orientalist Controversy," 151.

44. Ibid., 154.

45. Maneck, *Death of Ahriman*, 185.

46. Carson, "Golden Casket or Pebbles and Trash?," 153.

47. Rev. James Gray, *Life in Bombay and the Neighboring Out-Stations*, 233–34.

48. Ibid., 237–38.

49. Ibid., 239.

50. Wilson to Rev. G. White in 1835, reprinted in Smith, *Life of John Wilson*, 152–53.

51. Max Müller cited in Murzban, *Parsis in India*, 1:344.

52. Ibid., 2:330.

53. Henry George Briggs, *The Parsis; or, Modern Zerdusthians: A Sketch*, 18–19.

54. Dinshaw Edulji Wacha, *Shells from the Sands of Bombay: Being My Recollections and Reminiscences, 1860–1875*, 694–95.

55. Henry Moses, *Sketches of India: With Notes on the Seasons, Scenery, and Society of Bombay, Elephanta, and Salsette*, 254. The first Parsi to attend a British school frequently alludes to the adoption of new forms of sociability along English lines as a result of her British education. See Jessawalla, *My Life*.

56. See excerpts from John Wilson's memoirs quoted in Smith, *Life of John Wilson*, 44, 57, 122, 259.

57. Palsetia, *Parsis of India*, 138.

58. Framjee, *Parsees*, 197.

59. Ibid., 204. After one year of volunteer teachers from the society, the wealthy Cama family donated the money to hire teachers and provide more suitable buildings.

60. Kulke, *Parsees in India*, 84–85. The first Indian girl, a Parsi, to attend a British school was D. C. Jessawalla, whose mother sent her to Mrs. Ward's school in 1842. See Jessawalla, *My Life*.

61. M. J., *The Parsis and Their Religion*, 1.

62. Quoted in Framjee, *Parsees*, 204.

63. Extract from Professor Sinclair's address to the governor, cited in ibid., 208.

64. Ibid., 212–13 (emphasis added).

65. Ibid., 216–17.

66. Framji Bomajii, *Lights and Shades of the East*, 94, as cited in Kulke, *Parsis in India*, 105.

67. Wacha, *Shells from the Sands of Bombay*, 684–85.

68. *Cricket Chat* (1887), as cited in M. E. Pavri, *Parsi Cricket, with Hints on Bowling, Batting, Fielding, Captaincy, Explanation of Laws of Cricket, &*, 8–9.

69. On the phenomenon of Parsi elites adopting British yardsticks of "culture" and "civilization" and the dilemma doing so placed them in as ultimately unable to become fully British, see T. M. Luhrmann, *The Good Parsi: The Fate of a Colonial Elite in a Postcolonial Society*.

70. Briggs, *Parsis*, 27.

2. The Protestant Challenge to Zoroastrianism

1. Hinnells, "Parsis and the British," 2.

2. *A Voyage to East India &tc.* (London, 1625, reprinted 1655), 336ff, quoted in ibid., 23.

3. *A Display of Two Forraigne Sects in the East Indies, the Sect of the Banians, the Ancient Natives of India, and the Sect of the Persees, the Ancient Inhabitants of Persia* (London, 1630), chap. 8, as cited in ibid., 24. Lord was chaplain at Surat in 1630.

4. Hyde was rumored to have believed in Zoroastrianism. Sir William Erskine, in a "letter to Sir John Malcolm," noted that Hyde "apparently was more than half a believer." See Erskine, "On the Sacred Books and Religion of the Parsis," 2:319. Apparently, it was Rev. John Wilson who believed Hyde to be "nearly as much a Zoroastrian as a Christian." J. Duchesne-Guillemin repeats this rumor in *The Western Response to Zoroaster*, 9. I am grateful to Hinnells for pointing out this rumor and for the sources. See Hinnells, "Parsis and the British," 29.

5. See Duchesne-Guillemin, *Western Response*, 10–11.

6. Anquetil Du Perron studied Zand and Pahlavi with Dastur Darab. He reportedly collected more than 180 manuscripts. See Smith, *Life of John Wilson*, 125. His translations of the Avesta were first published in 1770.

7. Voltaire, Diderot, Goethe, Byron, and Wordsworth, among others, saw in Zoroastrianism a "model of a natural, reasonable religion, later corrupted by priestly fanaticism." See Duchesne-Guillemin, *Western Response,* 14–15.

8. Linguistic origins and family relationships inaugurated the use of language as a tool for interpreting religious history. See ibid., 19–20.

9. Erskine, in dialogue with Hyde and Malcolm, opined that "there are no good grounds for ascribing the *Zend-Avesta* to Zoroaster. Erskine, "Sacred Books," 302. John Wilson would also insist on the later provenance of the Avesta, a position that subsequently became standard in academic and Zoroastrian circles.

10. *A Voyage to the East Indies* (London, 1750), 1:340, as quoted in Hinnells, "Parsis and the British," 29.

11. Quoted in ibid., 33.

12. Erskine, "Sacred Books," 295–341.

13. Ibid., 319.

14. Ibid., 325.

15. Ibid.

16. Ibid., 335.

17. Ibid., 327, 335.

18. Ibid., 334–35.

19. Ibid., 331.

20. Ibid., 336.

21. According Philip Stern, the change in policy was partly owing to a change toward a more Anglicizing form of governing that was supported by evangelicals and also partly owing to an erosion of the East India Company's monopoly on trade and government in India. Private communication with Philip Stern, summer 2008. See also Penelope Carson, "An Imperial Dilemma."

22. The Americans were the first Protestant missionaries to work in India. The London Missionary Society began work in 1815, and in 1820 and 1822, respectively, the (British) Church Missionary Society and the Scottish Missionary Society began operations. See Smith, *Life of John Wilson,* 35. Smith attributes the continued official anxiety about "offending the Brahmins" as an obstacle in the way of missionary activity.

23. One of the most vehement of the British government's critics on this issue was John Wilson. He, however, did admit that the government did not prevent missionary activity or the promotion of Christianity by government officials in their private capacities. Wilson hoped, however, that the government would actively support Christianity and conversion away from "false religions." See ibid., 283, 353. See in particular Wilson's sermon "The British Sovereignty in India," delivered on November 8, 1835. On the changes in governing approaches to India between the East India Company and the British government, see also Palsetia's history of legal reforms in *Parsis of India,* 197–276.

24. Smith, *Life of John Wilson,* 60–61. This particular battle concerned the conversion controversy, considered below, although it is indicative of Wilson's overall sense of purpose in the larger mission of proselytization.

25. On Wilson's dialogues with the Parsis, see Susan Stiles Maneck, "The Presbyterian and the Parsis."

26. Wilson received ample recognition of his scholarship in his lifetime. He was elected president of the Bombay branch of the Royal Asiatic Society in 1835, served as secretary to the different translation committees of the Bombay Bible Society for twelve years, and in 1836 was awarded an honorary diploma from the University of Edinburg. See Smith, *Life of John Wilson*, 121, 181, 220. He was also involved in the establishment of the University of Bombay and became vice chancellor in 1868. See M. D. David, *John Wilson and His Institution*, 40.

27. Smith, *Life of John Wilson*, 60.

28. Ibid., 196.

29. For some correspondence between Wilson and Livingstone, see ibid., 329–30.

30. Maneck, *Death of Ahriman*, 185. The Bombay and other stations of the Scottish Free Church founded by Wilson had reportedly accepted 1,071 converts by 1877 and taught 2,877 students in as many as fifty-six schools. Smith, *Life of John Wilson*, 350.

31. Wilson, *The Parsi Religion*, 265.

32. Ibid., 180.

33. Ibid., 7.

34. Ibid., 64.

35. Ibid., 65.

36. Ibid., 106.

37. John Wilson, *Oriental Christian Spectator* 2, no. 7 (1831): 235–36.

38. Smith, *Life of John Wilson*, 5.

39. John Wilson, "Correspondence with the Parsis of Bombay," *Oriental Christian Spectator* (July–Aug. 1831): 331–35.

40. Ibid., 331.

41. *Oriental Christian Spectator* (July–Aug. 1831): 386, 426.

42. *Oriental Christian Spectator* (July–Aug. 1831): 387.

43. See, for example, the minutes of the World's Parliament of Religions in John Henry Barrows, ed., *The World's Parliament of Religions*.

44. John Wilson, *The British Sovereignty in India: A Sermon Preached in St. Andrew's Church, Bombay, Delivered on Behalf of the Bombay Auxiliary Scottish Missionary Society in St. Andrews Church on Sunday, 8 November 1835*, 198–99, 207–8.

45. John Wilson, *The Star of Bethlehem and the Magi from the East: A Sermon Preached on the Occasion of the Baptism of a Parsi Youth, August 31, 1856*, 35.

46. Despite differences of opinion, Haug was also a friend of Wilson's. Wilson visited Haug in Germany, where he was treated to a "right good German supper." See Smith, *Life of John Wilson*, 344–45.

47. Haug, *Essays on the Parsis*, 300–301.

48. Ibid., 302.

49. Ibid., 302, 311–13.

50. Ibid., 303.

51. According to Wilson, there was another instance of a Parsi boy who announced his intention to convert but recanted in a letter dated April 1, 1848. Wilson, commenting on this case, wrote in a letter, "That promising neophyte has, I am most sorry to mention, made shipwreck, for the present at least, of his Christian profession, and returned to the bosom of his caste. This he has done under powerful influences and temptations, arising from Parsees, Hindoos, and Muhammadans confederated together." Letter to Mir Tweedie, convener of the Foreign Mission Committee in Edinburgh, quoted in Smith, *Life of John Wilson*, 243–44. It is noteworthy that issues of conversion elicited cooperation among Indian religious communities.

52. Wilson claimed that this person was not, in fact, the first Parsi to desire to convert. He does not provide the name or circumstances of the first mentioned individual. See Smith, *Life of John Wilson*, 134. For another account of the conversion incident, see the autobiography of Dhanjibhai Nauroji, *From Zoroaster to Christ: An Autobiographical Sketch of the Rev. Dhanjibhai Nauroji, the First Modern Convert to Christianity from the Zoroastrian Religion.*

53. Dhanjibhai Nauroji as quoted in Wilson, *The Parsi Religion*, 85. The same account appears in testimony before the Supreme Court of Judicature at Bombay on May 3, 1839. The Vendidad text mentioned here by Nauroji was the subject of an attack on its origin and authenticity by Wilson and later generally accepted as not dating from the time of Zoroaster.

54. Nauroji, *From Zoroaster to Christ*, 20–21.

55. John Wilson, "Conversion of Two Parsis and Prosecution of the Rev. John Wilson, D.D., on a Writ of Habeas Corpus, Before the Supreme Court of Judicature of Bombay."

56. The only information on this boy is his first name. According to Nauroji, he came to study at Wilson's school in 1835. He was kidnapped and held in Navsari to prevent his conversion. Although he was eventually brought back to Bombay, he died shortly thereafter. Nauroji, *From Zoroaster to Christ*, 43, 61–63.

57. The court testimony differs somewhat from Nauroji's later autobiography where he mentions that it was *on the occasion of his baptism* that he removed his *kusti* (sacred knotted rope belt). See ibid., 48.

58. This incident is not recorded in other sources. See ibid., 56.

59. Ibid., 65; Palsetia, *Parsis of India*, 120, 126–27, 84–85.

60. See Wilson's account of the events surrounding the "anti-conversion memorial" in *The Parsi Religion*, 85.

61. Maneck, *Death of Ahriman*, 199.

62. The letter was signed by Behramji Kersasji, Darasha Rattonji, Bhikaji Ardaserji, and Nassarwanji Barjorji. The letter is reprinted in *Star of Bethlehem*, 5–6 (emphasis in the original).

63. For this account, see ibid., 9–12.

64. "The Personal Statement of Behramji Kersasji," in ibid., 70–72.

65. Ibid.

66. On the phenomena of conversion to Christianity in India, see Van der Veer, *Conversion to Modernities*. On religious belief as individual consciousness, rather than political identification, see

Peter van Rooden, "Nineteenth-Century Representations of Missionary Conversion and the Transformation of Western Christianity," in ibid., 65–87.

67. Jeejeebhoy is named as the sponsor of the tract in Smith, *Life of John Wilson*, 131.

68. For a discussion of this book, see Maneck, *Death of Ahriman*, 205–10. Her reading and citations are from what she deems a "poor" English translation by T. R. Sethna, published in Bombay in 1970.

69. One of these youths, Dhanjibhai Nauroji, is discussed above. The other was named Hormusji Pestonji and converted at the same time as Nauroji. See John Wilson, *The Doctrine of Jehovah Addressed to the Parsis: A Sermon Preached on the Occasion of the Baptism of Two Youths of That Tribe.*

70. Dosabhoy Sohrabji, *Talim-i Zurtoosht on Vundidad*, cited in Maneck, *Death of Ahriman*, 205.

71. Ibid.

72. These conclusions are Maneck's on the basis of her reading of the text. See ibid.

73. Ibid., 215.

74. Pestonji was editor of the journal *Jam-i Jamshid*. On this text, I am relying on Maneck's discussion in ibid., 211–14.

75. Maneckji Pestonji, *Rahnuma-i Zartusht* [The Way/Guide of Zoroastrians] (Jan. 1843), quoted in ibid., 213–14.

76. Maneckji Pestonji, *Discussion of Christian Religion as Contained in the Bible and Propounded by Christian Clergymen*. For this quotation and others from this text, I am using citations in Maneck, *Death of Ahriman*, 219–20 (emphasis in the original).

77. Maneckji, *Discussion of Christian Religion*, cited in Maneck, *Death of Ahriman*, 219–20.

78. Sohrabji, *Talim*, cited in ibid., 206.

79. These unusual events were recorded in the *Bombay Telegraph and Carrier* and later reprinted in the *Oriental Christian Spectator*. I am relying on Maneck's account in ibid., 225–27.

80. At Behramji's urging, Maneckji agreed to return home and read the earlier refutation of Christian superiority, *Talim-i Zurtoosht on Vundidad*, written in 1840 by Dosabhoy Sohrabji, as discussed above.

81. This account of Maneckji's rationale for converting is reprinted in the *Oriental Christian Spectator* 19 (Mar. 1848) and quoted in Maneck, *Death of Ahriman*, 225.

82. Behramji as cited in the *Oriental Christian Spectator* 19 (Mar. 1848) and quoted in Maneck, *Death of Ahriman*, 226.

83. Maneckji as cited in the *Oriental Christian Spectator* 19 (Mar. 1848) and quoted in Maneck, *Death of Ahriman*, 227.

84. The *Bundahishn* ("The Founding" or "The Creation") is a cosmological and eschatological text that purports to reproduce an earlier, now lost, Avestan text.

85. "Dispute with Parsis," *Oriental Christian Spectator*, 418–22, signed Goosequill, Sept. 20, 1831.

86. Ibid., 385.

87. Ibid., 384–85.

88. N. J. Girardot, "Max Müller's *Sacred Books* and the Nineteenth-Century Production of the Comparative Science of Religions," *History of Religions* 41, no. 3 (2002): 213–50.

3. The Parsi Response: Rational Religion and the Rethinking of Tradition

1. Davar, *History of the Parsi Punchayet,* 32–38. See also Kulke, *Parsees in India,* 93.

2. Sati was "the most definite sign of Hindu depravity and Christian moral superiority," in the eyes of British evangelicals opposed to this practice. Rammohan Roy, founder of the Hindu reform movement the Brahmo Samaj, was also a staunch opponent and wrote much on the subject. See Van der Veer, *Imperial Encounters,* esp. 43–44. See also Parekh, *Brahma Samaj.*

3. For an early reformist view on the dissolution of the Parsi priesthood, see Framjee, *Parsees,* 277–78.

4. For an outline of this emerging controversy, see Kulke, *Parsis in India,* 96–98.

5. Framjee, *Parsees,* 279.

6. Kulke, *Parsis in India,* 99.

7. Such prominent priests included Dastur Peshotan Sanjana, J. J. Modi, G. K. Nariman, S. K. Hodivala, M. N. Dhalla, S. Bharucha, and T. Anklesaria. See Kulke, *Parsis in India,* 96.

8. Framjee also wrote under the name D. F. Karaka.

9. Framjee, *Parsees,* 251.

10. Ibid., 250, 266. Deism is the belief, based solely on reason, in a God who created the universe and then abandoned it, assuming no control over life, exerting no influence on natural phenomena, and giving no supernatural revelation. *The American Heritage Dictionary,* s.v. "deism."

11. Framjee, *Parsees,* 260–61.

12. Ibid., 274.

13. Ibid., 283.

14. Ibid., 281–82.

15. Ibid., 283–84.

16. Ibid., 286.

17. Ervad Sheriarji Dadabhai Bharucha, *A Brief Sketch of the Zoroastrian Religion and Customs: An Essay Written for the Rahnumai Mazdayasnan Sabha;* S. A. Kapadia, *The Teachings of Zoroaster and the Philosophy of the Parsi Religion.*

18. Bahmanji Framji Billimoria, *A Warning Word to Parsees.*

19. Ibid., 3.

20. Ibid., 4.

21. Ibid., 5.

22. Ibid., 3.

23. Ibid., 5.

24. Ibid., 2.

25. Ibid., 11.

26. Ibid., 15.

27. Ibid., 16.

28. Ibid., 17.

29. Ibid.

30. Ibid., 20.

31. Ibid., 21.

32. Ibid.

33. According to John Hinnells, Barucha's paper was accepted for the conference, but he did not attend, and it was not read in his absence. Private correspondence.

34. Bharucha, *Brief Sketch*, 6.

35. Ibid., 13, 11. Theism is the belief in the existence of a god or gods, especially belief in a personal God as creator and ruler of the world. *American Heritage Dictionary*, s.v. "theism."

36. Bharucha, *Brief Sketch*, 15.

37. Ibid., 34.

38. Ibid., 23–29. Loyalty to the Crown was particularly valued by the British as a desirable quality among their Indian subjects following the Mutiny of 1857–58. See Bernard S. Cohn, "Representing Authority in Victorian India," 167.

39. Bharucha, *Brief Sketch*, 38, 43, 46–47.

40. Although Zoroastrian reformers blamed "backward" practices as the adoption of Hindu customs, Hindu reformers, too, at this time sought to eliminate them as inauthentic. See Kenneth W. Jones, *Socio-religious Reform Movements*.

41. Kapadia, *Teachings of Zoroaster*, 17–18.

42. Ibid., 18–19.

43. Ibid., 49–50.

44. Ibid., 50.

45. Dastur Erachji Sohrabji Dastur Meherjirana, *Rehbar-e Din-e Zarthushti*, reprinted as Dastur Firoze M. Kotwal, *A Guide to the Zoroastrian Religion: A Nineteenth Century Catechism with Modern Commentary*. Erachji later wrote a similar catechism in Persian for the sake of Iranian Zoroastrians.

46. Ibid., 1.

47. Ibid., 12, 21, 37.

48. Ibid., 22, 23, 27.

49. Ibid., 52, 53.

50. Ibid., 181. See also the introduction to the text, xvii, xx, xix.

51. Ibid., 3.

52. Kotwal and Boyd's introduction to ibid., xxvii.

53. Ibid., xxxii.

54. Framjee intimates that he was present at the time of the lecture, but he may also have read accounts of it that were printed subsequently. See Framjee, *Parsees*, 217–18.

4. Western Religious Studies Scholarship: Historicism and Evolutionism

1. No fewer than two representatives of the Hindu reform movement, the Bramho Samaj, were invited to participate in the World's Parliament of Religions in Chicago in 1893. Protap Chunder Mozoomdar, "The Principles of the Brahmo-Somaj," 1:428–33; B. Nagarkar, "The Spiritual Ideas of the Brahmo-Somaj," 1:435–40.

2. Müller dedicated his *Sacred Books of the East* to the Very Reverend H. G. Liddell, dean of Christ Church, in addition to the Marquis of Salisbury (chancellor of Oxford and formerly secretary of state for India), and Sir Henry J. S. Maine (member of the Council of India). A. C. De Vooys described Müller as "at heart a believer" and a pietistic and "sentimental Lutheran" who "identified with the classy social and intellectual pretensions of Oxonian Broad Church Anglicanism." Quoted in Girardot, "Max Müller's *Sacred Books*," 219n12.

3. As pointed out by Girardot, Müller's greatness was in large part a function of his ability to popularize his ideas and reach out to the general public; he was "in many ways the first 'celebrity' academician." *Vanity Fair* even featured him in their "Men of the Day" of 1875 and noted that he was "known to the Many." See ibid., 214–15.

4. Max Müller, "Lectures on the Science of Religion" (1870), as quoted in Jon R. Stone, *The Essential Max Müller: On Language, Mythology, and Religion*, 113.

5. Ibid.

6. Max Müller, "Biographies of Words and the Home of the Aryas" (1888), as quoted in ibid., 6.

7. Max Müller, *My Autobiography: A Fragment* (1901), quoted in ibid., 11.

8. Max F. Müller, ed., *Sacred Books of the East*, 1:ix.

9. Müller, *My Autobiography: A Fragment* (1901), as quoted in Stone, *Max Müller*, 11.

10. Albert Réville, *Prolegomena of the History of Religions*, 8.

11. Ibid., 10.

12. Ibid., 25.

13. Albert Réville, *Histoire des réligions*, 1:v.

14. Réville, *Prolegomena*, 95, 204–6.

15. Ibid., 166.

16. Ibid., 185.

17. Ibid., 222–23.

18. See the excellent discussion of this connection in Girardot, "Max Müller's *Sacred Books*," 213–50.

19. Ibid., 218.

20. In keeping with the British project of educating, civilizing, and consequently revising Indian religious practice, the Prince of Wales took several copies of *Sacred Books of the East* with him to India as presents for Indian rajas. See Van der Veer, *Imperial Encounters*, 112.

21. According to Van der Veer, Müller believed that "religious reform movements in Hinduism were the most enduring result of the missionary efforts in India." Although Müller never traveled to India, he met Dwarkanath Tagore, father of Debendranath Tagor, who was a leader of the Hindu

reform movement Brahmo Samaj. Müller preferred the Brahmo Samaj over another reform movement, the Arya Samaj, since it was closer to his own rational religion. See ibid., 110, 114, 117.

22. Ibid., 117.

23. Oberlin College archives, biography of John Henry Barrows. Barrows resigned from the First Presbyterian Church in Chicago in order to travel on his lecture tour in India and Japan. Upon his return, he assumed the position of president of Oberlin College.

24. Richard Hughes Seager, *The World's Parliament of Religions: The East/West Encounter, Chicago, 1893*, xvii.

25. Ibid., xxi.

26. See the introduction in Eric J. Ziolkowski, ed., *A Museum of Faiths: Histories and Legacies of the 1893 World's Parliament of Religions*.

27. John Henry Barrows, *Christianity, the World-Religion*, 311–12.

28. Merwin-Marie Snell, "Service of the Science of Religions to the Cause of Religious Unity," 71.

29. Professor Thayer is quoted in Barrows, *Christianity*, 306.

30. His name, however, was misrecorded as *Jinanji* Jamshedji Modi in the congress proceedings.

31. Jinanji Jamshedji Modi, "Belief and Ceremonies of the Followers of Zoroaster," paper presented at the World's Parliament of Religions and included in Barrows, *Parliament of Religions*, 452–65.

32. Barrows, *Christianity*.

33. Ibid., 96.

34. Ibid., 93–94.

35. Ibid., 75–76.

36. Ibid., 26.

37. The English version of the lectures appeared as *The Teaching of Zarathushtra: Eight Lectures and Addresses Delivered to Parsis in Bombay* (Bombay: Captain Printing Works, 1917). The Gujarati version was translated by Jehangir K. Daji, an orthodox Parsi. See Moulton, *Treasure of the Magi*, 220.

38. Moulton, *Treasure of the Magi*, 224–25.

39. Ibid., 9.

40. Ibid., 36.

41. Ibid., 40.

42. Ibid., 48, 15.

43. Ibid., 9.

44. Ibid., 60.

45. Ibid., 64.

46. Ibid., 60.

47. Ibid., 65.

48. Ibid., 221.

49. Moulton, *Teaching of Zarathushtra*, 57.

50. Ibid., 59–60.

51. Moulton, *Treasure of the Magi*, 238.

52. Ibid., 109–10.

53. Ibid., 108.

54. Ibid., 225.

55. Ibid., 141.

56. Ibid., 175.

57. Ibid., 61.

58. Ibid., 227.

59. Ibid., 2–3.

60. Ibid., 11.

61. Ibid., 232.

62. Ibid., 195, 200–202.

63. Ibid., 199.

64. Ibid., 212.

65. The most famous of his Parsi students was Maneckji Nusserwanji Dhalla, a leading Reformist and high priest of the Zoroastrian community in Karachi. Another of his students, Leo J. Frachtenberg, was a specialist in the anthropological analysis of superstitions as historical clues to "our pre-historical, savage ancestors" in the method of E. B. Tylor, J. G. Frazer, and J. J. Modi. See Leo J. Frachtenberg, "Allusions to Witchcraft and Other Primitive Beliefs in the Zoroastrian Literature," 399–453.

66. On Jackson's biography, see Louis H. Gray, "A. V. Williams Jackson in Memoriam."

67. Ibid.

68. A. V. W. Jackson, *Zoroastrian Studies: The Iranian Religion and Various Monographs*, 3–4.

69. Ibid., 8.

70. Ibid., 140.

71. Ibid., 183.

72. Ibid., 139.

73. Ibid., 137.

74. Ibid., 20.

75. Ibid., 141.

76. Ibid., 186.

77. Ibid., 30.

78. His history of Zoroaster, for example, evinces very little historicism and is in fact a compendium of all textual references, rather than an attempt at excavating Zoroaster's "true" message. See A. V. W. Jackson, *Zoroaster, the Prophet of Ancient Iran*. His travelogue is also a record of information, without the attempt to evaluate or distill that is so typical of many of his predecessors. See Jackson, *Persia, Past and Present*.

79. Jackson, *Zoroastrian Studies*, for example, 3–4, 6–7, 13–14, 41, 141, 173.

5. Parsi Religious Reform in the Second Generation:
The Recovery of "True" Religion

1. *The Dastur Hoshang Memorial Volume: Being Papers on Iranian Subjects Written by Various Scholars in Honour of the Late Shams ul-Ulama Sardar Dastur Hoshang Jamasp, M.A., Ph.d., C.I.E.*, xi.

2. Dhanjishah Meherjibhai Madan, *Revelation Considered as a Source of Religious Knowledge*. First presented to the "Convention of Religions in India," held in April 1909.

3. Ibid., 4.

4. Ibid., 6.

5. Ibid., 13.

6. Ibid., 7.

7. Ibid., 4, 8.

8. Ibid., 7 (emphasis added).

9. Ibid., 16.

10. Ibid., 17.

11. Modi frequently collaborated with Western colleagues on books and served as the Parsi representative to the World's Parliament of Religions in 1893.

12. Jivanji Jamshedji Modi, *A Catechism of the Zoroastrian Religion*. This was an English translation of the original Gujarati version published in 1907 under the auspices of the Society for the Promotion of Zoroastrian Religious Education and Knowledge. According to Modi, this one was the first Zoroastrian catechism to appear in English.

13. Jivanji Jamshedji Modi, *Moral Extracts from Zoroastrian Books for the Use of Teachers in Schools*. The quote is from the introduction, xiii, written by R. E. Enthoven.

14. Modi, *Catechism*, 7–8.

15. Ibid., 5.

16. Ibid., 1.

17. Modi, *Moral Extracts*, 36.

18. Modi, *Catechism*, 46.

19. Ibid., 14.

20. Ibid., 18.

21. Modi, *Moral Extracts*, 6.

22. Modi, *Catechism*, 15.

23. Modi, *Moral Extracts*, 43.

24. Ibid., 22.

25. Modi, *Catechism*, 32.

26. Modi, *Moral Extracts*, 25–27.

27. Modi, *Catechism*, 25.

28. Modi, *Moral Extracts*, 9, 44, citing the Denkard, 1:54–55, translated by Dastur Dr. Peshotan.

29. Modi, *Catechism*, 1.

30. Ibid., 23.

31. Ibid., 37.

32. Ibid., 23.

33. Ibid., 27.

34. Ibid., 36.

35. Rastamji Edulji Dastoor Peshotan Sanjana, *The Parsi Book of Books: The Zend-Avesta*, 113.

36. Ibid.

37. Ibid., 122.

38. Ibid., 121.

39. Ibid., 108.

40. Ibid., 117.

41. Ibid., 118.

42. Ibid., 82.

43. Ibid., 109.

44. Ibid., 112.

45. Ibid., 113.

46. Ibid., 116.

47. Ibid., 114.

48. Ibid., 115 (emphasis added).

49. Ibid., 39.

50. Ibid., 5.

51. Ibid., 66.

52. Ibid., 18.

53. Ibid., 67.

54. Ibid.

55. Ibid., 87.

56. Ibid.

57. Ibid., 92.

58. Ibid., 121.

59. Rastamji Edulji Dastoor Peshotan Sanjana, *Zarathushtra and Zarathushtrianism in the Avesta*, 115.

60. Ibid., 191.

61. Ibid., 196–97.

62. In his discussion of the purpose of prayer, Sanjana cites Driscoll, Tennyson, Emerson, and Jeremy Taylor on the value of prayer in spurring greater spirituality. See ibid., 196–97.

63. Ibid., 221.

64. Ibid., 237 (emphasis added).

65. Ibid.

66. Ibid., 139.

67. Sanjana, *Book of Books,* 93.

68. Sanjana, *Zarathushtra,* 260.

69. Sanjana, *Book of Books,* 18.

70. Ibid.

71. Ibid., 23.

72. Miss B. A. Engineer, "Advancement of Religion."

73. Ibid., 5.

74. Ibid., 10.

75. Ibid., 11.

76. Ibid., 14.

77. Ibid., 15.

78. Maneckji Nusservanji Dhalla, *Dastur Dhalla: The Saga of a Soul, an Autobiography of Shams ul-Ulama Dastur Dr. Maneckji Nusserwanji Dhalla,* 158.

79. Maneckji Nusservanji Dhalla, *The History of Zoroastrianism.* See the chapter titled "Introduction of the Western Method of Iranian Scholarship in India," esp. 486–88.

80. Dhalla, *Dastur Dhalla,* 157.

81. Ibid., 197.

82. Dhalla, *Zoroastrianism,* xxxi–xxxii.

83. Ibid., 19.

84. Ibid., 14–15.

85. Ibid., 17.

86. Ibid., 31.

87. Ibid., 13.

88. Ibid., 14.

89. Dhalla frequently alludes to his own religious transformation in his autobiography. These quotes are taken from Dhalla, *Saga of a Soul,* 67–68, 198.

90. Ibid., 203–4.

91. Ibid.

92. Ibid., 199.

93. Ibid., 187–88.

94. Ibid., xiii.

95. Dhalla, *Zoroastrianism,* 125–26.

96. Ibid., 481–82.

97. Ibid.

98. Ibid., 197.

99. Ibid., 69.

100. Ibid., 68.

101. Ibid., 73.

102. Ibid., 484–85.

103. Ibid., 484.

104. In particular, see Ardaser Sorabjee N. Wadia, *The Message of Zoroaster*.

105. Ibid., 17.

106. Jivanji Jamshedji Modi, *The Religious Ceremonies and Customs of the Parsees*, vii.

107. Ibid., ix.

108. Sanjana, *Book of Books*, 58.

109. Ibid., 92–93.

110. Sanjana, *Zarathushtra*, 60.

111. Ibid., 61.

112. Ibid., 210.

113. Sanjana, *Book of Books*, 11–12.

114. Darab Dastur Peshotan Sanjana, *The Position of Zoroastrian Women in Remote Antiquity, as Illustrated in the Avesta, the Sacred Books of the Parsees; Being a Lecture Delivered at Bombay on the 18th of April 1892, by Darab Sastur Peshotan Sanjana, B.A.*, 4.

115. Ibid., 5.

116. Ibid., 5–6.

117. Ibid., preface.

118. Ibid., 38.

119. Ibid., 30. In the same article, Sanjana sought to put to rest the commonly held belief that ancient Zoroastrianism promoted incestuous marriage.

120. Dhalla, *Saga of a Soul*, 191–94.

121. Ibid.

122. Ibid., xiv.

123. Ibid.

124. Ibid., 217–18.

125. Ibid., 197–98.

126. Ibid., 241. It would be interesting to consider the similarities here in Ziya Gökalp's conception of the difference between civilization and culture.

127. On the several conversion cases of the early twentieth century, see Palsetia, *Parsis of India*, 227–50. For fresh insights into the 1906–8 case using notes from the judges, see Mitra Sharafi, "Judging Conversion to Zoroastrianism: Behind the Scenes of the Parsi Panchayat Case (1908)."

128. Dhalla, *Saga of a Soul*, 197.

6. The Parsi Rediscovery of Ancient Iran

1. This chapter owes its title to Michael Stausberg's article "Manekji Limji Hataria and the Rediscovery of Ancient Iran." Parts of this chapter have been previously published as Monica M. Ringer, "Reform Transplanted: Parsi Agents of Change among Zoroastrians in Nineteenth-Century Iran," available at http://informaworld.com. I am grateful for permission from the publisher to reprint sections of this earlier article here.

2. Dastur Vilayati trained Dastur Darab Kumana (later teacher of Anquetil du Perron), Dastur Jamasp Asa, and Dastur Fardunji. See Maneck, *Death of Ahriman*, 130. The Nirangestan, at the time believed to be an authentic religious text on ritual matters, was later disclosed as a later Sassanian text of uncertain, possibly even Muslim, authorship.

3. This last *rivayat* is called the *Ithoter*. See Vitalone, *Persian "Revayat" "Ithoter."* For Mulla Kaus's travels, see the account written subsequently by his son, Mulla Feroze, and discussed in Maneck, *Death of Ahriman*, 142–44.

4. In 1828 Mulla Kaus published ulama opinions concerning the Zoroastrian calendar in a manuscript titled "Risaleh-i Istishahad." See Maneck, *Death of Ahriman*, 143–44.

5. Quotes from this issue of the *Oriental Christian Spectator* are from ibid., 147–48.

6. Ibid.

7. There is an oft-repeated story associated with this first fund, which tends to take precedence in the historiography of Parsi activities in Iran and obscures the novelty and larger context of the establishment of the society. Briefly, an Iranian Zoroastrian fled Iran with his daughter to prevent her from being abducted and married to a Muslim in 1796. The daughter in question subsequently married Framji Panday, a Zoroastrian merchant in Bombay, and together they helped other refugees from Iran. One of their sons established a fund for this purpose in 1834, and a second son was responsible for helping to found the society. Among other sources, see Boyce, *Zoroastrians*, 209–10. On the establishment of the society, see also Amighi, *Zoroastrians of Iran*, 129–31.

8. In an article titled "Explanation of the Imposition and End of Jazieh on Zoroastrians," in the Zoroastrian journal *Pandarha*, written by Mobed Firuz Azargoshasp, Iranians are recalled as having requested assistance from the Parsis. Whether this reason was the initial impetus or not is unclear since Parsi sources do not confirm an Iranian request for assistance.

9. On Hataria, see Mary Boyce, "Maneckji Limji Hataria in Iran"; and Stausberg, "Hataria and the Rediscovery of Ancient Iran."

10. Mobed Firuz Azargoshasp, "Explanation of the Imposition." Azargoshasp cites the figure of 8,450 *tomans* as the official *jazieh* and notes that local officials required payment of three times as much.

11. Maneckji Hataria's figures are cited in Dr. Jahangir Ashidari, "A Corner of History," 59.

12. For compilations of Maneckji's correspondence, see the selection of letters in the *Ketab-khaneh-ye Meyhanparastan-e vagozari-ye Nasr al-Din Shah* in Tehran. See also T. Amini, ed., *Some Records on the Iranian Contemporary Zoroastrians, 1879–1959*, 1–90.

13. Haji Zaher al-Dowlah was the son-in-law of Qajar prince Mirza Ali Khan Qajar.

14. The translation is replicated in a letter from the president of the committee, Persian Zoroastrian Amelioration Fund, Dinshaw Manockji Petit, to His Excellency Ronald F. Thomson, Esq., C.I.E., dated Bombay, Dec. 4, 1882.

15. See, for example, Petit's letter to Sir A. C. Lyall, K.C.B.

16. Amighi, *Zoroastrians of Iran*, 130.

17. Jackson, *Persia, Past and Present*, 2:375.

18. Amighi, *Zoroastrians of Iran*, 104, 135.

19. Ashidari, "A Corner of History," 40–41, 59.

20. Ibid., 64.

21. Michael Fisher, "Zoroastrian Iran: Between Myth and Praxis," 97.

22. Amighi, *Zoroastrians of Iran*, 134. Amighi claims that the Zoroastrian literacy rate was "high" compared to the Muslim population. See *Zoroastrians of Iran*, 136.

23. Hataria notes that some benefactors' names had been lost, but specifically cites the following individuals as having provided funds for projects in Iran: Sir Jamshidji Jeejeebhoy, the first Baronet; Framji Cawasji Banaji; Merwanji Framji Panday; Minocherji Hormusji Kama; Rustomji Ruttonji Wadia; Behramji Noshirwan Datra; Ardeshir Dadiseth; Noshirwan Koyaji; Khurshedji Cawasji Banaji; and Cowasji Jehangir. See Hataria, *Parsi Mission to Iran*.

24. Ibid.

25. Fisher, "Zoroastrian Iran," 100, quoting Rashid Shahmardan, *Farzanegan-e Zartoshti*.

26. Hataria, *Parsi Mission to Iran*. See also Fisher, "Zoroastrian Iran," 100, quoting Shahmardan, *Farzanegan-e Zartoshti*.

27. For Jackson's remarks on Iranian Zoroastrian practice, see *Persia, Past and Present*, 337, 363, 372, 380–81, 383–87.

28. He was correct. Sir Jamshedji Jeejeebhoy supplied Parsi religious books to Zoroastrians in Iran. See Hataria, *Parsi Mission to Iran*.

29. For Jackson's remarks comparing Iranian and Indian Zoroastrian practice, see *Persia, Past and Present*, 337, 363, 372, 380–81, 383–87.

30. Ibid., 356.

31. Ibid., 376.

32. Framjee, *Parsees*, x–xi.

33. Ibid., 2.

34. Ibid., 4–5.

35. Ibid., 5–6.

36. The debate surrounding the veracity of the *Qisseh* remains unresolved. See in particular Williams, *Zoroastrian Myth of Migration*. See also M. Irani, "Story of Sanjan."

37. Framjee, *Parsees*, 6–7.

38. Ibid., 9.

39. Ibid., 9–10.

40. Williams, *Zoroastrian Myth of Migration*, 75, 77.

41. Framjee, *Parsees*, 14.

42. Ibid., 47–48 (emphasis added).

43. Stausberg, "Maneckji Limji Hataria," 440.

44. Hataria, *Parsi Mission to Iran*, 2.

45. See Mangol Bayat, *Mysticism and Dissent: Socioreligious Thought in Qajar Iran*; Afshin Marashi, *Nationalizing Iran: Culture, Power, and the State, 1870–1940*; and Stausberg, "Maneckji Limji Hataria."

46. Hataria, *Parsi Mission to Iran,* 1.

47. Ibid., 5.

48. Ibid., 15.

49. Hataria is very concerned to find a suitable museum in which to protect and further his collection. See ibid., 26–28.

50. See Dinyar Patel, "The Iran League of Bombay: Parsis, Iran, and the Appeal of Iranian Nationalism, 1922–1942"; and T. M. Luhrmann, *The Good Parsi: The Fate of a Colonial Elite in a Postcolonial Society.*

51. On the Iran League in particular, see Patel, "Iran League of Bombay."

52. Sir Jehangir C. Coyajee, "A Brief Life-Sketch of the Late Mr. Dinshah Jeejeebhoy Irani."

53. Irani's letter is quoted in ibid.

7. Iranian Nationalism and the Zoroastrian Past

1. In 1900 it was still easier to travel to Bombay than the overland dangerous route to Tehran. To give an example of the difficulty of travel overland in the absence of both roads and dependable security, it took between three and four weeks to travel between Yazd and Tehran and as much as three weeks to travel between Yazd and Kerman. See Boyce, *Zoroastrians,* 218.

2. In 1900 Yazd and the surrounding villages had a Zoroastrian population of 10,000 according to Boyce. Ibid.

3. Ibid. The figure of 50 merchants was estimated by Hataria.

4. Amighi, *Zoroastrians of Iran.*

5. In 1880 General Schindler (1881) estimated there to be 150 Zoroastrian merchants in Tehran. Cited in Amighi, *Zoroastrians of Iran,* 147–48.

6. J. Bharier, *Economic Development in Iran, 1900–1970,* as cited in Amighi, *Zoroastrians of Iran,* 144.

7. In 1912 the Zoroastrian council reported 500. See *Hukht* (1973), quoted in ibid., 148.

8. Ibid., 154.

9. Ibid., 146.

10. A. Reza Arasteh, *Education and Social Awakening in Iran, 1850–1968* (Leiden: E. J. Brill, 1969), cited in Amighi, *Zoroastrians of Iran,* 146.

11. Parsis joined with the Yazdi merchant house of Shah Jahan Brothers in the formation of a bank in Tehran. See R. Shahmardon, *Parasteshgah-e Zartoshtian,* cited in Amighi, *Zoroastrians of Iran,* 150.

12. Amighi, *Zoroastrians of Iran,* 150–51.

13. *Mahnameh* (1977), quoted in ibid., 152.

14. Ibid.

15. Ibid., 151.

16. Boyce, *Zoroastrians,* 218.

17. *Mahnameh* (1972), cited in Amighi, *Zoroastrians of Iran,* 156.

18. Malcolm, *Five Years*, 52.

19. Amighi, *Zoroastrians of Iran*, 158.

20. Farhang Mehr, *Sahm-e Zartoshtiyan dar Enghelab-e Mashruteh* (Tehran: Univ. of Tehran Press, 1970), cited in Amighi, *Zoroastrians of Iran*, 158.

21. Amighi, *Zoroastrians of Iran*, 159, citing Bamdad, "Tarikh-e Mashruteh" (June), 23–36.

22. Bayat, *Mysticism and Dissent*. See also Marashi, *Nationalizing Iran*.

23. "The Supplementary Fundamental Laws of October 7, 1907," in *The Persian Revolution of 1905–1909*, by Edward G. Browne, 372–73.

24. Ibid., 196.

25. Amighi, *Zoroastrians of Iran*, 158–60.

26. See Hamid Dabashi, ed. and trans., "Two Clerical Tracts on Constitutionalism."

27. On the deliberations concerning the establishment of the republic and ulama opposition, see Mohammad Faghfoory, "The Ulama-State Relations in Iran, 1921–1941."

28. The Tehran Anjoman had previously been established by the Bombay Amelioration Society representative in Iran, Kay Khosrow Saheb Tirandaz Kucheh Biouki, prior to the Constitutional Revolution. It languished, however, and did not function. The merchants agreed to raise their prices and donate the proceeds to the support of the *anjoman*. See Amighi, *Zoroastrians of Iran*, 162, who cites Timsar Oshidary, *Tarikh-e Zartoshtian*.

29. *Yearbook of the Anjoman*, 1906–8, 3–4, as quoted in Amighi, *Zoroastrians of Iran*, 162.

30. Amighi, *Zoroastrians of Iran*, 162.

31. Kay Khosrow Shahrokh had served as secretary of the Kerman Anjoman after his return from India. See Shahrokh, *The Memoirs of Keikhosrow Shahrokh*, 35–36.

32. *Mahnameh* (1972) and (1973), cited in Amighi, *Zoroastrians of Iran*, 163. The Tehran Anjoman had five separate funds, each designated for an area of activity: schools, poor relief, religious necessities, the *dakhmeh* and burial, and extraordinary community expenses. See Shahrokh, *Memoirs*, 187.

33. According to Fisher, "Zoroastrian-Bahais are convinced that [Khodabakhsh] was a Bahai. Zoroastrians are equally certain that what he advocated was that if Muslims became Bahai, life for everyone would become easier." Fisher, "Zoroastrian Iran," 436.

34. On the intellectual development of nationalism in Iran, see Marashi, *Nationalizing Iran*.

35. On the emergence and development of Iranian nationalism, see ibid.

36. On the possibility of an "indigenous solution" before World War I, see Ringer, *Education, Religion, and the Discourse of Cultural Reform*.

37. Marashi, *Nationalizing Iran*.

38. R. P. Masani, "With Dinshah Irani in New Iran," in *Dinshah Irani Memorial Volume: Papers on Zoroastrian and Iranian Subjects*, xv–xxiv.

39. US State Department, letter dated June 30, 1931, 1.

40. Ibid., Feb. 3, 1932, 2.

41. The parliament on May 20, 1928, authorized the government to enforce 955 articles of the new Civil Code. According to a foreign diplomat, "The effect was that in addition to brining into

play certain principles of modern jurisprudence, a *uniform basis was established for the application of Koranic law*, thereby eliminating personal and often conflicting interpretations and executions by individual clerics." Ibid., Jan. 16, 1939, 6.

42. Personal Status Law of July 22, 1933.

43. Incomplete legal secularization perpetuates religious-based identity, law, and patriarchy and thus the meaning of citizenship in the Middle East. See Suad Joseph, ed., *Gender and Citizenship in the Middle East*.

44. US State Department, letter dated May 31, 1927, RG 2, notes that Islamic legal principles were obliged to be taught to all Muslim students. These included the idea of apostasy from Islam as punishable by death, unequal legal consequences of killing non-Muslims, and unequal laws of inheritance.

45. See an expanded discussion of the uneasy relationship between Iranian nationalism and Zoroastrian identity in the Pahlavi period in Monica M. Ringer, "Modern Zoroastrian Identity: Between Cyrus and Zoroaster."

46. Talinn Grigor, "Recultivating 'Good Taste': The Early Pahlavi Modernists and Their Society for National Heritage," 37. See also Talinn Grigor, *Building Iran: Modernism, Architecture, and National Heritage under the Pahlavi Monarchs*.

47. Boyce, *Zoroastrians*, 219; Amighi, *Zoroastrians of Iran*, 170.

48. US State Department, letter by Rives Childes dated Apr. 26, 1935, 3.

49. P. Bharucha, "Mr. Irani's Concept of Religion," xxv–xxix.

8. Kay Khosrow Shahrokh: Rational Religion and Citizenship in Iran

1. Shahrokh, *Memoirs*, 3, 9.

2. Shahrokh was related to the prominent Parsi Petit family. This fact in part prompted his travel to Bombay and may have facilitated his acceptance into the Jeejeebhoy school. Ibid., 3.

3. Ibid., 19.

4. Ibid., 34–44.

5. Ibid., 35. According to Shahrokh, invited dignitaries included Deputy Governor Asadollah Mo'tazed, Mirza Mehdi Khan Kalantar, and, subsequently, Governor Farmanfarma, among others.

6. On "new" schools and their comparison to the tradition schools, see Ringer, *Education, Religion, and the Discourse of Cultural Reform*. On new forms of discipline in the new schools, see also Timothy Mitchell, *Colonizing Egypt*.

7. Shahrokh, *Memoirs*, 35–36.

8. See, for example, ibid., 36–46. Scholars have understood this dynamic as well. See, for example, the detailed accounts provided by Michael Fisher on violence against Bahais, Jews, and Zoroastrians in "Zoroastrian Iran."

9. Khaikhosrow's speech to the Majles, dispatch 979 by Smith Murray, US Embassy, Iran, 1925, vol. 73, RG 84/350/6/34/4, 2.

10. Shahrokh, *Memoirs*, 10–11.

11. Ibid., 9.

12. Interestingly, Sheikh Yayha's concern was that Shahrokh *not* convert to Christianity. It is also noteworthy that Sheikh Yayha was in a position, or at least believed himself to be in a position, to instruct Shahrokh on the basic doctrines of Zoroastrianism. Ibid., 10–11. I have found no evidence corroborating this story, but it does not strike me as inherently unbelievable.

13. Ibid., 10.

14. Ibid., 11.

15. Ibid., 55, 10.

16. Amighi, *Zoroastrians of Iran,* 147.

17. See Shahrokh's own account of the establishment of the Zoroastrian cemetery and the debate surrounding the abandonment of the *dakhmeh* in Shahrokh, *Memoirs,* 11–16.

18. Ibid., 11.

19. The Zoroastrian population of Tehran tripled in the ten years 1925–35, from 450 to 1,300. Only five years later in 1940 it had reached 1,800. See ibid., 172; and Amighi, *Zoroastrians of Iran,* 172.

20. Farhang Mehr also believed that the establishment of the medical school at Tehran University in 1934 and the Islamic prohibition on dissection led to the pillaging of the *dakhmeh* for corpses. See Farhang Mehr, "Zoroastrians in Twentieth Century Iran," 287, 291.

21. Of the three hundred members of the Zoroastrian community assembled at Shahrokh's proposal of the cemetery, he managed to collect a sum of twenty-three thousand *tomans.* Shahrokh subsequently requested that Arbob Rostam Giv build a reception hall, which he generously agreed to do. See Shahrokh, *Memoirs,* 15.

22. Mehr, "Zoroastrians in Twentieth Century Iran," 291.

23. Patel, "Iran League of Bombay."

24. Iran League, "Dokhma: A Scientific Method of Disposal of the Dead Among Zoroastrians," iv.

25. Ibid., 7.

26. Ibid., 24.

27. Ibid., 6–7.

28. Ibid., 21–22 (emphasis added). Lord Randolph Henry Spencer Churchill (1849–95) was a British statesman and father of Sir Winston Churchill (1874–1965). It remains a mystery where this quotation is taken from or the origins of Churchill's expertise in the matter of Zoroastrian funeral customs.

29. Ibid., v–vi.

30. Mehr, "Zoroastrians in Twentieth Century Iran," 291.

31. The 1907 edition was printed in seven thousand copies and the 1921 edition an additional three thousand. Kay Khosrow Shahrokh, *A'ineh-ye A'in-e Mazdasna.*

32. Shahrokh, *Memoirs,* 26–28. On page 27 Shahrokh specifically mentions that the famous scholar of Zoroastrianism (and possible convert) Ibrahim Pur Davud began his interest as a result of these books.

33. Kay Khosrow Shahrokh, *Zartosht: Payghambari keh as now bayad shenakht (Forough-e Mazdisna).* Martin Haug was one of the first scholars to insist on Zoroastrianism's essential monotheism. His conclusions were eagerly embraced by the Parsi community in Bombay. See chapter 2 above.

34. The question of whether Zoroastrianism was or was not understood to be or practiced as a monotheistic religion in Iran at the time is much more difficult to answer. However, what was being argued was Zoroastrianism's "essential" nature, irrespective of how it was actually understood and practiced. Maneck argues in her book *Death of Ahriman* that in the Islamic period, Zoroastrianism certainly claimed to be monotheistic, although many other scholars disagree, at least in terms of practice. Certainly, one of the issues that spurred Parsi intervention in Iran was the Iranians' presumed failure to practice "true" Zoroastrianism. This failure, however, occurred after the beginning of the Parsi reform movement and was therefore influenced by their visions of reform.

Conclusion: Religion and the Creation of Pious Citizens

1. A dominant theme in various Hindu reform movements was the emphasis on religious unity as a substitute for national unity.

2. Karkaria, *India,* 17.

3. Ibid., 17 (emphasis added).

4. Darab Dastur Peshotan Sanjana, "The Position of Zoroastrian Women in Remote Antiquity, as Illustrated in the Avesta, the Sacred Books of the Parsis," lecture delivered at Bombay, April 18, 1892, in *Position of Zoroastrian Women,* 47–48 (emphasis added).

5. By this statement I mean that Iran did not implement fully secular law, nor were all members of religious communities allowed equal access to political life, and Islam as the religion of state was not eliminated from the constitution.

6. US State Department, letter from Teymourtache to the German minister, Jan. 16, 1939 (emphasis added).

7. *Iranshahr* was published in Berlin in the years 1922–27 by Hosain Kazemzadeh. This quote cited in Ervand Abrahamian, *A History of Modern Iran,* 123 (emphasis added).

8. Shahrokh, *Memoirs,* 10.

9. On the problem of community loss through intermarriage, see ibid., 6.

10. Karkaria, *India,* 7.

11. On the mutual attractions of the Parsis and British and their developing relationship in Bombay, see Hinnells, "Parsis and the British."

12. Captain Hamilton, quoted in ibid., 28.

13. George Viscount Valencia, cited in ibid., 12.

14. Karkaria, *India,* 51. Karkaria earlier wrote under the name Dosabhoy Framjee.

15. Ibid., 50.

16. On the history of Indian religious reform movements, see Jones, *Socio-religious Reform Movements,* esp. 30–39, 137–51; and Dobbin, *Urban Leadership,* 65–76, 248–54. On the Brahmo Samaj in particular, see Parekh, *Brahma Samaj.*

17. Mozoomdar, "Principles of the Brahmo-Somaj," 1:428–29.

18. Parekh, *Brahma Samaj,* 18.

19. Ibid., 6–7. See also Van der Veer, *Imperial Encounters,* 7, 44–45.

20. Parekh, *Brahma Samaj*, 21.

21. Mozoomdar, "Principles of the Brahmo-Somaj," 1:430.

22. Parekh, *Brahma Samaj*, 10.

23. An example of an Islamic reformer for whom political objectives were paramount is Jamal al-Din al-Afghani. As Nikki R. Keddie points out, "The political unification and strengthening of the Islamic world and the ending of Western incursions there were his primary goals, while the reform of Islam was secondary." Keddie, *An Islamic Response to Imperialism: Political and Religious Writings of Sayyid Jamal ad-Din 'al-Afghani*, 39.

24. This title is from the Quran, Sura 3, verse 159. Namık Kemal, "Wa Shawirhum fi'l-amr" [And Seek Their Counsel in the Matter].

25. Ibid., 144.

26. Ibid.

27. Qasim Amin, *The Liberation of Women: A Document in the History of Egyptian Feminism (1899)*, 65 (emphasis added).

28. Al-Afghani, "Lecture on Teaching and Learning," in *Islamic Response to Imperialism*, by Keddie, 102. Originally presented as a public lecture, November 8, 1882, in Albert Hall, Calcutta.

29. Ibid., 106–7.

30. On the challenge that "new" secular education posed to the ulama, see Ringer, *Education, Religion, and the Discourse of Cultural Change*. On Islamic legal change, specifically with reference to Qasim Amin, see Talal Asad, *Formations of the Secular: Christianity, Islam, Modernity*, specifically the chapter "Reconfigurations of Law and Ethics in Colonial Egypt," 205–56.

31. Van der Veer posits that Indian and British modernities were constructed in relationship with each other. The same holds true for the development of other Middle Eastern modernities, whether they involved colonialism or not. See Van der Veer, *Imperial Encounters*. See also Van der Veer, *Conversion to Modernities*.

32. I term this conundrum faced by reformers the "modernization dilemma." See Ringer, *Education, Religion, and the Discourse of Cultural Change*. On the use of binaries of tradition and modernity in internal struggles, and as "deployed against a nation's internal "foes," see Tavakoli-Targhi, *Refashioning Iran*, 1–2.

33. As Mehta theorizes, "The will to power that liberals do express for the empire is always as a beneficent compensation for someone else's powerlessness relative to a more elevated order. As its corollary, the rights that liberals do assert are supported by a higher order of things: a superior knowledge, a more credible science, a more consistent morality, and a more just and free politics. These relative valuations all follow from, and undergird, the claim of the provisionality of other people's experiences." Mehta, *Liberalism and Empire*, 191.

34. See, for example, the pioneering works by Jenny B. White, *Islamist Mobilization in Turkey: A Study in Vernacular Politics*; and Saba Mahmood, *Politics of Piety: The Islamic Revival and the Feminist Subject*.

Bibliography

Abdi, Kamyar. "Nationalism, Politics, and the Development of Archeology in Iran." *American Journal of Archeology* 105, no. 1 (2001): 51–76.

Abrahamian, Ervand. *A History of Modern Iran.* Cambridge: Cambridge Univ. Press, 2008.

Algar, Hamid. *Mirza Malkum Khan: A Study in the History of Iranian Modernism.* Berkeley and Los Angeles: Univ. of California Press, 1973.

Amanat, Abbas. *Pivot of the Universe: Nasir al-Din Shah Qajar and the Iranian Monarchy, 1831–1896.* Berkeley and Los Angeles: Univ. of California Press, 1997.

Amighi, Janet Kestenberg. *The Zoroastrians of Iran: Conversion, Assimilation, or Persistence.* New York: AMS Press, 1990.

Amin, Qasim. *The Liberation of Women: A Document in the History of Egyptian Feminism.* Translated by Samiha Sidhom Peterson. Cairo: American Univ. in Cairo Press, 1992.

Amini, T., ed. *Some Records on the Iranian Contemporary Zoroastrians, 1879–1959.* Tehran: Records Research Center, Iran National Archives Organization, 2001.

Anderson, Benedict. *Imagined Communities: Reflections on the Origins and Spread of Nationalism.* London: Verso, 1983.

Arjomand, Said Amir, ed. *Authority and Political Culture in Shi'ism.* Albany: State Univ. of New York Press, 1988.

Asad, Talal. *Formations of the Secular: Christianity, Islam, Modernity.* Stanford: Stanford Univ. Press, 2003.

Ashidari, Dr. Jahangir. "A Corner of History." *Mahnameh-ye Zartoshtian* (Nowruz 2535) (March 1976): 59.

Azargoshasp, Ardeshir. *Adab va Rosum-e Zartoshtiyan* [Ceremonies and Customs of Zoroastrians]. Tehran: Fravahar, 1973.

Azargoshasp, Mobed Firuz. "Explanation of the Imposition and End of Jazieh on Zoroastrians." *Pandarha* 2, no. 8 (1940): 15–18.

Bakhash, Shaul. *Iran: Monarchy, Bureaucracy, and Reform under the Qajars, 1856–1896.* Ithaca: Cornell Univ. Press, 1978.

Barrows, John Henry. *Christianity, the World-Religion: Lectures Delivered in India and Japan.* Chicago: A. C. McClurg, 1897.

———, ed. *The World's Parliament of Religions.* 2 vols. Chicago: Parliament, 1893.

Bassett, James. *Persia, the Land of the Imams: A Narrative of Travel and Residence, 1871–1885.* 1887. Reprint, n.p.: Elibron Classics, 2001.

Bastani Parizi, M. Ibrahim. "Principes de l'évolution de la tolérance dans l'histoire de Kerman." In *Contacts Between Cultures,* edited by A. Harrak, 374–83. Lewiston, NY: Edwin Mellen Press, 1992.

Bayat, Mangol. *Mysticism and Dissent: Socioreligious Thought in Qajar Iran.* Syracuse: Syracuse Univ. Press, 1982.

Behdad, Ali. *Belated Travelers: Orientalism in the Age of Colonial Dissolution.* Durham: Duke Univ. Press, 1994.

Bekhradnia, Shahin. "The Decline of the Zoroastrian Priesthood and Its Effect on the Iranian Zoroastrian Community in the Twentieth Century." *Journal of the Anthropological Society of Oxford* 23, no. 1 (1992): 37–47.

Berkes, Niyazi. *The Development of Secularism in Turkey.* Montreal: McGill Univ. Press, 1964.

Bharucha, Ervad Sheriarji Dadabhai. *A Brief Sketch of Zoroastrian Religion and Customs: An Essay Written for the Rahnumai Mazdayasnan Sabha.* Bombay: Duftur Ashkara Press, 1903.

———. "Is Zoroastrianism Preached to All Mankind or One Particular Race?" In *Dastur Hoshang Memorial Volume,* 248–57. Bombay: Fort Printing Press, 1918.

Bharucha, P. "Mr. Irani's Concept of Religion." In *Dinshah Irani Memorial Volume: Papers on Zoroastrian and Iranian Subjects.* Bombay: Dinshah J. Irani Memorial Fund Committee, 1948.

Bhattacharya, S. "Paradigms Lost: Notes on Social History of India." *Economic and Political Weekly* 17 (Apr. 14, 1982): 690–96.

Bilimoriya, Bahmanji Framji. *A Warning Word to Parsees.* Bombay: Meher Printing Works, 1900.

Bourdieu, Pierre. "Cultural Reproduction and Social Reproduction." In *Knowledge, Education, and Cultural Change,* edited by Richard Brown, 71–112. London: Taylor and Francis, 1973.

———. "The Genesis of the Concepts of Habitus and Field." *Sociocriticism* 2 (1985): 11–24.

Boyce, Mary. "Manekji Limji Hataria in Iran." In *K. R. Cama Oriental Institute Golden Jubilee Volume,* edited by N. D. Minochehr-Homji and M. F. Kanga, 19–31. Bombay: K. R. Cama Oriental Institute, 1969.

———. "Parsis in Iran after the Arab Conquest." In *A Zoroastrian Tapestry*, edited by Firoza Punthakey Mistree and Pheroza J. Godrej, 228–45. Usmanpura: Mapin, 2002.

———. *A Persian Stronghold of Zoroastrianism*. Oxford: Clarendon Press, 1977.

———. "The Zoroastrian Houses of Yazd." In *Iran and Islam*, edited by C. E. Bosworth, 125–47. Edinburgh: Edinburgh Univ. Press, 1971.

———. *Zoroastrians: Their Religious Beliefs and Practices*. London: Routledge, 1979.

Briggs, Henry George. *The Parsis; or, Modern Zerdusthians: A Sketch*. Edinburgh: Oliver and Boyd, 1852.

Browne, Edward G. *The Persian Revolution of 1905–1909*. Edited by Abbas Amanat. Washington, DC: Mage, 1995.

———. *A Year Amongst the Persians: Impressions as to the Life, Character, and Thought of the People of Persia Received During Twelve Months' Residence in That Country in the Year 1887–1888*. 2 vols. 1893. Reprint, n.p.: Elibron Classics, 2001.

Bulsara, Sohrab Jamshedjee. *The Religion of Zarathushtra as Taught by Himself and His Apostles*. Bombay: Fort Printing Press, 1938.

Cama, Kharshedji Rustamji. *The Collected Works of K. R. Cama*. 2 vols. Bombay: K. R. Cama Oriental Institute, 1968.

Carson, Penelope. "Golden Casket or Pebbles and Trash? J. S. Mill and the Anglicist/Orientalist Controversy." In *J. S. Mill's Encounter with India*, edited by Martin I. Moir, Douglas M. Peers, and Lynn Zastoupil, 149–72. Toronto: Univ. of Toronto Press, 1999.

———. "An Imperial Dilemma: The Propagation of Christianity in Early Colonial India." *Journal of Imperial and Commonwealth History* 18, no. 2 (May 1990): 169–90.

Chosky, Jamsheed. *Conflict and Cooperation: Zoroastrian Subalterns and Muslim Elites in Medieval Iranian Society*. New York: Columbia Univ. Press, 1997,

Coats, Thomas. "Notes Respecting the Trial by Punchiet, and the Administration of Justice at Poona, under the Late Paishwa." In *Transactions of the Literary Society of Bombay*, 2:273–80. London: Richard and Arthur Taylor, 1820.

Cohn, Bernard S. "Representing Authority in Victorian India." In *The Invention of Tradition*, edited by Eric Hobsbawm and Terence Ranger, 165–209. Cambridge: Cambridge Univ. Press, 1983.

Coyajee, Sir Jehangir C. "A Brief Life-Sketch of the Late Mr. Dinshah Jeejeebhoy Irani." In *Dinshah Irani Memorial Volume: Papers on Zoroastrian and Iranian Subjects*, i–xiii. Bombay: Dinshah J. Irani Memorial Fund Committee, 1948.

Cursetjee, Manockjee. *A Few Passing Ideas for the Benefit of India and Indians Addressed to the Bombay Association*. Bombay: Bombay Education Society's Press, 1853.

Curzon, George N. *Persia and the Persian Question*. 2 vols. 1892. Reprint, n.p.: Elibron Classics, 2001.

Dabashi, Hamid, ed. and trans. "Two Clerical Tracts on Constitutionalism." In *Authority and Political Culture in Shi'ism,* edited by Said Amir Arjomand, 334–70. Albany: State Univ. of New York Press, 1988.

Darrow, William R. "The Zoroaster Legend: Its Historical and Religious Significance." PhD thesis, Harvard Univ., 1981.

Davar, Sohrab P. *The History of the Parsi Punchayet of Bombay.* Bombay: New Book, 1949.

David, M. D. *John Wilson and His Institution.* Bombay: John Wilson Educational Society, 1975.

Davis, Natalie Zemon. "The Sacred and the Body Social in Sixteenth-Century Lyon." *Past and Present* 90 (1981): 40–70.

De Gobineau, Comte. *Trois ans en Asia.* 2 vols. 7th ed. Paris: Bernard Grasset, 1923.

Desai, Sapur Faredun. *The Parsi Panchayet and Its Working.* Bombay: Godrej Memorial Printing Press, 1963.

Dhabhar, Ervad Bamanji Nusserwanji. *The Persian Rivayats of Hormazyar Framarz and Others: Their Version with Introduction and Notes.* Bombay: K. R. Cama Oriental Institute, 1932.

Dhalla, Maneckji Nusservanji. *Dastur Dhalla, the Saga of a Soul: An Autobiography of Shams ul-Ulama Dastur Dr. Maneckji Nusserwanji Dhalla High Priest of the Parsis of Pakistan.* Translated by Behram Sohrab H. J. Rustomji. Karachi: Dastur Dr. Dhalla Memorial Institute, 1975.

Dhalla, N. H. *History of Zoroastrianism.* Bombay: K. R. Cama Oriental Institute, 1963.

———. *Zoroastrian Theology: From Earliest Times to the Present.* 1914. Reprint, New York: AMS Press, 1972.

Dobbin, Christine. "The Parsi Panchayat in Bombay City in the Nineteenth Century." *Modern Asian Studies* 4, no. 2 (1970): 149–64.

———. *Urban Leadership in Western India: Politics and Communities in Bombay City, 1840–1885.* London: Oxford Univ. Press, 1972.

Drummond, J. G. *Panchayats in India.* London: Oxford Univ. Press, 1937.

Duchesne-Guillemin, J. *The Western Response to Zoroaster.* 1956. Reprint, Westport, CT: Greenwood Press, 1973.

Eastwick, Edward Backhouse. *Journal of a Diplomate's Three Years' Residence in Persia.* 2 vols. 1864. Reprint, n.p.: Elibron Classics, 2001.

Edwardes, S. M. *Kharshedji Rustamji Cama, 1831–1909: A Memoir.* Oxford: Oxford Univ. Press, 1923.

Elias, Norbert. *The History of Manners: The Civilizing Process.* New York: Pantheon Books.

Engineer, Miss B. A. "Advancement of Religion." In *Dastur Hoshang Memorial Volume,* 1–15. Bombay: Fort Printing Press, 1918.

Erskine, William. "On the Authenticity of the Desatir, with Remarks on the Account of the Mahabadi Religion Contained in the Dabistan." In *Transactions of the Literary Society of Bombay*, 2:342–44. London: Richard and Arthur Taylor, 1820.

———. "On the Sacred Books and Religion of the Parsis." In *Transactions of the Literary Society of Bombay*, 2:295–341. London: Richard and Arthur Taylor, 1820.

Faghfoory, Mohammad H. "The Impact of Modernization on the Ulama in Iran, 1925–1941." *Iranian Studies* 26, nos. 3–4 (1993): 277–312.

———. "The Ulama-State Relations in Iran, 1921–1941." *International Journal of Middle East Studies* 19, no. 4 (1987): 413–32.

Farquhar, J. N. *Modern Religious Movements in India*. New York: Macmillan, 1915.

Filmer, Henry. *The Pageant of Persia*. Indianapolis: Bobbs-Merrill, 1936.

Firby, N. K. *European Travellers and Their Perceptions of Zoroastrians in the 17th and 18th Centuries*. Berlin: D. Reimer Verlag, 1988.

Fischer, Michael. "Zoroastrian Iran: Between Myth and Praxis." PhD diss., Univ. of Chicago, 1973.

Frachtenberg, Leo J. "Allusions to Witchcraft and Other Primitive Beliefs in the Zoroastrian Literature." In *The Dastur Hoshang Memorial Volume: Being Papers on Iranian Subjects Written by Various Scholars in Honour of the Late Shams ul-Ulama Sardar Dastur Hoshang Jamasp, M.A., Ph.d., C.I.E.*, 399–453. Bombay: Fort Printing Press, 1918.

Framjee, Dosabhoy. *Parsees: Their History, Manners, Customs, and Religion*. London: Smith, Elder, 1858.

Girardot, N. J. "Max Müller's *Sacred Books* and the Nineteenth-Century Production of the Comparative Science of Religions." *History of Religions* 41, no. 3 (2002): 213–50.

Göçek, Fatma Müge. *Rise of the Bourgeoisie, Demise of Empire: Ottoman Westernization and Social Change*. Oxford: Oxford Univ. Press, 1996.

Gordon, Thomas Edward. *Persia Revisited (1895)*. 1896. Reprint, n.p.: Elibron Classics, 2002.

Gray, James. *Life in Bombay, and the Neighboring Out-Stations*. Bombay: Richard Bentley, 1852.

Gray, Louis H. "A. V. Williams Jackson in Memoriam." *Bulletin of the American Schools of Oriental Research* 68 (Dec. 1937): 5–7.

Grigor, Talinn. *Building Iran: Modernism, Architecture, and National Heritage under the Pahlavi Monarchs*. New York: Periscope, 2009.

———. "Recultivating 'Good Taste': The Early Pahlavi Modernists and Their Society for National Heritage." *Iranian Studies* 37, no. 1 (2004): 17–45.

Hartman, Sven S. *Parsism: The Religion of Zoroaster*. Leiden: E. J. Brill, 1980.

Hataria, Maneckji Limji. *Social and Economic Life of Zoroastrians in the Last Century: The Jezya Problem*. Translated by H. Razi. Tehran: Fravahar, 1975.

——. *Travels to Iran: A Parsi Mission to Iran (1865)*. Apr. 6, 2007. http://www.fravahr .org/spip.php?article61.

Haug, Martin. *Essays on the Sacred Language, Writings, and Religion of the Parsis*. Edited by E. W. West. Boston: Houghton, Osgood, 1878.

Heater, Derek. *A Brief History of Citizenship*. New York: New York Univ. Press, 2004.

Hinnells, John R. "Bombay Parsis and the Diaspora in the 18th and 19th Centuries." In *A Zoroastrian Tapestry*, edited by Firoza Punthakey Mistree and Pheroza J. Godrej, 458–77. Usmanpura: Mapin, 2002.

——. "The Parsis: A Bibliographical Survey." *Journal of Mithraic Studies* 3 (1980): 100–149.

——. "Parsis and the British." *Journal of the K. R. Cama Oriental Institute* 46 (1978): 2–93.

——. "Social Change and Religious Transformation among Bombay Parsis in the Early Twentieth Century." In *Traditions in Contact and Change: Selected Proceedings of the XIVth Congress of the International Association for the History of Religions*, 105–25. Ontario: Canadian Corporation for Studies in Religion, 1983.

——. *Zoroastrian and Parsi Studies: Selected Works of John R. Hinnells*. Aldershot: Ashgate, 2000.

Hinnells, John R., and Alan Williams, eds. *Parsis in India and the Diaspora*. London: Routledge, 2007.

Hobsbawm, Eric, and Terence Ranger, eds. *The Invention of Tradition*. Cambridge: Univ. of Cambridge, 1983.

Hodivala, Shahpurshah Hormasji. *Studies in Parsi History*. Bombay, 1920.

Inostrantsev, K. "The Emigration of the Parsis to India and the Musulman World in the Middle of the VIII Century." Translated by L. Bogdanov. *Journal of the K. R. Cama Oriental Institute* 1 (1922): 33–70.

Irani, D. J. *The Path to Happiness; or, The Ethical Teachings of Zoroaster*. Bombay: Jehangir B. Karani's Sons, 1939.

Irani, M. S. "The Story of Sanjan: The History of Parsi Migration to India, a Critical Study." In *Proceedings and Transactions of the All-India Oriental Conference*, 68–85. Patna: Bihar and Orissa Resear, 1940.

Iran League. *Dokhma: A Scientific Method of Disposal of the Dead among Zoroastrians*. Bombay: Fort Printing Press, 1936.

J., M. *The Parsis and Their Religion*. London: N.p., 1900.

Jackson, A. V. W. "The Modern Zoroastrians of Persia." *Momiletic Review* 48 (1904): 14–19.

———. *Persia, Past and Present: A Book of Travel and Research.* 2 vols. 1909. Reprint, n.p.: Elibron Classics, 2002.

———. *Zoroaster, the Prophet of Ancient Iran.* New York: Macmillan, 1899.

———. *Zoroastrian Studies: The Iranian Religion and Various Monographs.* New York: Columbia Univ. Press, 1928.

Jacob, Margaret C. *The Radical Enlightenment: Pantheists, Freemasons, and Republicans.* London: George Allen and Unwin, 1981.

Jessawalla, D. C. *The Story of My Life.* Bombay, 1911.

Jones, Kenneth W. *Socio-religious Reform Movements in British India.* Vol. 3, bk. 1 of *The New Cambridge History of India.* Cambridge: Cambridge Univ. Press, 1989.

Joseph, Suad, ed. *Gender and Citizenship in the Middle East.* Syracuse: Syracuse Univ. Press, 2000.

Kamerkar, Mani Dhunjisha Soonu. "From the Iranian Plateau to the Shores of Gujerat: The Story of Parsi Settlement and Absorption in India." *South Asia* 27, no. 1 (2004): 120–21.

Kapadia, S. A. *The Teachings of Zoroaster and the Philosophy of the Parsi Religion.* The Wisdom of the East Series. New York: E. P. Dutton, 1908.

Karaka, Framji Dosabhai. *The Parsis: Their History, Manners, Customs, and Religion.* 1858. Reprint, n.p.: Elibron Classics, 2003.

Karkaria, Rustomji Pestonji. *India: Forty Years of Progress and Reform, Being a Sketch of the Life and Times of Behramji M. Malabari.* London: Henry Frowde Oxford Univ. Press Warehouse, 1896.

Katrak, Sohrab K. H. *Who Are the Parsees?* Karachi: Pakistan Herald Press, n.d.

Keddie, Nikki R. *An Islamic Response to Imperialism: Political and Religious Writings of Sayyid Jamal ad-Din 'al-Afghani.* Berkeley and Los Angeles: Univ. of Californian Press, 1983.

———. *Modern Iran: Roots and Results of Revolution.* New Haven: Yale Univ. Press, 2003.

Kemal, Namık. "Wa Shawirhum fi'l-amr" [And Seek Their Counsel in the Matter]. *Hürriyet* [Liberty] (London) 4 (July 20, 1869): 1–4. Translation from the Turkish by M. Şükrü Hanioğlu. In *Modernist Islam, 1840–1940: A Sourcebook,* edited by Charles Kurzman. Oxford: Oxford Univ. Press, 2002.

Kennedy, Robert E., Jr. "The Protestant Ethic and the Parsis." *American Journal of Sociology* 68, no. 1 (1962): 11–20.

Kitagawa, Joseph M., and John S. Strong. "Friedrich Max Müller and the Comparative Study of Religion." In *Nineteenth Century Religious Thought in the West,* edited by Ninian Smart et al., 3:179–304. Cambridge: Cambridge Univ. Press, 1985.

Knanishu, Joseph. *About Persia and Its People.* 1899. Reprint, Piscataway, NJ: Gorgias Press, 2001.

Kotwal, Dastur Firoze M. "The Authenticity of the Parsi Priestly Tradition." *Journal of the K. R. Cama Oriental Institute* 45 (1976): 24–33.

———. "A Brief History of the Parsi Priesthood." *Indo-Iranian Journal* 33, no. 3 (1990): 165–75.

Kotwal, Dastur Firoze M., and James W. Boyd, eds. and trans. *A Guide to the Zoroastrian Religion: A Nineteenth Century Catechism with Modern Commentary.* Harvard Univ. Center for the Study of World Religions Studies in World Religions Series. Chico, CA: Scholars Press, 1982.

Kraminick, Isaac, ed. *The Portable Enlightenment Reader.* New York: Penguin Books, 1995.

Kulke, Eckehard. *The Parsees in India: A Minority as Agent of Social Change.* Munich: Weltforum Verlag, 1974.

Kurzman, Charles, ed. *Modernist Islam, 1840–1940: A Sourcebook.* Oxford: Oxford Univ. Press, 2002.

Luhrman, T. M. *The Good Parsi: The Fate of a Colonial Elite in a Postcolonial Society.* Cambridge: Harvard Univ. Press, 1996.

Macfie, Alexander Lyon, ed. *Orientalism: A Reader.* New York: New York Univ. Press, 2000.

Madan, Dhanjishah Meherjibhai. *Revelation Considered as a Source of Religious Knowledge: With Special Reference to the Zoroastrian Religion.* Bombay: British India Press, 1909.

Mahmood, Saba. *Politics of Piety: The Islamic Revival and the Feminist Subject.* Princeton: Princeton Univ. Press, 2005.

Majeed, Javeed. "James Mill's *The History of British India:* A Reevaluation." In *J. S. Mill's Encounter with India,* edited by Martin I. Moir, Douglas M. Peers, and Lynn Zastoupil, 53–71. Toronto: Univ. of Toronto Press, 1999.

Malcolm, Napier. *Five Years in a Persian Town.* London: John Murray, 1905.

Maneck, Susan Stiles. *The Death of Ahriman: Culture, Identity, and Theological Change among the Parsis of India.* Bombay: K. R. Cama Oriental Institute, 1997.

———. "The Presbyterian and the Parsis." *Fides et Historia* 21, no. 2 (1989): 51–60.

Marashi, Afshin. "Imagining Hafez: Rabindranath Tagor in Iran, 1932." *Journal of Persianate Studies* 3 (2010): 46–77.

———. *Nationalizing Iran: Culture, Power, and the State, 1870–1940.* Seattle: Univ. of Washington Press, 2008.

———. "The Nation's Poet: Ferdowsi and the Iranian National Imagination." In *Iran in the Twentieth Century: Historiography and Political Culture,* edited by Touraj Atabaki, 93–111. New York: I. B. Tauris Press and the Iran Heritage Foundation, 2009.

———. "Performing the Nation: The Shah's Official State Visit to Kemalist Turkey, June to July 1934." In *The Making of Modern Iran: State and Society under Riza Shah, 1921–1941,* edited by Stephanie Cronin. London: Routledge, 2003.

Masani, Ervad Phiroze Shapurji. *Zoroastrianism Ancient and Modern Comprising a Review of Dr. Dhalla's Book on Zoroastrian Theology.* Bombay: Ardeshir Bhicaji Dubash, 1917.

Masani, R. P. *Dadabhai Naoroji: The Grand Old Man of India.* Mysore: Kavyalaya, 1957.

———. "With Dinshah Irani in New Iran." Introduction to *Dinshah Irani Memorial Volume: Papers on Zoroastrian and Iranian Subjects.* Bombay: Dinshah J. Irani Memorial Fund Committee, 1948.

Matthee, Rudi. "Transforming Dangerous Nomads into Useful Artisans, Technicians, Agriculturalists: Education in the Reza Shah Period." *Iranian Studies* 26, nos. 3–4 (1993): 313–36.

Mehr, Farhang. *Sham-e Zartoshtian Dar Engeleb-e Mashrutiat-e Iran.* Isfahan: Univ. of Isfahan, 1969.

———. "Zoroastrians in Twentieth Century Iran." In *A Zoroastrian Tapestry,* edited by Firoza Punthakey Mistree and Pheroza J. Godrej. Usmanpura: Mapin, 2002.

Mehta, Uday Singh. *Liberalism and Empire: A Study in Nineteenth-Century British Liberal Thought.* Chicago: Univ. of Chicago Press, 1999.

Mirza, Hormazdyar Dastur Kayoji. *Outlines of Parsi History.* Bombay: Industrial Press, 1974.

Mistree, Khojeste. "The Breakdown of the Zoroastrian Tradition as Viewed from a Contemporary Perspective." In *Irano-Judaica II: Studies Relating to Jewish Contacts with Persian Culture Throughout the Ages,* edited by Shaul Shaked and Amnon Netzer, 27–254. Jerusalem: Ben-Zvi Institute, 1990.

———. "Parsi Arrival and Early Settlements in India." In *A Zoroastrian Tapestry,* edited by Firoza Punthakey Mistree and Pheroza J. Godrej, 410–33. Usmanpura: Mapin, 2002.

Mistree, Khojeste, and Pheroza J. Godrej, eds. *A Zoroastrian Tapestry.* Usmanpura: Mapin, 2002.

Mitchell, Timothy. *Colonising Egypt.* Cambridge: Cambridge Univ. Press, 1988.

Modi, Jivanji Jamshedji. "Beliefs and Ceremonies of the Followers of Zoroaster." In *The World's Parliament of Religions,* edited by John Henry Barrows, 452–65. Chicago: Parliament, 1893.

———. *A Catechism of the Zoroastrian Religion.* Bombay: J. N. Petit Parsi Orphanage Captain Printing Works, 1911.

———. *A Glimpse into the History and Work of the Zarthoshti Din-ni Khol-Karnari Mandli.* Bombay: M. B. Mithaivala, 1922.

———, ed. *The K. R. Cama Memorial Volume: Essays on Iranian Subjects Written by Various Scholars in Honour of Mr. Karshedji Rustamji Cama on the Occasion of His Seventieth Birth-Day.* Bombay: Fort Printing Press, 1900.

———. *Moral Extracts from Zoroastrian Books for the Use of Teachers in Schools.* Bombay: British India Press, 1914.

———. "Notes on Anquetil DuPerron on King Akbar and Dastur Meherji Rana." *Journal of the Bombay Branch of the Royal Asiatic Society* 21 (1901): 537–51.

———. "The Parsees at the Court of Akbar and Dastur Meherji Rana." *Journal of the Bombay Branch of the Royal Asiatic Society* 21 (1901): 69–245.

———. *The Religious Ceremonies and Customs of the Parsees.* 1922. Reprint, New York: Garland, 1979.

Moir, Martin I., Douglas M. Peers, and Lynn Zastoupil, eds. *J. S. Mill's Encounter with India.* Toronto: Univ. of Toronto Press, 1999.

Monod, Paul Kléber. *The Power of Kings: Monarchy and Religion in Europe, 1589–1715.* New Haven: Yale Univ. Press, 1999.

Moore, Robin. "John Stuart Mill and Royal India." In *J. S. Mill's Encounter with India,* edited by Martin I. Moir, Douglas M. Peers, and Lynn Zastoupil, 87–110. Toronto: Univ. of Toronto Press, 1999.

Moses, Henry. *Sketches of India: With Notes on the Seasons, Scenery, and Society of Bombay, Elephanta, and Salsette.* London: Simpkin, Marshall, 1850.

Motivalla, Jahangir Jamshedji, and Bahmanji Navrojji Sahiar. *Enlightened Non-Zoroastrians on Mazdayasnism, the Excellent Religion.* Bombay: Mistry Printing Works, 1897–99.

Moulton, James Hope. *The Teaching of Zarathushtra: Eight Lectures and Addresses Delivered to Parsis in Bombay.* 2nd ed. Bombay: Captain Printing Works, 1917.

———. *The Treasure of the Magi: A Study of Modern Zoroastrianism.* London: Humphrey Milford Oxford Univ. Press, 1917.

Mozoomdar, Protap Chunder. "The Principles of the Brahmo-Somaj." In *The World's Parliament of Religions,* edited by John Henry Barrows, 428–33. 2 vols. Chicago: Parliament, 1893.

Müller, F. Max, ed. *Sacred Books of the East.* 50 vols. Oxford: Clarendon Press, 1879.

Murzban, M. M. *The Parsis in India, Being an Enlarged and Copiously Annotated, Up to Date English Edition of Mlle. Delphine Menant's "Les Parsis."* 2 vols. N.p., 1917.

Nagarkar, B. "The Spiritual Ideas of the Brahmo-Somaj." In *The World's Parliament of Religions,* edited by John Henry Barrows, 435–40. 2 vols. Chicago: Parliament, 1893.

Najmabadi, Afsaneh. "Hazards of Modernity and Morality: Women, State, and Ideology in Contemporary Iran." In *Women, Islam, and the State,* edited by Deniz Kandiyoti, 48–76. Philadelphia: Temple Univ. Press, 1991.

Naoroji, Dadabhai. *The Manners and Customs of the Parsees: A Paper Read Before the Liverpool Philomathic Society, 13th March, 1861*. London: S. Straker and Sons, 1864.

———. *Speeches and Writings of Dadabhai Naoroji*. Madras: G. A. Natesan, n.d.

Nariman, G. K. "Was It Religious Persecution Which Compelled the Parsis to Migrate from Persia into India?" *Islamic Culture* 7 (1933): 277–80.

Nauroji, Dhanjibhai. *From Zoroaster to Christ: An Autobiographical Sketch of the Rev. Dhanjibhai Nauroji, the First Modern Convert to Christianity from the Zoroastrian Religion*. Edinburgh: Oliphant, Anderson, and Ferrier, 1909.

Oshidari, Timsar. *Tarikh-e Zartoshtiyan* [History of Zoroastrians]. Tehran: Fravahar, 1976.

Palsetia, Jesse S. "Parsi and Hindu Traditional and Nontraditional Responses to Christian Conversion in Bombay, 1839–45." *Journal of the American Academy of Religion* 74, no. 3 (2006): 615–45.

———. *The Parsis of India: Preservation of Identity in Bombay City*. Leiden: Brill, 2001.

———. "Partner in Empire: Jamsetjee Jejeebhoy and the Public Culture of Nineteenth-Century Bombay." In *Parsis in India and the Diaspora*, edited by John R. Hinnells and Alan Williams, 81–99. London: Routledge, 2007.

Parekh, Manilal C. *The Brahma Samaj: A Short History*. Bombay: Bombay Vaibhave Press, 1929.

Patel, Dinyar. "The Iran League of Bombay: Parsis, Iran, and the Appeal of Iranian Nationalism, 1922–1942." Master's thesis, Harvard Univ., 2008.

Patel, Simin. "Passages and Perspectives: Travel Writing by Parsis in English." Master's thesis, School of Oriental and African Studies, Univ. of London, 2008.

Pavri, M. E. *Parsi Cricket with Hints on Bowling, Batting, Fielding, Captaincy, Explanation of Laws of Cricket, &*. Bombay: J. B. Marzban, 1901.

Paymaster, Rustom Burjorji. *Early History of the Parsees in India: From Their Landing in Sanjan to 1700 A.D.* Bombay: Zartoshti Dharam Sambandhi Kelavni Apnari Ane Ndyan Felavnari Mandli, 1954.

Réville, Albert. *Histoire des réligions*. 4 vols. Paris: Librairie Fischbacher, 1889.

———. *Prolegomena of the History of Religions*. Translated by A. S. Squire. London: Williams and Norgate, 1884.

Ringer, Monica M. *Education, Religion, and the Discourse of Cultural Reform in Qajar Iran*. Costa Mesa: Mazda, 2001.

———. "Iranian Nationalism and Zoroastrian Identity." In *Iran Facing Others: Identity Boundaries in a Historical Perspective*, edited by Abbas Amanat and Farzin Vejdani. New York: Palgrave Macmillan, 2012.

———. "Reform Transplanted: Parsi Agents of Change among Zoroastrians in Nineteenth-Century Iran." *Iranian Studies* 42, no. 4 (2009): 549–60.

————. "Rethinking Religion: Progress and Morality in the Early Twentieth-Century Iranian Women's Press." *Comparative Studies of South Asia, Africa, and the Middle East* 24, no. 1 (2004): 49–57.

Rose, Jennifer. "The Traditional Role of Women in the Iranian and Indian (Parsi) Zoroastrian Communities from the Nineteenth to the Twentieth Century." *Journal of the K. R. Cama Oriental Institute,* no. 56 (1989): 1–102.

Said, Edward. *Orientalism.* London: Pantheon Books, 1978.

Sanjana, Darab Dastur Peshotan. *The Position of Zoroastrian Women in Remote Antiquity, as Illustrated in the Avesta, the Sacred Books of the Parsees, Being a Lecture Delivered at Bombay on the 18th of April 1892, by Darab Dastur Peshotan Sanjana, B.A.* Bombay: Education Society's Steam Press, 1892.

Sanjana, K. "Zoroastrianism in the Light of Modern Science." In *Dastur Hoshang Memorial Volume,* 239–47. Bombay: Fort Printing Press, 1918.

Sanjana, Rastamji Edulji Dastoor Peshotan. *The Parsi Book of Books: The Zend-Avesta.* Bombay: New Art Printing Press, 1924.

————. *Zarathushtra and Zarathushtrianism in the Avesta.* Leipzig: Otto Harrosowitz, 1906.

Seager, Richard Hughes. *The World's Parliament of Religions: The East/West Encounter, Chicago, 1893.* Bloomington: Indiana Univ. Press, 1995.

Shahmardan, Rashid. *Farzanegan-e Zartoshti.* Tehran: Rasti, 1960.

Shahrokh, Kay Khosrow. *A'ineh-ye A'in-e Mazdasna.* 2nd ed. Bombay: Mozzafari Publishers, 1921.

————. *Forough-e Mazdisna.* Tehran: Jami, 1380.

————. *The Memoirs of Keikhosrow Shahrokh.* Translated and edited by Shahrokh Shahrokh and Rashna Writer. Lewiston, NY: Edwin Mellen Press, 1994.

————. *Zartosht: Payghambari keh as now bayad shenakht (Forough-e Mazdisna).* Edited by Farzan Kayani. Tehran: Jami, 1380.

Sharafi, Mitra. "Judging Conversion to Zoroastrianism: Behind the Scenes of the Parsi Panchayat Case (1908)." In *Parsis in India and the Diaspora,* edited by John R. Hinnells and Alan Williams, 159–80. London: Routledge, 2007.

Shissler, A. Holly. *Between Two Empires: Ahmet Ağaoğlu and the New Turkey.* London: I. B. Tauris, 2003.

Shotwell, James T. *The Religious Revolution of To-day.* The William Brewster Clark Memorial Lectures, Amherst College, 1913. Boston: Houghton Mifflin, 1913.

Shroff, Phiroze J. "A Note on the History and Activities of the K. R. Cama Oriental Institute." In *K. R. Cama Oriental Institute Golden Jubilee Volume,* i–xxii. Bombay: K. R. Cama Oriental Institute, 1969.

Smart, Ninian, John Clayton, Steven Katz, and Patrick Sherry, eds. *Nineteenth Century Religious Thought in the West*. Vol. 3. Cambridge: Cambridge Univ. Press, 1985.

Smith, George. *The Life of John Wilson, D.D., F.R.S.: For Fifty Years Philanthropist and Scholar in the East*. 2nd ed. London: John Murray, 1879.

Snell, Merwin-Marie. "Service of the Science of Religions to the Cause of Religious Unity." In *Museum of Faiths: Histories and Legacies of the 1893 World's Parliament of Religions*, edited by Eric J. Ziolkowski, 69–74. Atlanta: Scholars Press, 1993.

Sorushian, Jamshid. *Farhang-e Behdinan* [Zoroastrian Culture]. Tehran, 1956.

Stausberg, Michael. *Faszination Zarathushtra: Zoroaster und die Europeaische Religionsgeschichte der Frühen Neuzeit*. Religionsgeschichtliche Versuche und Vorarbeiten 42. 2 vols. Berlin: Walter de Gruyter, 1998.

———. "Manekji Limji Hataria and the Rediscovery of Ancient Iran." In *Atas-e Dorun: The Fire Within*, edited by Carlo G. Cereti and Farrokh Vajifdar, 2:439–46. Jamshid Soroush Soroushian Commemorative Volume. Bloomington: 1st Books Library, 2003.

Stavorinus, J. S. *Voyages to the East Indies*. Translated by S. H. Wilcocke. Vol. 2. London: Dawsons, 1969.

Stone, Jon R., ed. *The Essential Max Müller: On Language, Mythology, and Religion*. New York: Palgrave, 2002.

Sykes, Ella Constance. *Persia and Its People*. 1910. Reprint, n.p.: Elibron Classics, 2001.

Tarapore, J. C., ed. *The Collected Works of the Late Dastur Darab Peshotan Sanjana*. Bombay: British India Press, 1932.

Tavakoli-Targhi, Mohamad. *Refashioning Iran: Orientalism, Occidentalism, and Historiography*. New York: Palgrave, 2001.

———. "Women of the West Imagined: Persian Occidentalism, Euro-Eroticism, and Modernity." *CIRA Bulletin* 13, no. 1 (1997): 19–200.

Taylor, Charles. *Sources of the Self: The Making of the Modern Identity*. Cambridge: Harvard Univ. Press, 1989.

Tibawi, A. L. "English-Speaking Orientalist." *Islamic Quarterly* 8, nos. 1–4 (1964): 25–45.

Tsadik, Daniel. *Between Foreigners and Shi'is: Nineteenth-Century Iran and Its Jewish Minority*. Stanford: Stanford Univ. Press, 2007.

US State Department. Letter dated May 31, 1927. RG 59/250, file 891.42/10. National Archives.

———. Letter dated June 30, 1931. RG 59/250, file 891.404/23. National Archives.

———. Letter dated Feb. 3, 1932. RG 59/250, file 891.404/24. National Archives.

———. Letter dated Apr. 26, 1935. RG 59/250, file 891.402/18. National Archives.

———. Letter dated Jan. 16, 1939. National Archives.

Vahman, Fereydun. "The Conversion of Zoroastrians to the Baha'i Faith." In *The Baha'is of Iran: Socio-historical Studies,* edited by Dominic Parviz Brookshaw and Seena B. Fazel. London: Routledge, 2008.

Van den Bosch, Lourens Peter. "Theosophy or Pantheism? Friedrich Max Müller's Gifford Lectures on Natural Religion." http://www.here-now4u.de/eng/theosophy_or_pantheism_friedr.htm.

Van der Veer, Peter, ed. *Conversion to Modernities: The Globalization of Christianity.* New York: Routledge, 1996.

———. *Imperial Encounters: Religion and Modernity in India.* Princeton: Princeton Univ. Press, 2001.

———. "Syncretism, Multiculturalism, and the Discourse of Tolerance." In *Syncretism/Anti-Syncretism: The Politics of Religious Synthesis,* edited by Charles Stewart and Rosalind Shaw, 196–212. London: Routledge, 1994.

Van Rooden, Peter. "Nineteenth-Century Representations of Missionary Conversion and the Transformation of Western Christianity." In *Conversion to Modernities: The Globalization of Christianity,* edited by Peter van der Veer, 65–87. London: Routledge, 1996.

Vevaina, Yuhan Sohrab-Dinshaw. "'Surely the Prophet Intended . . .': Authority and Legitimation in the Study of Zoroastrianism." Unpublished paper.

Vitalone, Mario. *The Persian "Revayat" "Ithoter": Zoroastrian Rituals in the Eighteenth Century.* Naples: Istituto Universitario Orientale, 1996.

Voekel, Pamela. *Alone Before God: The Religious Origins of Modernity in Mexico.* Durham: Duke Univ. Press, 2002.

Wacha, Dinshaw Edulji. *Shells from the Sands of Bombay: Being My Recollections and Reminiscences, 1860–1875.* Bombay: Bombay Chronicle Press, 1920.

Wadia, Ardaser Sorabjee N. *The Message of Zoroaster.* 2nd ed. London: J. M. Dent and Sons, 1924.

Wadia, Rusheed R. "Bombay Parsi Merchants in the Eighteenth and Nineteenth Centuries." In *Parsis in India and the Diaspora,* edited by John R. Hinnells and Alan Williams, 119–35. London: Routledge, 2007.

White, Jenny B. *Islamist Mobilization in Turkey: A Study in Vernacular Politics.* Seattle: Univ. of Washington Press, 2002.

Williams, Alan. *The Zoroastrian Myth of Migration from Iran and Settlement in the Indian Diaspora: Text, Translation, and Analysis of the 16th Century "Qesse-ye Sanjan," "The Story of Sanjan."* Leiden: Brill, 2009.

Williams, David, ed. *The Enlightenment.* Cambridge: Cambridge Univ. Press, 1999.

Wills, C. J. *Persia as It Is: Being Sketches of Modern Persian Life and Character.* 1886. Reprint, n.p.: Elibron Classics, 2002.

Wilson, John. *The British Sovereignty in India: A Sermon Preached in St. Andrew's Church, Bombay.* Edinburgh: William Whyte, 1835.

———. "Conversion of Two Parsis and Prosecution of the Rev. John Wilson, D.D., on a Writ of Habeas Corpus, Before the Supreme Court of Judiciature at Bombay." May 3, 1839.

———. *The Doctrine of Jehovah Addressed to the Parsis: A Sermon Preached on the Occasion of the Baptism of Two Youths of That Tribe.* Bombay: American Mission Press, 1839.

———. *The Parsi Religion.* Bombay: American Mission Press, 1843.

———. *The Star of Bethlehem and the Magi from the East: A Sermon Preached on the Occasion of the Baptism of a Parsi Youth, August 31, 1856.* Edinburgh: William Whyte, 1857.

Wilson, Rev. S. G. *Persian Life and Customs.* New York: Fleming H. Revell, 1899.

Wink, Andre. *Al-Hind: The Making of the Indo-Islamic World.* Vol. 1. Bombay: Oxford Univ. Press, 1990.

Yule, H., ed. and trans. *The Wonders of the East by Friar Jordanus.* 2 vols. London: Hakluyt Society, 1863.

Zastoupil, Lynn. "India, J. S. Mill, and 'Western' Culture." In *J. S. Mill's Encounter with India,* edited by Martin I. Moir, Douglas M. Peers, and Lynn Zastoupil, 111–48. Toronto: Univ. of Toronto Press, 1999.

Ziolkowski, Eric J., ed. Introduction to *A Museum of Faiths: Histories and Legacies of the 1893 World's Parliament of Religions.* Atlanta: Scholars Press, 1993.

Index

Italic page number denotes illustration.